RECONSTRUCTING THE WORLD

RECONSTRUCTING THE WORLD

Southern Fictions and

U.S. Imperialisms, 1898–1976

Harilaos Stecopoulos

CORNELL UNIVERSITY PRESS

Ithaca and London

First published 2008 by Cornell University Press
First printing, Cornell Paperbacks, 2008

Printed in the United States of America

Library of Congress Cataloging-in-Publication Data
Stecopoulos, Harry.
  Reconstructing the world : Southern fictions and U.S. imperialisms, 1898–1976 / Harilaos Stecopoulos.
     p. cm.
  Includes bibliographical references and index.
  ISBN 978-0-8014-4685-6 (cloth : alk. paper) — ISBN 978-0-8014-7502-3 (pbk. : alk. paper)
     1. American literature—Southern States—History and criticism.
  2. American literature—20th century—History and criticism.   3. Southern States—In literature.   4. Literature and history—Southern States—History—20th century.   5. Imperialism in literature.   6. Regionalism in literature.   I. Title.
     PS261.S73 2008
     810.9'35875—dc22   2008026509

Cornell University Press strives to use environmentally responsible suppliers and materials to the fullest extent possible in the publishing of its books. Such materials include vegetable-based, low-VOC inks and acid-free papers that are recycled, totally chlorine-free, or partly composed of nonwood fibers. For further information, visit our website at www.cornellpress.cornell.edu.

Cloth printing   10 9 8 7 6 5 4 3 2 1
Paperback printing   10 9 8 7 6 5 4 3 2 1

for Kathy Lavezzo

CONTENTS

ACKNOWLEDGMENTS

Let me begin these acknowledgments by thanking the amazing people at Cornell University Press: Peter Potter, Alison Kalett, Candace Akins, Susan Barnett, Sara Ferguson, Kay Scheuer, and Susan Specter. They give publishing a good name.

This book had its start many years ago at the University of Virginia where I learned from such exemplary scholars as Karen Chase, Pat Gill, Deborah McDowell, and Michael Levenson. Their instruction was complemented by the many conversations I had with such good friends as Brent Lanford, Andrea Levine, Michael Uebel, and Tim Wager. At the dissertation stage, my teachers Sara Blair and Teju Olaniyan proved to be brilliant (and patient) readers.

At the University of Iowa, I have benefited from vital relationships with a stunning array of colleagues and friends. Thanks must go to Kathleen Diffley whose invitation to join a writing group helped me get my project on track. The other members of that group, including Margaret Bass, Matt Brown, Corey Creekmur, Loren Glass, and the incomparable Tom Lutz, provided me with just the right mixture of flattery and critique necessary to focus the manuscript. My graduate student assistants Jo Davis-McElligatt, Amit Baishya, Rob McLoone, Eve Rosenbaum, and Dorothy Giannakouros delivered invaluable research assistance while the University of Iowa offered me financial support in the form of summer fellowships and a flexible load semester. Brooks Landon and Jon Wilcox, my two DEOs, gave me the release time needed for significant research and writing.

I also express my gratitude to fellow Iowa faculty Linda Bolton,

Huston Diehl, Barbara Eckstein, Mary Lou Emery, Naomi Greyser, Cheryl Herr, Kevin Mumford, Horace Porter, and Stephen Vlastos. They all have either read or discussed with me parts of the book. Three colleagues offered me extensive commentary on various portions of the project. I owe Bluford Adams, Claire Fox, and Laura Rigal a significant debt that will take years to repay.

I am no less obligated to my colleagues farther afield. I have been fortunate to forge intellectual ties with such extraordinary scholars as Herman Beavers, Ashley Dawson, Travis Foster, Matthew Jones, Richard King, John Lowe, Jack Matthews, Lawrence Oliver, Donald Pease, Lee Quinby, John Rowe, Malini Schueller, Jon Smith, Patricia Yaeger, Bryan Wagner, and Alys Weinbaum. John Rowe, in particular, continues to astound me with his intellectual and professional generosity. Above all, however, one professor has proven indispensable to the creation of this book: Eric Lott. Witty, learned, and brilliant, Eric provided me with a superb education at UVA and then supported me through good times and bad in the subsequent years. I feel fortunate to have been—to be—his student.

Closer to home, I thank my parents, Rena and Nicholas Stecopoulos, for all they have done for me. And I am delighted to celebrate my amazing daughter Nina—a six-year-old who takes her own efforts at book production seriously indeed. Her work will soon grace the shelves of the Lincoln Elementary School library in Iowa City.

The final "shout" must go out to my partner in intellectual crime, Kathy Lavezzo. Kathy has been with this book and its assorted false starts and missteps from the outset. She has helped with many aspects of this manuscript, from local points to historical research to overall organization. It is her book as much as it is mine.

RECONSTRUCTING THE WORLD

INTRODUCTION

The unending tragedy of Reconstruction is the utter inability
of the American mind to grasp its . . . national and worldwide
implications.

    W. E. B. Du Bois, *Black Reconstruction*

When film director Spike Lee posed before a crumbling New Orleans
house tagged with the name "Baghdad" during the shooting of *When
the Levees Broke* (2006), he created a startling image. Fixing the viewer
with a cold and slightly accusatory stare, the position of his hands di-
recting our attention to the graffiti behind him, Lee asks us to consider
how the much-fabled "Big Easy" has become strange to the United
States—how it seems a place not so much familiar as foreign (see Figure 1). For some viewers, this troubling photograph may recall what
reporters and pundits had emphasized two years earlier when the wa-
ter-logged city and its largely black homeless population resembled an
impoverished section of the developing world. News reports on Hurri-
cane Katrina and its aftermath often drew analogies between this portion of the domestic South and other places in the global South such as
Rwanda and Bangladesh.[1] What distinguishes Lee's photo from those
comments is the filmmaker's apparent refusal to assert a loose connection between a ravaged New Orleans and a generic site in the developing world, but on the contrary to insist that the terrible crisis in the
Crescent City has everything to do with a far bloodier tragedy in another impoverished metropolitan area. As both the photo and the documentary suggest, for Lee, New Orleans and its environs must be
understood as linked to a site of U.S. conquest thousands of miles away.
Reading "Baghdad" on a New Orleans wall isn't simply a matter of
reckoning unusual resemblances between first world and third; it is
also a matter of recognizing the presence of imperialism, at home and
abroad.

    Consciously or otherwise, both Lee and the reporters who chronicled

Figure 1. Spike Lee in New Orleans
Credit: Charlie Varley/Sipa

the aftermath of Katrina drew on a longstanding tradition: that of de-
picting the U.S. South as less a normative part of the republic than a
colonial region that stood apart from the imagined community.[2] To borrow from W. J. Cash, "There exists among us . . . a profound conviction
that the South is another land, sharply differentiated from the rest of the
American nation."[3] This "conviction" originated in the antebellum era
when, as Anne Norton has argued, U.S. intellectuals represented the
South as an "alternative America" variously coded as female, black, and
Indian.[4] And even as the figures asserting the idea of southern difference necessarily grew more diverse after Emancipation, the tradition itself persisted in various forms, from Appomattox to the New Deal and
beyond. Colonial Virginian Robert Beverly's proud assertion "I am an
Indian," became African American journalist Ida B. Wells's late nineteenth-century claim that white southern lynchers resembled "canni-
bals" and "savage Indians."[5] Wells's characterization of the region as
uncivilized adumbrated German-American H. L. Mencken's suggestion that the South is like the Sahara Desert, which, in turn, presaged

white New Yorker Carl Carmer's linkage of Alabama to another African space, the Congo.[6] By the time African American poet Yusef Komunyakaa drew connections between his native Louisiana and war-torn Vietnam in the 1980s, the notion that the domestic region was alien to the nation had been well established.[7] To many U.S. intellectuals, white and black, northern and southern, the South was, in the words of C. Vann Woodward, a region that seemed to have "rather more in common with the ironic and tragic experience of . . . the general run of mankind than have other parts of America."[8]

The more perspicacious of these intellectuals have understood, with Spike Lee, that to emphasize the South's alien status is not only to comment on the region's longstanding racism and poverty, but also to raise the linked questions of how "Uncle Sam" has managed the challenge of his "other province" and how that challenge intersected with the United States' charged relationship to other parts of the world.[9] Many Americans perceive the nation-state's historic relationship to the South as an inspiring parable of color and democracy, wherein benevolent federal forces have periodically intervened to uplift a tragically retrograde part of the nation. But the tradition of representing the South as a strange and colonial space urges us to reread its relationship to the federal government in a broader imperial context. To raise the question of the alien South is also to emphasize the nation-state's own frequent incapacity to uphold the ideals of liberal democracy on a variety of geographic scales; or, as W. E. B. Du Bois might claim, to highlight the tragedy of U.S. *reconstruction* in the broadest sense.[10]

I take Du Bois's emphasis on the "national and worldwide implications" of a failed Reconstruction in my epigraph as a mandate to consider how the federal government's decision to abandon the onerous task of building democracy in the region not only devastated the African American South, but also laid the groundwork for the U.S. betrayal of many other communities of color overseas. The "unending tragedy of Reconstruction" is, in my analysis, a sign of the United States' tendency over the twentieth century to impose its compromised, if not hollow, promises of freedom and modernization on a host of subaltern peoples.[11] The United States might have failed to meet its own democratic standard in the southland, leaving African Americans to the mercy of a violent Jim Crow regime, but that failure has hardly deterred the nation-state from making similarly false claims about liberty and democracy to other oppressed populations the world over.[12]

In this book, I engage with the long shadow of an incomplete Reconstruction as it informed the culture of U.S. imperialism from the sinking of the U.S.S. Maine (1898) to the fall of Saigon (1975). *Reconstructing the World: Southern Fictions and U.S. Imperialisms, 1898–1976* examines the

lives and works of Thomas Dixon, W. E. B. Du Bois, James Weldon Johnson, William Faulkner, Carson McCullers, Alice Walker, and other U.S.
writers sensitive to the mediatory status of the South for a nation looking at the world with imperial eyes. Reading these figures' rich writings
as political interventions, I argue that such texts as Johnson's *Autobiography of an Ex-Colored Man* (1912), Du Bois's *Dark Princess* (1928), and
McCullers's *Member of the Wedding* (1946) tend to portray the South as
an alien, backward, and un-American space. Those depictions of the
region have both illustrated the longstanding federal failure to foster
democracy in the U.S. southeast, and, at the same time, highlighted surprising connections among poor and usually black southerners and
people of color in the developing world. If these intellectuals argued
that the failure of Reconstruction helped render the South what Du Bois
dubbed "the gateway to the colored millions," they also understood that
this alternate geography stood perforce in complex relation to the imperial geography promulgated by the nation's power elite.[13]

Indeed, with the notable exception of Dixon, all of the figures examined in my book seized upon the South's peculiar reputation to posit
transnational and often cross-racial relationships that challenged the
putative coherence of an appetitive nation eager to claim the world as
its own. These challenges varied in intensity and meaning, to be sure.
As we shall see, Johnson's anti-imperialist identification with the Haitians hardly paralleled Faulkner's cold war bonding with the Japanese.
But most of these intellectuals understood that to view the South in international terms was to remap nation and empire, to unsettle the nationalist narrative that found in a chaotic world requisite justification for
American power, to recognize that the global hopes of democracy exceeded the dictatorial authority of any one imagined community, large
or small.

Post-Regionalist American Studies

In reading the South in the context of modern imperialism, I engage
with the emergent field of U.S. empire studies.[14] Unlike their academic
counterparts who specialize in European imperialism, scholars of U.S.
empire face certain challenges when attempting to define their object of
analysis. As many historians and political scientists have pointed out,
the fluid and ever-protean territorial, commercial, and ideological dimensions of U.S. empire often seem to defy a conventional understanding of imperialism, one that emphasizes, in Edward Said's words,
"the practice, the theory and the attitudes of a . . . metropolitan center
ruling a distant territory."[15] That many U.S. imperialists historically
have tended to disavow such territorial, indeed colonial, ambitions

even as they have pursued them makes the scholar's job still more difficult. Americanists confronted either by U.S. policymakers who sidestep "the use of terms that would hint at aggression or imperial domination" or by the multifarious dimensions of U.S. expansion, understandably have sought to define imperialism in as concrete a manner as possible.[16] One such method—and the method I will favor in this volume—has been to lay stress on state policies, particularly those regarding the judiciary and the military. Literary critic Amy Kaplan thus examines the Battle of San Juan Hill as a military action that sparked a racial debate over African American heroism, while historian Nikhil Singh foregrounds the overlaps between post–World War II foreign policy and the emergence of multiculturalism in his work on African American intellectuals.[17] This isn't to deny that U.S. empire studies scholars also focus on multinational corporations, non-governmental organizations (NGOs), cultural producers, or other non-state actors; they do. It is instead to claim that, for all the recent talk of the demise or irrelevance of the nation-state, much of the new scholarship attempts in one way or another to link the politics and poetics of U.S. imperialism to the U.S. government.[18] If the Trail of Tears, the Walt Disney Corporation, and United Fruit plantations all constitute different historic aspects of an oft-denied U.S. empire, emphasizing the nation-state and its variegated policies provides one way of grounding U.S. empire studies in some notion of a historical real.

To be sure, if the nation-state remains important to recent work on the culture of U.S. imperialism, it does so largely as an object of critique.[19] As in many contemporary academic disciplines that now stress transnational or hemispheric initiatives, the nation-state for many contemporary Americanists doesn't so much warrant respectful allegiance as provoke an impulse to transgress its boundaries and un-write its fictions. No longer content to limit themselves to an intellectual purview determined by normative notions of national belonging, such figures as Anna Brickhouse, Amy Kaplan, Lisa Lowe, Donald Pease, John Carlos Rowe, Ramón Saldívar, and Malini Schueller have redefined American studies in a post- *and* transnational frame.[20] At once foregrounding and challenging the limits of American Studies as it has been traditionally conceived, these scholars have accomplished two important interventions. First, they have urged us to examine how the dominant fiction of nationhood necessarily relies upon the exclusion of African Americans, Asian Americans, women, the working class, and other subaltern groups in order to function.[21] As Donald Pease puts it, "the national narrative produced national identities by way of a social symbolic order that systematically separated an abstract, disembodied subject from resistant materialities, such as race, class, and gender. . . . The universality of the national identity depends on their externality for its integrity."[22] For Pease, Rowe, Saldívar, and other post-nationalist Americanists, we should at once recognize the structural externationalization at work in this national narrative and at the same time understand that subaltern social agents have often rejected assimilation into that narrative in favor of destabilizing it.[23] Second, these scholars have insisted that any challenge to the nation-form must recognize the global reach of "America" and take seriously the obligation to examine U.S. culture and politics as they affect domestic *and* foreign populations. Fully aware that any forceful consideration of the cultural and political consequences of U.S. empire must manifest a willingness to transgress official borders and boundaries, new Americanists now write about such topics as Cuban activist José Marti, Filipino resistance to U.S. colonialism, and the Soviet response to African American writer Claude McKay.[24] In a similar vein, these Americanists also tend to emphasize the past and present contributions of non-U.S.–based scholars of U.S. studies, a mission that has over the past ten years greatly diversified stateside academic conferences. Thanks to these linked efforts at unmaking the national narrative from within and without, the meaning of the word "American" in "American Studies" has never been more fruitfully interrogated.[25]

Reconstructing the World is a work that seeks to contribute to post-nationalist American studies. I will, for example, examine W. E. B. Du Bois's complicated post–World War I involvement in Liberian politics and Carson McCullers's horrified response to total war in the 1940s. Yet my book also seeks to recognize and address a potential Achilles heel of the new methodology: a tendency to push aside traditional conceptions of space and subjectivity, to label them insignificant or, worse yet, reactionary. The impulse to celebrate all that transgresses customary geopolitical boundaries can render certain geographic formations, particularly sub-national geographic formations, less than worthy objects of analysis. Thus even as scholars of U.S. imperialism attend regularly to some lower-scale spaces—metropoles such as Los Angeles, for example—they have for the most part proven less interested in the region.[26] This is in part a matter of academic fashion. In an era when many scholars in the humanities find alluring the topics of the global and the transnational, issues of the region and the regional often seem passé. Yet there is a more important reason for the shunning of the region in recent post- and transnationalist American Studies: the idea that regionalism represents the worst aspects of nationalism writ small.

Contemporary cultural geographers tend to define the region largely in terms of mode of production—consider Neil Smith's claim that regional identity is "constructed disproportionately around the kinds of work performed there."[27] However, contemporary scholars of literature and culture often understand the region in terms of retrograde and exclusionary political affiliations, ascribing to regional subjects the same disturbing desire for homogeneity and similitude typically associated with the nation-form.[28] "Is the region trying to imagine yet again a *Volksgeist* or 'Spirit of Place,'" writes Robert Dianotto, "whose boundaries protect a community from the political and cultural negotiations imposed by differences of 'economics, gender, race, creed'?" For Dianotto, as for so many post-nationalist Americanists, the answer is typically "yes." To challenge the nationalist narrative of U.S. studies demands that we leave not only the nation, but also the region behind. Post-*nationalist* Americanists are post-*regionalist* Americanists.

For some contemporary scholars, of course, the traditional notion of the region has been supplanted by a more contemporary and seemingly relevant geographic formation. As John Carlos Rowe has recently argued, post-nationalist American Studies tends to focus not on "older, more discrete regional identities," but rather on "new regionalisms established by the different demographies, ethnicities, and global economic and cultural affiliations characterizing such important border or contact zones as Southern California's relation to Asia, Mexico, Central America, and the Caribbean."[29] Rowe's astute comment captures a contemporary intellectual viewpoint, one that informs much of my work. He emphasizes rightly how a transnational notion of region has grown extraordinarily important to scholars who seek in a new idea of internationalized community some possibility of resistance to the power of nation-states and multinational corporations.[30] At the same time, his invocation of "new regionalisms" both invites us to reconsider how the old regionalisms might still resonate productively for U.S. empire studies, and challenges us to produce a new post-nationalist reading of an imagined New England or an imagined West that resists reification.

Post-nationalist Americanists will be repaid richly by attending more carefully to the import of regionalism. These seemingly outmoded geographic fictions not only yield indispensable historical information about the economic, bureaucratic, and military mechanisms of power; they also offer us insight into the relationships that obtain between center and periphery. Indeed, for the scholar interested in the state's capacity to make and unmake geographic formations with and through capital, studying the region proves arguably the best means of identifying those strategies and the resistance they inevitably provoke. Americanists interested in U.S. empire studies don't have to look far for examples of how one might integrate a revisionist approach to regionalism into a post-nationalist methodology. In the 1970s historian Richard Slotkin pioneered a version of such scholarship in his study of the U.S. West and Manifest Destiny while a few years later critical theorist Kenneth Frampton offered a more philosophical rationale for similar work in his essay on critical regionalism and the universalizing tendencies of global capital.[31] More recently, the group of scholars loosely affiliated with what Houston Baker has dubbed "the new southern studies" has powerfully deployed a traditional notion of region in a distinctly transnational critical mode. Emphasizing how a shared plantation past—and in some cases a neoplantation present—bind together much of the U.S. South and the Caribbean islands and portions of Central and South America, such scholars as Baker, Trudier Harris, Barbara Ladd, Caroline Levander, John Lowe, John Matthews, and Patricia Yaeger have demonstrated how "Uncle Sam's other province" functioned as a hemispheric formation for politicians and intellectuals, activists and artists in the United States and much of Latin America. Thus Caroline Levander has recently recovered the history of nineteenth-century white southern fantasies of acquiring Cuba, while John Matthews has traced a genealogy of Caribbean and Central American colonial spaces in Faulkner's oeuvre from little-known short stories featuring the port of Rincon to *Absalom, Absalom*'s famous representation of the West Indies.[32]

The new southern studies has taught us that seemingly normative conceptions of region can still offer us valuable insights into the historic relationships that obtain among sub-national, national, and global geographic formations. Yet these scholars have also made a particular argument for the South's importance as a region that seems at once integral to the nation and alien to it. While understandably hesitant to make exceptional claims about this geographic formation, many of the academics affiliated with this new methodology do suggest that the South's peculiar national status renders it especially valuable for a postnationalist American studies eager to question and destabilize normative boundaries. As Jon Smith and Deborah Cohn have argued, contemporary scholars have much to learn from the notion of "a liminal south, one that troubles essentialist narratives both of global-southern decline and of unproblematic global-northern national or regional unity, of American or southern exceptionalism."[33] To recognize that this arguably most marginalized of U.S. regions has been linked through its very hybrid national status to foreign communities and places is to challenge at some basic level the hegemonic geography that demands a separation of the nation's notorious racial problems from its celebrated leadership of the world. Indeed, one might claim that to read U.S. expansion through the lens of the alien South is to confound the fantastic distinction between "home and away" that so often structures and enables imperialism in the first place.

Yet if the new southern studies has proven invaluable in reminding us that a much-maligned region has long served as something of a light-ning rod for crucial national and international debates about race, space, and power, it also true that this iconoclastic approach to region and re-gionalism might benefit from a greater engagement with U.S. empire studies, particularly with respect to questions of territory and state power. Geography is particularly important here. While hemispheric re-lations have been fruitfully examined in the new southern studies, the region's complex relations with other parts of the world remain largely unanalyzed. Possibilities for future scholarship include the South's con-nection to China—a subject of much fascination to such turn-of-the-cen-tury expansionists as Alabama senator John Tyler Morgan and North Carolina manufacturer Daniel Augustus Tompkins—and the commod-ification and marketing of U.S. southern culture in contemporary Eu-rope. The U.S. South's proximity to Cuba and Mexico hardly means that other more global deployments of the imagined region are insignificant.

Similarly, the emphasis on state juridical and military policies in U.S. empire studies offers a great deal to new southern studies scholars who tend by and large to emphasize historical and cultural issues and downplay the significance of both the repressive state apparatus and the ideological state apparatus.[34] Any attempt to read the South in the transnational frame demands some attention to the U.S. government and its failed Reconstruction. When one considers that this abortive at-tempt at democratic reform often dovetailed with imperial policies of one kind or another—for example, the decision to send U.S. Army troops directly from the South to hunt down Chief Joseph and the Nez Perce in 1877—the need to focus on the state grows even more appar-ent.[35] Insofar as it takes up the South's importance as an imperial signi-fier, the new southern studies begs what we might call the Washington question: not to revive hoary laments about the Lost Cause, but to take seriously the U.S. government's capacity to make and unmake geo-graphic formations on a variety of spatial scales.

Literary Intellectuals and State Geographies

The relationship between the South and U.S. imperialism is longstand-ing, reaching back as far as President Thomas Jefferson's decision to au-thorize the Louisiana Purchase (1803) and more specifically to regional dreams of expanding a slave-holding empire into Central America and the Caribbean. A *New York Herald* cartoon from July 31, 1898, well cap-tures this relation when it renders the southland as the hungry mouth of an expansionist Uncle Sam (Figure 2). My project tracks the modern history of that relationship from the Spanish-American War to the Viet-nam War, or, to put it another way, from when, as C. Vann Woodward

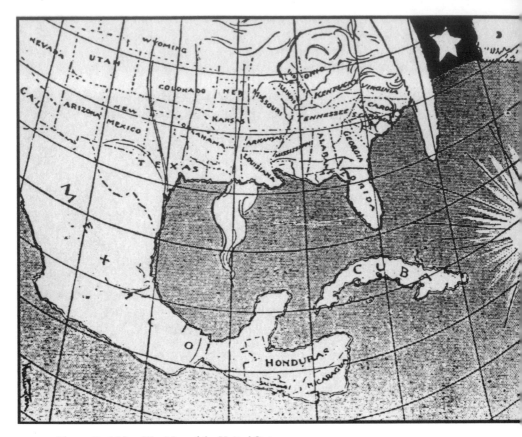

Figure 2. A New War Map of the United States
Credit: Charles Nelan, *New York Herald*, 1898

argues, the post-Reconstruction North looked "to Southern racial policy for national guidance in the new problems of imperialism" to when
the Nixon administration pursued a similar "southern strategy" during
another imperial conflict abroad and a crisis of "law and order" at
home.[36] I have decided to focus on this largely twentieth-century era not
because I think it is necessarily more significant than the earlier period,
but rather because it offers us an opportunity to see how the state understood the importance of the South at the very time the United States
was taking on the role of global hegemon. To focus on the complex entanglement of U.S. imperialism and U.S. regionalism is to recognize that
the strength and flexibility of the modern capitalist state depended
partly on its capacity to help produce colonial geographies within and

without the putative borders of the nation.[37] As we shall see, the U.S. South and certain locations in what is now called the global South often manifested disturbing similarities. That these similarities recall the connections linking persistent racist exploitation at home with new U.S. expansion abroad urges us to re-examine the rise and transformation of this imperial dynamic in the twentieth century.

Needless to say, I do not attempt to address all of the historical aspects of the South's role as a bearer of modern imperial meaning within the roughly eighty-year purview of the book.[38] Instead, I focus on a series of public intellectuals, most but not all from the South, who invoked the racially divided region as a means of intervening in contemporary debates about state power at home and abroad: Charles Chesnutt, Thomas Dixon, James Weldon Johnson, W. E. B. Du Bois, Carson McCullers, William Faulkner, Richard Wright, Alice Walker. That my list includes more African American than European American writers might strike some readers familiar with southern studies, old and new, as strange. Up until fairly recently, most scholarly works on the literature and culture of the South tended to the converse. Yet many studies of the South might adopt such a perspective; this is, after all, the region where, as Du Bois claimed in 1924, "[the Negro] is everything."[39] Furthermore, any attempt at reading the South in light of modern U.S. expansion demands greater attention to African American writers. More than the vast majority of their white counterparts, black writers felt the urge to link the empty promise of democracy in the region to the unfulfilled expectation of democracy in U.S. colonial spaces abroad. From Anna Julia Cooper's comments on Anglo-Saxon expansion in *A Voice from the South* to Robert Williams's transition in the early 1960s from an anti-racist Deacon for Defense and Justice to a North Vietnamese propagandist, African Americans long have combated regional, national, and global manifestations of white power. Any study that seeks to examine the South as a modern imperial signifier must attend carefully to black intellectuals and their often very public interventions.

I classify my eight black and white writers as public intellectuals for two reasons. First, each of them identified to varying degrees with a particular community for whom she felt she could speak, thus qualifying to some extent as what Antonio Gramsci would dub an organic intellectual.[40] Even Du Bois and Wright, the most overtly cosmopolitan of these figures, assumed the right, better, the obligation, to articulate the grievances and expectations of a group or groups—whether African Americans of the South, African Americans of the nation, or colored peoples of the world. Second, each of these intellectuals felt a responsibility to express their views in what were by and large accessible and well-disseminated forms. Thus the notoriously private Faulkner spent much of the 1950s speaking to reporters and publishing opinion pieces in mass-market magazines. All of these writers maintained some connection to the public sphere—whether through publishing best-sellers (Dixon's *The Leopard's Spots*), championing new political movements (Johnson's position as secretary of the NAACP), or maintaining an international celebrity profile (Wright); even McCullers and Walker, the two women in the group, had greater access to the public than one would expect, the former through urban women's culture of the 1940s, the latter through the civil rights culture of the 1960s and 1970s.

These public intellectuals are not particularly noteworthy for their interest in the racial politics of the southern question; such a category would after all include any number of politicians, activists, and journalists. However, they are unusual in that they proved especially responsive to the state's power to construct the South in a manner that resonated in global terms. Their sensitivity to the federal government was due in part to personal or professional relations with state officials or some element of the state apparatus. Dixon and Chesnutt had important personal links to the turn-of-the-century Republican party, the ruling party of the era; Johnson served as a U.S. State Department consul for over three years; Du Bois represented the United States at the 1924 presidential inauguration in Liberia; McCullers spent much of her youth taking piano lessons at an officer's home on a nearby U.S. military base and later married a career soldier; Faulkner worked as a State Department spokesman; and Wright found himself embroiled with various U.S. officials during his 1955 trip to the Bandung conference in Indonesia.

However inchoately, each of these intellectuals grasped that if the Civil War had, in the words of Eric Foner, helped stimulate "the birth of the modern American state," the federal government's postbellum size and power had hardly been focused on the construction of a democratic southland, but rather on the tacit maintenance of an internal colonial space where cheap labor and cheap land were readily available to capital.[41] The underdevelopment of the South, its delayed modernity, in other words, must be understood in light of federal policies and their elite capitalist supporters. That many members of the white southern elite, while to some degree dominated by a wealthy and powerful North, continued to oppress and exploit African Americans and poor whites only ensured the colonial state of the region.[42] To be sure, the liberal-to-left intellectuals I examine—Chesnutt, Johnson, Du Bois, McCullers, Wright, Walker—recognized and celebrated the government's enormous achievement in eliminating slavery. The fervent hope that the federal government would somehow return to the extraordinary feat of

Emancipation sustained African American intellectuals in particular, some of whom even sought to imagine how U.S. expansion might benefit colored peoples at home and abroad. At the same time, these intellectuals understood the important connection between the abandonment of Reconstruction and the rise of a powerful imperial state. Writers from Chesnutt to Wright proved acutely aware that the end of Reconstruction didn't so much mark the state's benign neglect of the region, as signal that a more powerful federal apparatus would through taxes, laws, and "pork" help produce the South as backward, impoverished, and alien—a fun-house mirror reflection of U.S. colonial spaces abroad. The American Century might not have been a Confederate Century, as Michael Lind has recently opined, but an unanswered southern question long has attended the expansion of U.S. global power.[43]

Yet if these intellectuals understood how the state and capital helped create, in the words of Stuart Hall, "not only . . . regional specificity and unevenness, but . . . [also] differential modes of incorporating so-called 'backward' sectors within the social regime of capital," they hardly accepted this realization as a death-knell for oppositional culture and politics.[44] To the contrary, the region's long history of social and political problems rendered it an exceptionally powerful goad to imagining new configurations of color and community during the high tide of U.S. power. Whatever their politics, whatever their image of the southland, all of these figures took seriously their own imaginative capacities to visualize new spaces and new cross-identifications that complicate the official interpellation of the South. Those new geographies expose and revise the hidden racial assumptions informing the state's role in making domestic southern and global southern spaces. Chesnutt thus imagines how a white southern woman finds in an imperial seascape a threat to her putative whiteness, while Walker explores how an African American in Georgia can redefine his farm as part of Native American territory and, in the process, suggest a new bond with First Peoples. By rewriting the region within the imperial frame, these intellectuals do not so much affirm the normative understanding of borders and spaces, races and communities, as imagine the fluid possibilities of such categories. When Mrs. Lamb links Mississippi blacks to Indonesians in Richard Wright's novel *The Long Dream*, one recognizes that a normative sense of cartography no longer obtains.

To examine configurations of U.S. imperialism and southern regionalism in the work of these intellectuals is to locate in a range of texts a rich political and literary response to the charged triangle of nation, region, and empire. While *Reconstructing the World* is not—and is not intended to be—a book of formalist analysis, each of the interpretations that appear in its pages carefully considers these writers' literary aesthetics. And with good reason: as many critics have taught us, literature, perhaps more accurately, narrative, has often played an important role in conceptualizing community for marginalized and disempowered people. At its best, the unfettered possibilities of the literary seem capable of giving shape to impossible solidarities and utopian yearnings difficult to articulate in more sober or restrictive genres. While I do not pursue a narrowly focused study of what Timothy Brennan might call a regional longing for form, I do consider how literary conceits invariably structured the political interventions under examination.[45] Toward that end, we will attend to figural language, meditate on plot structure, take up the question of genre, and generally pay close attention to how these intellectuals drew upon their artistic talents to fashion inspired literary counter-cartographies to the prevailing maps of U.S. imperialism. We will in sum examine how the imaginative writing of the modern U.S. South emerged in part through a dynamic engagement with an expansionist state.

My first chapter suggests as much. Recasting historian Nina Silber's famous phrase "the romance of reunion" in geographic terms, I examine how two major turn-of-the-century intellectuals, black integrationist Charles Chesnutt and white supremacist Thomas Dixon, responded to President William McKinley's argument that the imperial mission could inspire a new brotherhood of white southerners and white northerners. Both Dixon and Chesnutt criticized the GOP's global fantasy of sectional reunion by urging a reconsideration of the local. In *The Leopard's Spots*, Dixon urges the GOP elite to recognize the singular value of the white South in any attempt at imagining an expansionist basis for national coherence. Pushing McKinley's valuation of the region to a self-aggrandizing extreme, Dixon claims that the long-suffering South can teach the nation about the perils and promise of the white man's burden and help inaugurate a new era of American global power. By contrast, Chesnutt contends in *The Marrow of Tradition* that imperialism has revived white southern rebelliousness and thus threatened to unravel the fabric of the nation. Only a white Republican reunion with its erstwhile ally, the African American, Chesnutt implies, will ensure that expansion not lead to new sectional fragmentation at home and colonial disjuncture abroad. Profoundly opposed politically, these two literary intellectuals shared a fascination with how the most racially stratified of regions could render fluid the normative boundaries of "white" nation and "colored" colony at the inaugural moment of a new U.S. empire.

My second chapter picks up on Chesnutt's dream of a responsive GOP to focus on black Republican James Weldon Johnson and his literary engagement with the temptations of U.S. expansion. The centerpiece of this chapter is a reading of *The Autobiography of an Ex-Colored*

Man as a hemispheric text. Critics have often analyzed *The Autobiography* in light of such issues as narration, publishing history, and racial passing, but few have taken seriously the fact that Johnson wrote much of the novel while serving as a U.S. consul in Venezuela during the era of "big stick" diplomacy. In *The Autobiography,* Johnson meditates on themes important to fin-de-siècle U.S. expansion (e.g., the politics of the Cuban independence movement) in order to demonstrate his own belated realization that U.S. empire will never improve black life at home, least of all in the Jim Crow South. The picaresque titular character's eventual jettisoning of his own blackness and his work for a transnational investment firm represent the culmination of an imperialist approach to race and social aspiration that emerges early in the novel. From his manipulation of Latin Americans to his investment in the "world conquering" power of ragtime, the ex-colored man exemplifies the racial transgressions entailed by empire. For Johnson, U.S. imperialism both tempts African Americans with the enfranchisement they have been denied at home and threatens to undercut any sense of hemispheric racial solidarity. My reading of *The Autobiography* helps explain Johnson's subsequent decision to turn against imperialism and dedicate himself to NAACP activism in the South.

While the United States officially began to turn away from territorial imperialism in the 1920s, its efforts to secure global power continued unabated—a fact not lost on one of the most ardent anti-imperialists of the modern era, W. E. B. Du Bois. In my third chapter, I read Du Bois's legendary critique of Western empire from a regional perspective, by examining the central role of a global U.S. South in his two most important interwar texts: the novel *Dark Princess* and the history *Black Reconstruction.* Focusing on the coincidence of the intellectual's southern turn with his complex and largely disappointing experience promoting U.S. corporate investment in Liberia, I argue that the 1920s version of "dollar diplomacy" inadvertently inspired Du Bois to reconsider the geopolitical significance of the domestic region. While hardly jettisoning his longstanding devotion to Africa, Du Bois also began focusing on smaller spatial scales, a reorientation that taught him how local forms of attachment could help African Americans resist the oppressive allure of the nation-state and create ties to the world beyond U.S. borders. Du Bois's new geopolitical understanding of the U.S. South inspired him to reject anew Western imperialism for a radical reconstruction of global relations.

Chapter Four examines how Carson McCullers viewed the federal militarization of the South during the late 1930s and 1940s as a new way of linking the region to the U.S. imperium. Taking as my main text the classic novel *The Member of the Wedding,* I demonstrate how McCullers drew upon her own upbringing near Fort Benning, Georgia, to render the southern coming-of-age narrative a commentary on the geopolitical significance of an expanding U.S. Army. *Member* contrasts the cosmopolitan fantasies of Frankie, a white twelve-year-old who desperately wants to flee the South through military means, with the homespun commentaries of Berenice, a black housekeeper who recognizes that the dream of a (white) American Century depends on the oppression of people of color at home and abroad. The novel insists throughout that seemingly insignificant moments in humble spaces—a hot kitchen, a small southern town—can teach us home-truths about momentous international events. Namely, if Berenice's insights win the day, they don't indict only Frankie and the white South for racism, but rather all white Americans who find in the notion of an all-conquering Jim Crow military the key to a better world. The chapter concludes by linking McCullers's critical engagement with U.S. colonialism at home and abroad to contemporary geopolitical debates among such figures as Henry Luce, Henry Wallace, and Mary McLeod Bethune.

The creation of the term "third world" in the 1950s suggested that poor nations of color stood apart from the affluent and anti-Communist "first world," but William Faulkner and Richard Wright demonstrated that at least one U.S. region had an important, if vexed, relationship with those distant countries. Using *Faulkner at Nagano* and *The Color Curtain* as my major examples, but also drawing on Faulkner's *The Town* and Wright's *The Long Dream*, I demonstrate in my fifth chapter how each writer engaged with the dynamic relationship of the U.S. South and the cold war U.S. empire for very different purposes. For Faulkner, the South's experience of military defeat and occupation, longstanding poverty, and delayed modernization gives white southerners an affinity for another traditional people, the Japanese. In contrast, Wright uses the 1955 conference in Bandung, Indonesia, to query the notion that African Americans, citizens of a modern nation, would necessarily share any meaningful connection with the Indonesians, other than that of white oppression. Both interventions reveal how these two very different Mississippi modernists found in East Asian travel and travel writing a valuable opportunity to reexamine the racial politics of home.

The epilogue considers Walker's *Meridian* as a riposte to Richard Nixon's notorious "southern strategy." If the Nixon administration invoked the South via the newly completed Confederate memorial Stone Mountain for reactionary and imperialist ends, Walker reimagined the South through a Native American burial mound that endows the novel's black protagonist with a new awareness of colonial oppression. At once profoundly historical and wildly surreal, *Meridian*'s experience in the burial mound dislocates her, pushing her beyond a normative understanding of regional and racial politics to a visionary conception of a subaltern South resistant to white oppression. Walker's novel provides us with a powerful closing image of how this supposedly alien region can function as a third term that unsettles the binary thinking so often used to theorize the racial politics of nation and empire.

1

THE GEOGRAPHY OF REUNION

*Thomas Dixon, Charles Chesnutt,
and the McKinley Expansionists*

If you want to avoid civil war, you must become imperialists.
CECIL RHODES, 1895

During the Spanish-American War, the United States attempted to heal the lingering wounds of disunion through national expansion. President William McKinley led the charge to join North and South in the name of empire. He appointed ex-Confederate generals Joseph Wheeler and Fitzhugh Lee to important posts in the conquest and administration of Cuba; celebrated the heroism of white southern soldiers at Santiago and Manila; and even wore a Confederate badge during a tour promoting the proposed treaty with Spain.[1] If the likely addition of new lands and millions of new people to the Republic seemed to challenge the cohesion of the nation, the president argued precisely the opposite: expansion would transform old enemies into brothers and stimulate the birth of a stronger and more unified polity. As he put it at Antietam in 1899: "The followers of the Confederate generals with the followers of the Federal generals fought side by side in Cuba, in Porto Rico [sic], and in the Philippines, and together in those far-off islands are standing today fighting and dying for the flag they love, the flag that represents more than any other banner in the world the best hopes and aspirations of mankind."[2] Having forced the South to remain in the Union through military means more than thirty years before, McKinley and the Republicans now claimed that imperial war would complete the process of rebuilding the imagined community.

There is little doubt that many fin-de-siècle white Americans found the president's rhetoric of reconciliation through expansion appealing (see Figures 3 and 4). As historians David Blight, Paul Buck, Kathleen

Figure 3. The Confederate Soldier and the Spanish-American War
Credit: *New York Herald*, 1898

Diffley, Carol Reardon, and Nina Silber have taught us, calls for sectional reunion began during the war itself and then, after some interruption in the late 1860s, resumed with vigor during the virtual coincidence of the Centennial (1876) and the end of Reconstruction (1877).[3] In 1883, the Supreme Court declared the 1875 Civil Rights Act unconstitutional, thus releasing the white South from a legal obligation to respect the rights of African Americans. Two years later, the death of President Ulysses S. Grant prompted an outpouring of reconciliatory sentiment; several ex-Confederate generals served as pallbearers at Grant's funeral for which Mrs. Jefferson Davis wrote a eulogy widely reprinted in the North. And, in 1888, thousands of Union and Confederate veterans gathered together to commemorate the twenty-fifth an-

Figure 4. Union and Confederate Soldiers Defend Cuba
Credit: Fritz Guerin, Library of Congress

niversary of the battle of Gettysburg. When the Supreme Court decided in 1890 to uphold a Mississippi statute that demanded segregation on intrastate transportation and then reasserted this position in the notorious Plessy v. Ferguson decision (1896), the highest court in the land affirmed the way the white North and the white South had embraced the spirit of reunion. By the end of the century, white Americans were ready to hear President McKinley claim, "Sectional feeling no longer holds back the love we bear each other. Fraternity is the national anthem, sung by a chorus of 45 states and our Territories at home and beyond the seas" (158). Indeed, the spirit of sectional reunion proved so strong during the

Spanish-American War and its aftermath that prominent anti-imperialists found themselves at a loss. Unwilling to admit that imperialism could produce national cohesion, they insisted instead that, in the words of Stanford University president David Starr Jordan, "our present solidarity shows that the nation was sound already, else a month could not have welded it together."[4]

The success of such fin-de-siècle fantasies depended greatly on the fact that many white northerners had come to see the white South in a new light, abandoning the Reconstruction-era image of an occupied and shamed Dixie for a new vision of a defiantly Anglo-Saxon and proudly traditional American southland.[5] As is so often the case in U.S. history, the problem of alterity *above* the Mason-Dixon line helped inspire northern appreciation of southern racism. White northerners always had shared white southern racial attitudes far more than they were willing to admit, but massive southern and eastern European immigration at home and new encounters with people of color abroad at the end of the century made New Yorkers and Bostonians, for example, more sympathetic to Dixie.[6] The consequences of this anxious affirmation of white superiority were enormous indeed, particularly for African Americans in the South. When white northerners found themselves confronting what Lothrop Stoddard would later dub "the rising tide of color," they not only celebrated the supposed virtues of whiteness as loudly as possible, but also accelerated the process of abandoning their black fellow citizens to the cruelty of the Jim Crow regime.[7] Vestigial Reconstruction lost many of its remaining white supporters, and abolitionism became for most a dim memory.[8] White sectional rapprochement may have gained new traction in the imperial arena, as McKinley's rhetoric well suggests, but the northern decision to jettison the African American cause proved just as central to fantasies of a newly unified and increasingly rapacious nation. Or, as Howard Clapp, the racist white New Englander in Pauline Hopkins's *Contending Forces* (1900), claims in a typically jingoistic moment, "For the loyal white man there would be no greater joy in life than to see his poetic dream of superiority to all other governments realized. . . . He knows that this can never be while the Negro question keeps up the line of demarcation which marks the division of the North from the South."[9]

Of course, as the more historically informed Americans of the fin de siècle were aware, the nation often had dealt with social and political problems by turning to geographic expansion. So long as the United States had an open space into which it could expand, this fantasy went, all forms of discord, sectional and racial included, might be, if not resolved, ignored. The West would provide a sort of dumping ground–cum–utopian dream space to which those unhappy with civilization could turn. The official claim in the 1890 census that the frontier was closed seemed to signal the end of this quintessentially American myth; with the disappearance of an open continent came the elimination of the nation's geographic safety valve.[10] Yet the decision to pursue a new global empire changed this depressing conclusion forever.[11] Overseas expansion provided Americans with a way of extending the logic of the frontier into the new century, particularly with respect to the vexed problems of racial and sectional animosity. Demonstrating the international power of the nation and eliminating the divisive "Negro question" were mutually constitutive goals. Instead of creating new problems, as the anti-imperialists claimed, the conquest of distant lands would provide the nation with a new frontier where a unified and powerful (white) nation would be reborn.

For all the widespread appeal of imperial reunion, however, two of the populations most profoundly concerned with the legacy of the Civil War responded in a more guarded manner to the president's oratory.[12] Unlike McKinley and his allies, many African Americans and white southerners tended to resist the notion that expansion would somehow bond whites in the two sections and render the problem of the color line a thing of the past. And with good reason: these populations remembered all too well that the nation's expansion into the western portion of the continent during the antebellum years hadn't so much resolved as intensified the slavery question. Rather than inspire a desire for unity, imperialism could highlight, even exacerbate, the nation's persistent social problems. Few intellectuals of the era proved more sensitive to this dynamic than Thomas Dixon and Charles Chesnutt, two men of letters who intervened publicly in debates about the relationship between domestic racial politics and U.S. imperial expansion.[13] However opposed politically, one a white supremacist, the other a black integrationist, both intellectuals hoped to forge a special relationship with Republican Washington on behalf of their respective communities.[14] Dixon attempted to exploit the GOP's new spirit of sectional reunion to the advantage of the white South, while Chesnutt sought to revive a largely moribund Republican concern for African Americans. Yet for all their desire to sway the federal state on behalf of competing political agendas, neither Dixon nor Chesnutt completely endorsed the new imperial vision of an imagined community promulgated by McKinley and his Republican cohort. Neither accepted at face value the idea that U.S. expansion would prove mutually constitutive with a successful reunion of white South and white North.[15]

These politically opposed intellectuals shared more than North Carolina ancestry and a connection to the GOP; they shared an awareness of how prominently the South figured in the contemporary culture of

THE PRESENT: TO THE STARS AND STRIPES DEWEY OPENED A NEW WORLD.

Figure 5. To the Stars and Stripes Dewey Opened a New World
Credit: Charles Nelan, *New York Herald*

U.S. imperialism, and they worked that view into what are arguably their most important literary and political interventions, *The Leopard's Spots* (1902) and *The Marrow of Tradition* (1901). Both novels contend that a new unified nation, one intent on claiming the future as its own, would emerge not only through a new frontier, a third space physically distant from the domestic problem of the color line, but also through a new appreciation of the southland that would, in turn, teach the nation about the political ramifications of a new global mission. The dominant politics and culture of the era might have recognized the need for a "new world," to borrow from the caption to a contemporary cartoon of Admiral Dewey, in which the white nation could reunite and make itself anew (Figure 5). But Dixon and Chesnutt insisted in their respective ways that the U.S. South could provide the crucial space needed as the nation attempted to expand into a global power—a site where, contrary to stereotype, extraordinary manifestations of union were readily available as examples for the entire nation.

Needless to say, Dixon and Chesnutt had very different notions of how the fin-de-siècle South represents unity in the imperial frame, and their differences emanated not only from matters of race, as one would expect, but also from issues of gender and sexuality. Although President McKinley imagined imperial reunion in exclusively fraternal terms, both Dixon and Chesnutt seize on the question of the biological reproduction of the nation and use that question to redefine the South as pivotal to the American future.[16] In *The Leopard's Spots*, Dixon argues that the white southern man's wisdom in combating the terrible prospect of the black rapist and the defiled white woman shores up the importance of Dixie as a bulwark of white fraternal ideology. In triumphing over the divisions inflicted upon them by a violent North and its black allies, white southern men provided their white compatriots with an indispensable lesson in the importance of Anglo-Saxon male community—a lesson capable of sustaining the nation as it entered new global arenas.[17] For all Dixon's fear of interracial procreation, the white woman and her reproductive capacities are in the end most valuable to the author of *The Leopard's Spots* as a pretext for the creation of a new political geography. In his view, the South will help the nation sustain its racial values in imperial modernity by demonstrating how one can transform the vulnerability of white woman into the raison d'être for local and national manhood.[18]

Chesnutt, conversely, rejects the idea that biological reproduction might serve as little more than the justification of white imperial fraternity and pays far more attention to issues of maternity and family. The miscegenation that Dixon fears is for Chesnutt a longstanding and indeed unavoidable process of amalgamation that may make the nation strong. As Chesnutt contends in his essay "The Future American" and in *The Marrow of Tradition*, it is the prevalence of amalgamated people that renders the contemporary South exemplary as the nation aspires to imperial power. Inasmuch as U.S. expansion into foreign communities of color necessarily increases the chance of interracial union, the current vogue for empire may not so much bolster white unity as compromise the very fiction of white identity, thus making possible an eventual reevaluation of the southland's many mixed-race people. At his most hopeful, Chesnutt imagines that empire will inadvertently undermine discourses of racial purity and create the conditions for true national reunion across the sectional and the color lines. If Dixon finds in the small-town southern square and the rural southern county his exemplum for a distinctly American modernity, Chesnutt locates his southern pedagogy in the mixed race bloodline that will in his estimation survive centuries after whiteness has disappeared. While Dixon celebrates white fraternity, Chesnutt emphasizes amalgamated family. In both cases, however, the future consequences of U.S. empire cannot be fully comprehended without heeding the example of a region where, as Chesnutt puts it, "life . . . is like no other life under the sun."[19]

The White Southerner's Burden

As Eric Love, Walter Benn Michaels, and other scholars have argued, Republican expansionist policies hardly received an unqualified endorsement from the white South.[20] For most white residents of the former Confederate states, the Republicans still represented a hated political force that had engineered the defeat, occupation, and colonization of their region, destroying the sovereignty of their beloved southland in the name of northern capital and African American rights. The latter issue would prove pivotal, for some white southerners objected to the McKinley administration's expansionist designs by claiming that the Republicans were once again leading the nation into a racial morass, particularly when it came to the question of annexing the Philippines.[21] White northern anti-imperialists also feared the incorporation of new people of color into the body politic, but white southerners were particularly concerned with this issue given their longstanding anxieties over maintaining white supremacy in the region.[22] Mrs. Jefferson Davis worried publicly about the wisdom of allowing "fresh millions of foreign negroes" into the nation. South Carolina senator Ben Tillman would make a similar point on the floor of the U.S. Senate, arguing in February 1899 that as a white southerner he knew full well the folly of attempting to bring civilization to the "darker" races. Or, as he put it, "Why do we as a people want to incorporate into our citizenship ten millions more of different or of differing races?"[23] Nineteen of twenty-eight southern senators voted against the bill that would have annexed the Philippines because they feared the capacity of the Republicans to manage populations of color.[24] For these white southerners, the very idea of U.S. expansion into the Caribbean and the Pacific suggested nothing so much as the domineering ways of an affluent North indifferent to the seriousness of the black question—to, that is, what they saw as the real and immediate threat of an inferior race's presence within the nation's borders.

Yet even as many white southerners feared the GOP's lack of racial savvy at home and abroad, they also understood the close relationship of U.S. expansion to the Jim Crow regime. If northern aggression rendered white southerners de facto colonial subjects in their own nation, U.S. imperialism recognized white southerners as important members of an all-conquering Anglo-Saxon force destined to rule the world.[25] Empire had its racial rewards. Thus even as important white southerners resisted McKinley's plans, many others, in the words of C. Vann Woodward, "responded to . . . the upsurge of martial spirit and put aside sectional grievances."[26] Ultimately, southerners found appealing the president's vision of a world in which the United States treated the territory and markets of people of color as their own. The South might affirm anti-imperialist sentiments when its own interests were at stake, but it knew full well where the white man's profits lay.

Of all the white intellectuals of the era, no one understood better than Thomas Dixon that white southerners wanted both to claim a part of the nation's imperial success and to accuse the North of colonization—both to revel in Anglo-Saxon triumphalism and to indulge in white sectional ressentiment.[27] And no one grasped more completely than Dixon that such a complex response to the new imperialism placed the white South in a potentially advantageous political position at the beginning of the modern era. Born in 1864, in the rural Piedmont area of North Carolina, Dixon experienced firsthand the poverty, hunger, and violence of Reconstruction and early in life learned to resent the power of the North. A patriotic white southerner who "had long felt that the South was misunderstood and maligned," Dixon was passionate enough about his embattled region that at the age of twenty-three he stood up in a Boston church and castigated a minister preaching about "the southern problem."[28] Indeed, his thorough identification with the community of his birth may be the most consistent thing about him during a period in which he changed careers on an almost annual basis, switching from actor to politician to lawyer to reverend during the 1880s alone. Yet Dixon was also an opportunist of the first order and his longstanding dislike for Yankee colonization did not stop him from accepting lucrative ministerial posts in the North and adopting a new and largely Republican circle of friends and acquaintances. Dixon took a job first in Massachusetts, and then in New York, where he earned a reputation as an extraordinary preacher and attracted the attention of such prominent figures as John D. Rockefeller and Theodore Roosevelt. His willingness to leave the region of his youth paid off handsomely indeed; by the early 1890s, Dixon was making twenty thousand dollars a year, an enormous salary for the time, and had raised over half a million dollars in an abortive attempt to build the biggest Baptist church in Manhattan.

In 1895, Dixon resigned his Baptist pulpit to begin his own non-denominational Church of the People, a change that enabled the already outspoken minister to lecture even more forcefully on the major social and political issues of the day. Dixon promoted a number of Progressive causes, denounced the Democratic candidacy of William Jennings

Bryan, and, most important for our purposes, celebrated the cause of Cuban liberation. Any New York parishioner who saw the Reverend Dixon condemn the perfidy of Spain on a stage decorated with Cuban and American flags in 1896 would hardly have been surprised to find him applauding the U.S. decision to invade the Caribbean island two years later.[29] During the Spanish-American War, Dixon proved an ardent expansionist, celebrating U.S. military victories and affirming the virtues of a powerful U.S. presence around the world. His published sermons from the era suggest as much. In "The Mightiest Navy in the World," Dixon cites U.S. expansionism as a brilliant example of American democracy: "This empire of the common people is something absolutely new and unique in the history of the world"—a point reiterated in "The Battle Cry of Freedom," where he claims that U.S. victories against the Spanish constitute nothing less than "the birth pangs of a new giant nation."[30]

Indeed, Dixon identified so strongly with U.S. expansion and its largely Republican advocates that while indisputably racist, his fin-de-siècle sermons suggest little or no resentment over the war and Reconstruction, both GOP enterprises. His white racism was, as we shall see, ideologically mobile, capable of addressing both local and national populist imperatives. When Dixon invoked the mid-century conflagration or sectional discord in his sermons, he sometimes argued, "the war between the States was fought for the simple reason that in her madness the South seceded and fired on the flag of the Republic" ("A Friendly Warning to the Negro" [116]). But more typically, he reminded his auditors of how the tragic conflict ended with Lee gallantly surrendering for the good of the nation ("The Battle Cry of Freedom" [5]); or claimed in a McKinley-like manner that, despite the suffering of the 1860s, both sides now fought together under one flag and saw each other as brothers: "From the graves of the country's dead, from the earth baptized in blood, rose the new nation to its new life—to solidarity, nationality, fraternity" ("The New Thanksgiving Day," [51]). Little wonder, then, that Dixon applauded the nation's chief executive as a hero who managed to reunite the nation. "Under McKinley's generous spirit the crisis of the war ended forever the bitterness of sectionalism," argued Dixon, and would go on in the same sermon to claim that the president "honored the ex-confederate with high command along side the union veteran. He grasped the extended hand of the new and loyal South with perfect faith" (75). McKinley and his allies could hardly have asked for a more ardent white southern supporter.

But precisely because he was a white southerner who recognized the linked regional and national meanings of empire, Dixon's passion for expansion led him to rediscover the sectional ressentiment of his youth—not as a reason to jettison his belief in U.S. expansion but rather as a justification for building that empire around an impregnable core of domestic white unity. For Dixon, we may imagine, a heartfelt identification with Republican expansion demanded that he share with the nation all of the valuable lessons about race, space, and power gleaned painfully from years of white subaltern status in those insular possessions known as the U.S. South. The growing power of U.S. Anglo-Saxonism at the fin de siècle inspired him to recall the virtues of southern experience as an important source of wisdom for white Americans eager to take up "the white man's burden," the line from the famous Rudyard Kipling poem that subtitles his first novel. To critique the Republicans of old was not to undercut their new plans for an American imperium, but rather to ensure that their inheritors recognized how important the nineteenth-century trials of the white South were to any vision of national expansion.[31]

Given Dixon's insistence that the imperial designs of U.S. Anglo-Saxonism necessitated a recovery and revaluation of regional Anglo-Saxonism, it is all too fitting that *The Leopard's Spots* both celebrates recent U.S. victories in the Caribbean and the Pacific and warns white Americans that these impressive conquests hardly guarantee a bright future for the white nation.[32] "Almost every problem of national life had been illumined and made more hopeful by the searchlight of war save one," the narrator argues, "the irrepressible conflict between the African and the Anglo-Saxon in the development of our civilization."[33] The ease with which Dixon had asserted the capacity of U.S. imperialism to stimulate a rebirth of the white nation in his sermons gives way in *The Leopard's Spots* to the claim that military victory alone cannot ensure a white racial future for the rising nation.[34] Only a complete repudiation of Reconstruction can accomplish that. And to dispel the vestiges of Reconstruction demands that the white nation confront the ugly events of that era as directly as possible, a task to which Dixon dedicated his first major literary effort.

For those seeking a white supremacist text imbued with southern ressentiment, *The Leopard's Spots* does not disappoint.[35] From the moment early in the novel when young Charlie Gaston, the novel's quasi-autobiographical hero, receives his dead Confederate's father's sword to the late scene in which he mounts the rostrum at the North Carolina Democratic convention to announce the birth of a new white nation, the novel chronicles the many horrors inflicted upon the white South by Radical Republicans and the carpetbaggers, scalawags, and upstart African Americans who followed in their wake. And it does so with all the melodrama it can muster, even going so far as to appropriate famous characters from *Uncle Tom's Cabin* in an effort to outdo Stowe at her own affective game.[36] Yet what renders *The Leopard's Spots* significant for my purposes is not its racist transformation of a sentimental classic—as interesting as that transformation is—but rather its extraordinary interest in the making and unmaking of the political geography of race. *The Leopard's Spots* offers the reader an extremely offensive, aesthetically confused, but nonetheless important disquisition on how the emergence of a powerful new America depends in large part on the white southern male capacity to remake local space under adverse circumstances. At once registering and complicating President McKinley's affirmation of reunion through expansion, Dixon emphasizes how Reconstruction destroyed the South and how white southern men have through fraternal bonding managed to redeem it. That Dixon's deep investment in territory demands an intense sensitivity to the interrelationship of spatial scales is one of the most surprising aspects of his novel; that this sensitivity in the end only contributes to a vicious affirmation of white southern racism reminds us that geography always should be read as a discourse of power.

While Dixon indulges in the usual modes of white southern ressentiment, he also takes pains to depict Reconstruction as the unmaking of white southern space in the name of black rights or, as the Preacher, the novel's main ideologue, puts it, as an attempt "to blot the Southern states from the map of the world" (96). In the "historical note" which inaugurates the narrative, Dixon invokes the fictional setting of Hambright, North Carolina, and writes, "the village is my birthplace, and is located near the center of 'Military District No. 2', comprising the Carolinas, which were destroyed as States by an Act of Congress in 1867." What was a North Carolina village of U.S. citizens becomes, by federal fiat, part of a redefined and occupied district. The Carolinas are forcibly consolidated into one colonized territory dominated by northern arms. Dixon's account continues to emphasize how the government's destruction of the Carolinas becomes, in turn, its unmaking of the white public space in the town of Hambright. Crowded with "vagrant negroes," the town's public places prove hostile to white southerners; in one telling scene, the Preacher finds himself stepping aside for "a burly negro on the sidewalk, dressed in an old federal uniform" (33).[37] And the destruction of the southern urban sphere gives way to something far more terrifying: the federally sanctioned unmaking of the southern home. Dixon emphasizes how Reconstruction licensed white northern carpetbaggers and their African American allies to invade, despoil, and appropriate southern domestic spaces. Thus black Republican Tim Shelby becomes the owner of "farm after farm and home after home" when the white owners are unable to pay the exorbitant new property taxes" (134). Old Tom, an elderly Confederate veteran of modest means, suffers this fate, as does Charlie Gaston, our younger and more well-born hero (133, 139).

Dixon elaborates on the destruction of these different white southern locales to dramatize for the reader how Reconstruction left virtually no aspect of antebellum white southern life untouched. Yet if these varied scales—region, state, town, home—all suffer the colonial violence of an interracial Republican invasion, their reterritorialization proves most important as a sign of the northern assault on the most vital and vulnerable scale of southern life, that of the body and the white female body in particular.[38] Dixon emphasizes that any assault on the white woman endangers the entire white southland. While the narrator suggests that the white South can endure the destruction of its states, towns, and homes, he also insists that it cannot tolerate the radical North's attempt to mandate mixed-race relations; for example, the case of a federal official in Charleston who "commanded intermarriage, and ordered the military to enforce the command at the point of the bayonet" (146). Suppressing the long history of white male assaults on black women, not to mention the large mixed-race population in the region, Dixon claims that the North has enabled the rise of the black male vagrant who poses a near-constant threat of rape and murder to white southern women. The North may view the white southern body as yet another spatial scale awaiting colonization, but to push the geography of domination to this register is to attempt a near-permanent occupation of territory. As the Preacher puts it, "this towering figure of the freed Negro had been growing more and more ominous, until its menace overshadowed the poverty, the hunger, the sorrow and the devastation of the South, throwing the blight of its shadow over future generations" (33). In forcing white women to endure the sexual attacks of black men, Dixon contends, the North has sought to corrupt the white South for the next hundred years, if not for all time. The resulting mixed-race people will only ensure that all of those once white southern spaces will remain blotted "from the map of the world"—the nefarious goal of mid-nineteenth-century Republican radicals.

Yet as Dixon insists throughout the novel, the white South hardly stands alone in its vulnerability before the menacing "freed Negro"; the entire nation confronts this threat, if only because the South has "enough Negro blood . . . to make mulatto the entire Republic" (244). The attack on the white southern body may eventually undermine the very possibility of a white nation. "This Republic can have no future if racial lines are broken, and its proud citizenship sinks to the level of a mongrel breed of Mulattoes," argues the Preacher (198). The colonial assault on the white southern woman becomes an assault on the white national body—the white southern body scaled up, if you will. Dixon's emphasis on this threat suggests a riposte, inadvertent or otherwise, to McKinley and the fin-de-siècle GOP. Dixon argues, after all, that regardless of imperial successes abroad, the danger of interracial *union* still threatens to eclipse the promise of sectional *reunion*. The conquest of foreign lands may have offered white southerners and northerners distant sites in which they may reunite, but it has not addressed the continuing capacity of southern blacks to unmake domestic spaces through the colonization of white blood and the production of mixed-race offspring. By allegedly advocating the black male colonization of the white southern woman, the radical Republicans of the 1860s and 1870s have set in motion a process that can potentially turn the entire nation into a mulatto community.[39] And as black Republican Tim Shelby's desire to turn "this mighty South" into "a more glorious San Domingo" suggests, this possibility carries with it a potent historical irony (93). If pushed to the extreme, the legacy of the radical Republican agenda raises the possibility that the United States, the rising Anglo-Saxon power of the fin de siècle, might eventually end up resembling the very hybrid Caribbean islands it seeks to control. Rather than conquering the miscegenated lands south of its border, the United States may come to join them.[40]

To suppress this threat, Dixon argues, the white woman must be defended from potential black male rapists at all costs—an imperative that licenses white racist violence of the most lethal and gruesome kind. Yet the white southern responsibility to guard against regional and national miscegenation, against what Charles Chesnutt would approvingly describe as an "amalgamated" "future American," has another social consequence as well. The need for a strong racial prophylaxis leads not only to various attempts to protect white women and kill black men, but also to a new sense of community among white males across North Carolina and the South. For all of Dixon's predictable racist concern over the defense of the white woman he is, in fact, no more worried about protecting her from black male attackers than he is fascinated by how this threat can generate powerful new bonds among white southern men. The radical Republicans may have endangered the white racial future through their Reconstruction policies, but it is precisely that threat of miscegenation that galvanizes defeated and divided white southern males into a new community capable of overcoming the many losses of the war and its aftermath. Dixon's response to the unmaking of southern space, in other words, isn't so much a celebration of the pure procreative capacities of white southern women—their ability to regenerate a community through reproduction—as it a celebration of how white southern men can recreate a virile South by banding together against the possibility of an attack on their racial future.

That the alleged black rapist and his potential white female victim serve as the inadvertent means of generating white male community becomes evident at several points in *The Leopard's Spots*. Consider, for example, how the narrator describes the white male reaction to the disappearance of Flora, a poor white girl who has just been seen talking to Dick, a local black man: "A great fear brooded over the hearts of the crowd, and soon the tumult was hushed into an awed silence. . . . In a moment the white race had fused into a homogeneous mass of love, sympathy, hate and revenge. The rich and the poor, the learned and the ignorant, the banker and the blacksmith, the great and the small, they were all one now" (372). The creation of this "homogeneous mass" results from a tragedy—Flora is indeed dead, raped and murdered by Dick—but the potential for white male southern community has grown enormously. As Amy Kaplan has argued, this passage suggests that inequalities of class and status—rich versus poor, learned versus ignorant—no longer matter with the emergence of this new homogeneous mass.[41] Dixon's novel offers us a classic example of how, in Dana Nelson's words, "calls to fraternity . . . rely on images that invoke relations not of male-male sameness, but male-female difference, and relations between men that function in turn to differentiate men."[42] The discourse of white southern brotherhood emerges through a capacity to invoke and exploit the linked alterities of the white woman and the black man.

That the black threat to white womanhood can underwrite a new white male fraternity also matters in relation to the traumatic memories of the Civil War. In another scene, Dixon takes pains to emphasize how the Ku Klux Klan appears in rural North Carolina as a response to a potential rape and in the process manages to reconnect white southern men long separated by their differences over the recent military conflict. When Judge Rivers dismisses a case against thousands of alleged Klansmen, releasing them from the local jail, the result is not retribution or recrimination, but a resonant affirmation of unity:

> When these prisoners were discharged, a great mass-meeting was called to give them a reception in the public square of Independence. . . . *Every discordant element of the old South's furious political passions was now melted into harmonious unity.* Whig and Democrat who had fought one another with relentless hatred sat side by side on that platform. *Secessionist and Unionist now clasped hands.* It was a White Man's Party, and against it stood in solid array the Black Man's Party. . . .
>
> Henceforth there could be but one issue, are you a White Man or a Negro? They declared there was but one question to be settled:—"Shall the future American be an Anglo-Saxon or a Mulatto?" . . . *The state burst into a flame of excitement that fused in its white heat the whole Anglo-Saxon race.* (161–62, emphasis added)

The capacity of the white citizens of Independence to melt "into har-monious unity" and thus oppose the Black Man's Party extends beyond the confines of their immediate town and area. "The public square of In-dependence" transmutes into the surrounding county, which, in turn, changes into the entire (white) state of North Carolina. Like wildfire, white male unity jumps up spatial scales. A small local rebellion has the capacity to inform far greater white solidarity, the prospect of a unified "whole Anglo-Saxon race." Passion no longer leads to biological repro-duction with all its attendant worries about miscegenation but instead to a "*white* heat" that fuses together the Anglo-Saxon race in a fantasy of exclusively male political reproduction (162, emphasis added). The reclaiming of public space (e.g., the small-town square) attests to the ca-pacity of white southern men to generate a new geography and the polity it demands.

In emphasizing the capacity of white southern men to confront that most "dire" of threats, racial death, and emerge a unified fraternal com-munity, Dixon makes his case for regional exceptionalism. In this argu-ment, the South is a place where terrible white suffering and loss lead not to recrimination and division but to a greater strengthening of white unity and power. To borrow from Sandra Gunning, "the national site of racial conflict and white suffering . . . would be the site of national white healing."[43] The South, in other words, already has accomplished on a regional scale the national reunion President McKinley identifies as a consequence of the imperial project. One hardly needs to move to an ex-tra-national arena to find a site where white men could assert their be-lief in white fraternity and white solidarity; such a space can be found in the domestic South itself. If the South was, in Michael Rogin's phrase, "not a defeated part of the American past, but a prophecy of its future," for Dixon that transformation stems from an unrivaled white southern capacity to represent the national ideal of fragments shored against their ruin even as the United States takes on new territories and new peoples that further tax the imagined community.[44] Those who worry about the effect of annexing the Philippines have no appreciation of how the white South can anchor the nation in its new imperial phase.

Yet if the white South is supposed to stand as a political exemplum for the nation because it recreates itself as white and whole in the face of overwhelming forces to the contrary, the specter of the white south-ern mob raises an alternate possibility: that "the homogeneous mass" of white southern men won't so much provide the example for a new white imagined community as revitalize the aging northern stereotype of the white South as monstrous and degenerate. Dixon already had be-gun to make this case in his sermon "A Friendly Warning to the Negro" (1899) where for all his criticism of "Negro agitators" in Wilmington,

North Carolina, he also argued that "no rational man can justify mobs or mob violence" and described Senator Ben Tillman as "a freak" for endorsing lynching (118; 112; 117). Dixon pushes this point even further in *The Leopard's Spots* by having Charlie Gaston observe how the "homogeneous mass" of white southerners cited above can within hours change into a terrifying lynch mob. Arguing unsuccessfully that burning a man alive will "disgrace" the "town . . . county, and . . . state," Gaston watches in horror as the group of white men before him "melt[s] into a great crawling, swaying creature, half reptile, half beast, half dragon, half man, with a thousand legs, and a thousand eyes, and ten thousand gleaming teeth, and with no ear to hear and no heart to pity" (383–84). The men's refusal to accede to the imperatives of civilization takes physical shape as a creature whose multiple halves—reptile, beast, dragon, man—defy normal cognition. A violation of categories, a conglomeration of excess, the white southern mob is nothing if not an abject sign of degeneration.

Instead of demonstrating how white southern men can respond to the threat of the black rapist in a lethal but orderly manner, the lynch mob suggests instead the eruption of chaos and savagery. Or, as Robyn Wiegman puts it in her discussion of Ben Tillman's pro-lynching discourse, "a racialized opposition between civilization and primitivity . . . significantly breaks down, in the face of the black brute, as the white man loses his civilized veneer."[45] The terrifying thousand-legged and thousand-eyed creature cannot reclaim the public square of Independence in a civilized manner that generates local and national respect. To the contrary, this ghastly form of white southern abjection sullies the reputation of the town, county, and state. "The lynching at Hambright . . . stirred the whole nation into unusual indignant interest," states the narrator (385). Even as Dixon defends the white southern vogue for vigilante justice, that is, he also insists that the grotesque nature of white lynching will not so much ensure a white racial future as undermine the fragile reputation of white southern civilization and thus destroy the possibility of a new connection between Dixie and Republican Washington. Indeed, the publicity surrounding such violence might have the potential to reunite African Americans with their erstwhile Northern protectors. Whatever it might accomplish in the short term, the spectacle of bestial mob murder is less likely to ensure the birth of a strong white community than undo the white South's gains at the national level.[46]

Needless to say, Dixon hardly shared the opinion of anti-lynching activists such as Ida B. Wells that white mob murder in the region demands a new federally mandated and well-armed "civilizing mission" from without. As Gunning has noted, Dixon supports the oxymoronic notion of a civilized (and civilizing) Ku Klux Klan as a solution to the problem of white southern savagery.[47] Yet the Klan makes only a brief appearance in *The Leopard's Spots;* in this novel, it is the nation-state that plays the role of much-needed disciplinary regime.[48] The nation-state may not yet fully appreciate the white South's racial and geographic wisdom, but it does have a keener sense than many working-class white southerners of the larger issues at stake in local incidences of racial crisis. To guard against the possibility of white degeneration and advance his region's interests, in other words, Dixon emphasizes the importance of white southerners taking the lessons of the state to heart.[49] The white southern woman must be defended, but in a way that doesn't limit the white South's potential to defend future white southern women more successfully still. The only way to create a New South is to attend to the national and global scales, a project that necessarily involves a new identification with the federal state and its rapacious militarism. If, as Gaston explains to General Worth, a fellow white southerner, "the State is now the only organ through which the whole people can search for righteousness," that faith in Washington has less to do with federal domestic policy than it does with the fact that the State has, in its imperial mission, provided a new opportunity for white southern men to unite with their white brethren in other sections (284). Dixon makes much the same point in his sermon "The Nation's Call," when he argues, "The Nation is the only possible center of the organization of the people's faith and energy. We dream of solidarity and social unity. Here alone we approach the realization of that dream" (32). The fin de siècle, the moment of Santiago and Manila, offers the white South the occasion to rewrite Reconstruction history as part of the nation-state's expansionist designs.

In a chapter entitled "The New America," Dixon first has his narrator explain that the war with Spain united Catholic and Protestant, rich and poor, and, most important, North and South (409–10). But this McKinley-like argument serves only as a prelude to a larger claim about the South's unique position in the conflict and the rise of U.S. power:

> From the James to the Rio Grande the children of the Confederacy rushed with eager, flushed faces to defend the flag their fathers had once fought.
>
> And God reserved in this hour for the South, land of ashes and tombs and tears, the pain and the glory of the first offering of life on the altar of the new nation. Our first and only officer who fell dead on the deck of a warship, with the flag above him, was Worth Bagley, of North Carolina, son of a Confederate soldier. (410–11)

McKinley and the Republican expansionists had suggested that new military conquests enabled white sectional reunion. Dixon implies instead that the regional suffering of "a land of ashes and tears and tombs" takes on new national meaning through the contemporary white southern sacrifice during the Cuban campaign. The triumphs in Cuba and the Philippines inspire thoughts of sectional reunion, in other words, because they provide a place where the wounded or dead white southern male (but neither the white southern woman nor, needless to say, the black southerner, male or female) can serve as a retroactive signifier of all the region has endured over the past thirty-odd years. Thanks to the sacrifices of such men as Ensign Worth Bagley, the only U.S. naval officer to die in the Spanish-American War and an object of regional *and* national mourning, the fin-de-siècle conflict offers white southerners an opportunity to celebrate their resilient unity in a manner that affirms white supremacy without slipping into white monstrosity.[50]

Dixon, that is, intends to preserve his southern localism and lay claim to an exceptional role in the nation's imperial design at the same time. Indeed, he argues that because the white South has suffered and recovered, because the South knows the value of defending a mythic whiteness against all odds, this regional culture will provide a reliable cornerstone of "Americanness" for the nation moving into a new globalized modernity. As the Preacher explains to a Boston deacon, "Against the possible day when a flood of foreign anarchy threatens the foundations of the Republic and men shall laugh at the faiths of your fathers . . . until it mocks at honour, love and God—against that day we will preserve the South" (337). To make this case, however, Dixon feels compelled to reassure white northerners that the notion of a southern heart of the U.S. empire does not signal a revival of white southern aggression. Toward the end of the novel, he has Charles Gaston deliver a speech at the North Carolina Democratic convention that speaks forcefully to this concern by sharply differentiating between the ambitions of the old South and those of the new: "The Old South fought against . . . the resistless tides of the rising consciousness of Nationality and World-Mission. . . . He joins his voice in the cheers of triumph which are ushering in this all-conquering Saxon. Our old men dreamed of local supremacy. We dream of the conquest of the globe" (439). The "old men" of the South are, in Gaston's view, mistaken both to have fought against "the rising consciousness of Nationality and World-Mission" and to have invested so passionately in "local supremacy"; for Gaston, as, we may assume, for his creator, this error suggests the political limitations of these venerable southern leaders. To dream of white supremacy in exclusively local terms creates the conditions for the sort of defeat and disorganization endured by the white South at the hands of the North. Moreover, an overemphasis on the local may lead to precisely that sort of white southern internal collapse vivified by the lynch mob monster.[51]

Following the indictment of the southern "old men" and their obsession with local supremacy, Gaston reaches a new height in using the contemporary debates over the annexation of the Philippines to justify white supremacy, old and new:

> In this hour of crisis, our flag has been raised over ten millions of semi-barbaric black men in the foulest slave pen of the Orient. Shall we repeat the farce of '67, reverse the order of nature, and make these black people our rulers? If not, why should the African here, who is not their equal, be allowed to imperil our life? (439)

Rendering the imperialism debate an opportunity for a freewheeling engagement with historical, geographic, and racial difference, Gaston suggests that to relinquish control over the newly conquered archipelago is somehow to sanction once more the crime committed by the Republicans during Reconstruction: that of allowing black to rule over white.[52] The islands may lie some four thousand miles away from the continental United States, but to abandon them to "semi-barbaric black men" would be to undermine white American autonomy. What renders this contemporary failure of imperial nerve a retroactive signifier of Reconstruction is, needless to say, Dixon's assumption that Filipinos and African Americans are both inferior to whites, even if the former are in his racist estimation somewhat more civilized than the latter. That color links the two subaltern peoples suggests to Dixon that the fin-de-siècle debate over annexing the Philippines might have the potential to revive white northern concern for African Americans in the domestic southland—a possibility he finds profoundly worrisome.[53] (Mark Twain's contemporary interest in drawing a mutually complimentary comparison between Filipino leader Emile Aguinaldo and a rebellious African American suggests that Dixon's anxieties were hardly misplaced.) For the author of *The Leopard's Spots*, all white southerners, indeed all white Americans, must recognize such attempts to manipulate race, space, and history in the Philippines debate, and respond accordingly. To ignore the potential connections between the U.S. South and the Pacific archipelago, between African Americans and Filipinos, between Reconstruction and empire, was to limit the future potential of their beloved nation. Implicitly lumping southern anti-imperialists such as Ben Tillman and Mrs. Jefferson Davis with the older generation whose geographic imagination was limited by a shortsighted parochialism, Dixon advocates a new spatial and historical flexibility on the part of white southerners and their northern brethren. If white America was to benefit from the Republicans' turn to Anglo-Saxon imperialism, it had to recognize that the South was a community whose fabled valuation of local whiteness paradoxically rendered it indispensable to a nation intent on claiming the colored world as its own.

Local Color in the Imperial Frame

Most African Americans responded to the advent of a new imperial sensibility with far more skepticism than whites, including white southerners. While prominent black intellectuals and activists supported the liberation of Cuba from the Spanish yoke—Ida B. Wells, for example, traveled to an Army camp to encourage black soldiers in training—the McKinley administration's subsequent decision to attack the Filipinos reminded African Americans that U.S. expansion was little more than Jim Crow performed on a Pacific stage.[54] Sensitive to the parallels between white violence against people of color abroad and at home, many prominent black intellectuals decried the new vogue for the white man's burden and demanded greater federal attention to the racial crisis in the southland. In the "Open Letter to President McKinley," for example, Archibald Grimke and a group of prominent black Bostonians, all Republican, indicted the Anglo-Saxonist priorities of the current administration: "We, sir, at this crisis and extremity in the life of our race in the South, and in this crisis and extremity of the republic as well, in the presence of the civilized world, cry to you to pause, if but for an hour, in pursuit of your national policy of 'criminal aggression' abroad to consider the 'criminal aggression' at home against humanity and American citizenship."[55] Grimke and his associates argued in effect that whatever the moral achievements of their mid-century predecessors, fin-de-siècle white Republicans had through expansion offered a tacit northern endorsement of white racist violence in the South. Their willingness to condemn President McKinley and the GOP was hardly unusual. From powerful critiques of southern lynching and impassioned attacks on imperial brutality, African Americans didn't shy away from criticizing the chief executive's red record. Challenging the president might produce no visible change in policy, but conscience allowed for no other course.

Or so it seemed. Other black Republican intellectuals, while equally disturbed by the GOP's passion for empire, adopted a less confrontational attitude toward their erstwhile white allies and sought instead to explore how contemporary geopolitics might augur a new future for African Americans. Charles Chesnutt was one such figure: an intellectual of longstanding Republican affiliation whose commitment to African American rights inspired him to consider how the McKinley administration's expansionism might produce unusual, indeed, surprising racial consequences.[56] Well aware of the intimate connections between U.S.

empire abroad and Jim Crow at home, intensely conscious of the arguments promulgated by Thomas Dixon and other white supremacists, Chesnutt nonetheless attempted the difficult task of imagining how the new desire to take up the white man's burden might undo or challenge hegemonic white identity. If most pro- and anti-imperialists of the era would likely find in McKinley expansionism a new means of shoring up whiteness, Chesnutt worked assiduously to consider the various ways in which imperialism might undermine the prevailing racial ideology and create the future possibility of new interracial connection. Unlike so many of his contemporaries, black and white, Chesnutt dared to hope that expansion might not so much shore up as eliminate whiteness, a possibility that suggested the birth of a very different nation indeed.

Born in Cleveland, Ohio, in 1858 of mixed-race southern parents, Chesnutt spent much of his childhood and early adulthood in Fayetteville, North Carolina, where he witnessed the steady elimination of African Americans rights as Reconstruction capitulated to Redemption. Unwilling to live under the emerging Jim Crow regime, Chesnutt returned to Cleveland in 1883 where, newly trained as a lawyer, he began a successful stenography firm. The business would provide him with a middle-class income from the mid-1880s until his death in 1932, but it also would offer him the means to craft a literary and political identity on the national stage at the turn of the century. A talented man with bourgeois security and some leisure time, Chesnutt began publishing local color fiction in the mid-1880s. His plantation tales of Uncle Julius soon won the admiration of major literary figures such as George Washington Cable and William Dean Howells, the latter including some of Chesnutt's work in the *Atlantic Monthly*. Middle-class readers proved equally susceptible to Chesnutt's charms, and the publication of *The Conjure Woman* (1899) made clear that dialect fiction, once a genre monopolized by such white writers as Joel Chandler Harris, now had a brilliant black practitioner. The appearance of *The Wife of His Youth and Other Stories* (1899) emphasized all the more that Chesnutt had the vision and skill to make an important contribution to the growing body of literature associated with the U.S. South.

Thanks to his new cultural capital, Chesnutt gained a public voice that he soon put to use commenting on matters both racial and imperial. By publishing such texts as the essay "The Future American" (1900) and the novel *The Marrow of Tradition* (1901) the writer attempted to reestablish the African American connection with the North. As Chesnutt put it in a contemporary letter to Booker T. Washington, *Marrow* could help "win back or help retain the popular sympathy of the Northern people."[57] In certain respects, both "The Future American" and *Mar-*

row do seem well suited to such a task. Evincing a notably calm and balanced approach to the race question, neither text condemns all white southerners and celebrates all African Americans. *Marrow* does point out that Republicans have forsaken African Americans in the southland, but it does so with a note of poignant regret that suggests that the break between the GOP and black America might still be bridged. Indeed, both works affirm interracial reunion and rapprochement far more than they promote confrontations of the kind evinced by the Grimke letter. But therein lies the strangeness of Chesnutt's interventions. For if "The Future American" and *Marrow* affirm the importance of interracial connection, they do so in a manner guaranteed to disturb the vast majority of southern and northern whites. These are, after all, both integrationist and amalgamationist texts. Chesnutt's works look toward the day when the various races of the region and the nation will come together into one composite bloodline. Indeed, as we shall see, Chesnutt found in the very products of interracial procreation so feared by Dixon a vision of a new and stronger America. This African American writer dreamed of more than resurgent white Republican support for black rights; he dreamed of a future nation in which race seemed no less outmoded than section.

That a very light-skinned African American might argue such a radical racial thesis isn't that surprising. The author of many works about miscegenation and mulattoes, Chesnutt, we may speculate, sought a nation, a world, in which his ambiguous position as "neither fish, flesh, nor fowl ... neither 'nigger,' white, nor 'buckrah'" no longer mattered.[58] Yet even as we acknowledge the biographical imperative driving Chesnutt's investment in amalgamation, we also must wonder how he imagined the idea might appeal to contemporary white readers, his main audience. Intermarriage, let alone reproduction, among people of different races seemed anathema to most whites during this era. Chesnutt's rhetorical burden proved particularly challenging in "The Future American," a text that hazards the inflammatory claim that amalgamation in the United States is "a foregone conclusion." While Chesnutt reassures his white readers that amalgamation will most likely result in a race that "will call itself white" and "will conform closely to the white type," he does not disguise the fact that this future citizen "will have absorbed and assimilated the blood of the other two races" (123). White she may appear, but the future American will bear a lineage of color. And while Chesnutt insists that the disappearance of racial difference would augur a new age of national achievement, he was no doubt canny enough to realize that the deferred promise of vague rewards would hardly pacify contemporary readers anxious over interracial procreation.

Yet even as Chesnutt could hardly rebut the claim offered by white southerner C. Alfonso Smith that "the author's panacea would seem to be intermarriage for the races," the African American writer sought to redefine the issue of amalgamation by rendering it a likely consequence of U.S. expansion.[59] Arguing that the domestic problem of the color line must be understood within the international frame, Chesnutt points out in "The Future American" that any contemporary predictions of future race relations would have to acknowledge the capacity of U.S. imperialism to transform hemispheric geography:

> The future American race—the future American ethnic type—will be formed of a mingling, in a yet to be ascertained proportion, of the various racial varieties which make up the present population of the United States; or, to extend the area a little farther, of the various peoples of the northern hemisphere of the western continent; for, if certain recent tendencies are an index of the future, it is not safe to fix the boundaries of the future United States anywhere short of the Arctic Ocean on the north and the Isthmus of Panama on the South.[60]

Frederick Wegener has argued that the euphemistic reference to "certain recent tendencies" suggests Chesnutt's anti-imperialism in muted form, but the entire passage in fact sidesteps the question of critique in order to address the racial implications of a changing hemisphere.[61] If these expansionist "tendencies are an index of the future," Chesnutt is willing to invoke that index in support of an amalgamationist thesis whatever his feelings about imperialism may be. He thus emphasizes how the nation's likely conquest of the hemisphere portends a new national geography that will produce a very different type of American:

> The adding to our territories of large areas populated by dark races, some of them liberally dowered with Negro blood, will enhance the relative importance of the non-Caucasian elements of the population, and largely increase the flow of dark blood to the white race, until the time shall come when distinctions of color shall lose their importance, which will be but the prelude to a complete racial fusion. (135)

Rather than claiming that empire would not add to the likelihood of race-mixing at home, the standard GOP position of the time, Chesnutt contends to the contrary that the addition of mixed-race peoples through U.S. imperialism would in fact result in the eventual elimination of the color line. As he puts it elsewhere in "The Future American," "If now and then, for a few generations, an occasional trace of the black ancestor should crop out, no one would care, for all would be tarred from the same stick" (125). Through expansion into the hemispheric

South, United States would follow the examples of "South America, parts of Mexico and . . . the West Indies" and eliminate "the elements of racial discord which troubled our civil life so gravely and still threaten our free institutions" (125). In Chesnutt's scenario, the United States comes to resemble some of the very hybrid nations and communities it has conquered. Dixon's fear that the South and the nation might turn into a second Santo Domingo becomes a reality not because mid-century Reconstruction had promoted interracial procreation, but because fin-de-siècle Republican expansion has initiated a process of absorbing millions of new people of color into the body politic.

To argue that empire would lead to increased interracial union was, as Chesnutt no doubt knew, an argument maintained by such anti-imperialist white southerners as Georgia senator Augustus Bacon and South Carolina senator Ben Tillman. For such figures, as we have seen, the amalgamated consequences of imperialism provided sufficient reason to abandon all thoughts of annexing foreign lands populated by the darker races. Chesnutt's bold and brilliant stroke is to wholeheartedly concur: not to shore up the power of racist southerners, needless to say, but to redirect their thesis toward a new democratic goal. Expansion will lead to amalgamation, he agrees, and all citizens should eagerly anticipate this result; "racial fusion" would eliminate the problem of the color line and enable the nation to move toward a bright future of unity and strength. President McKinley located in expansion the fruits of white sectional reunion; Chesnutt found in expansion the rewards of (eventual) black and white racial union.[62] The nation's imperialism foreshadowed the long-term demise of whiteness.

The Marrow of Tradition also explores how expansion might inadvertently destabilize whiteness and thus generate new political possibilities for African Americans, but in a far more complex manner, attending to both the destructive effects of domestic and imperial racism and the potentially benevolent future that might arise from a validation of interracial ties. *Marrow* takes as its historic touchstone the Wilmington, North Carolina, white riot of 1898—one of the most notorious racial conflagrations of the fin de siècle and an event built upon white hysteria over the perceived threat of the black rapist. The revolution, as it was known, resulted from the machinations of Alfred Moore Waddell and other local white supremacists who sought to "redeem" their town by purging it of Republicans and Fusion party members, many of them black. The white supremacist strategy was clever and brutal: by publicizing African American journalist Alexander Manly's courageous rebuttal of lynching discourse—a rebuttal that addressed the reality of *consensual* white female and black male relations—Moore and his co-

conspirators fomented the racist fears of white men and generated a mob that laid waste to the African American community.[63] White hysteria over interracial union led to a crime wave of murder and arson that for generations rendered Wilmington synonymous with white terrorism. Few riots of the era better illustrate the explicit connections between the discourse of the black rapist and the white monopolization of political power.

Eric Sundquist has argued persuasively that Chesnutt uses the riot and other manifestations of white racist brutality to demonstrate through his novel how the "national reunion" of North and South was "built upon an escalation of racial discrimination and violence."[64] Chesnutt makes evident how the white takeover of Wellington and the white American attempt to redefine the nation in Anglo-Saxonist terms nourished each other. If Dixon dramatizes how postbellum Republican administrations licensed the destruction of white southern spaces in their zeal to promote African American rights, Chesnutt depicts the converse situation, describing in detail how whites murder African Americans, old and young, burn black buildings, drive most black professionals from the town, and generally claim the right to reterritorialize Wellington in a manner that jibed with contemporary U.S. affirmations of white supremacy (274–322). Yet even as he attended carefully to the relationship between the South and the nation, Chesnutt also recognized that the appeal of white sectional reconciliation depended on the "escalation of racial discrimination and violence" in the global arena. It wasn't only that, as the narrator puts it, in "the North, a new Pharaoh had risen, who knew not Israel," but also that the rise of a new northern appetite for world empire rendered the defense of African American rights contrary to the white zeitgeist (238). "The nation was rushing forward with giant strides toward colossal wealth and world-dominion," explains the narrator of *Marrow.* "The same argument that justified the conquest of an inferior nation could not be denied to those who sought the suppression of an inferior race" (238). Chesnutt devotes the majority of his novel to a regional chronicle of how white southerners attempt to suppress the possibility of any meaningful connection to African Americans, but he also proves sensitive to how the northern appetite for expansion encourages such self-destructive beliefs—licensing the disenfranchisement and brutalization of African Americans in the same breath that it authorizes the invasion and occupation of the Filipino and Cuban communities. For this African American intellectual, the imperialist notion that "the white man was to inherit the earth and hold all other races under his heel" had much to do with the horrors of the Wilmington riot (244).

Major Carteret, General Belmont, and Captain McBane, the white supremacist leaders who provoke the urban violence in *Marrow*, variously demonstrate how the rise of Anglo-Saxon expansionism has informed their plans to make the "town fit to live in" (33). For Major Carteret, "schemes of empire" prove mutually constitutive with "dreams of his child's future" (141), while for General Belmont, the example of imperial Rome offers valuable lessons for white southerners eager to reclaim their power (182–83). Chesnutt makes particularly manifest the connection between local white supremacy and U.S. expansionism in the case of Captain McBane. The unlettered McBane doesn't comment on empire directly, but Chesnutt has him appear just as Dr. Miller, our black bourgeois hero, attempts to repress the indignities of a Jim Crow railway car by reading a newspaper editorial on "the inestimable advantages which would follow to certain recently acquired islands by the introduction of American liberty" (57). The entry of U.S. forces into Cuba and the Philippines discussed in Dr. Miller's newspaper appears in miniature as Captain McBane's entrance into an ostensibly African American conveyance. The space of domestic segregation proves mutually constitutive with—and no less vulnerable than—the space of colonialism. For Chesnutt, to comment on the diffusion of "American liberty" is to recall the bitter fact that contemporary whites have laid claim to virtually all places populated by people of color.

That such an ironic citation of "American liberty" questions the very idea of U.S. exceptionalism cannot be overstated. If Chesnutt had in "The Future American" attempted in loyalist fashion to find some silver lining in the GOP's new expansionism, he seems to abandon that quest here in favor of subdued but palpable opposition. He takes particular issue with the notion that white sectional unity would emerge over the broken bodies of the African American, the Cuban, and the Filipino, emphasizing in various ways throughout *Marrow* that such violence redounds to destructive effect in and among the white communities of the United States as well. As one white character puts it, "it is no longer safe to assume what white men will or will not do" (215). Rather than accept the turn-of-the-century argument that Anglo-Saxon fraternity constitutes civilization by another name, Chesnutt indicts the idea that desirable unity and order—"a promise of good things for the future"—can come from such white racist hatred and bloodletting (310). Toward that end, *Marrow* attempts to supplant the contemporary discourse of black degeneration with a discourse of white decline. Matthew Wilson has argued that *Marrow* offers ample evidence of white degeneracy—from the dissolute Tom to the sociopathic McBane to the mob that threatens to murder the innocent Sandy, a long-time servant of the aristocratic Mr. Delamere.[65] As that scion of the old ancestral order explains to Major Carteret, "I have lived to hear of white men, the most favored of races, the heirs of civilization, the conservators of liberty, howling like red Indians around a human being slowly roasting at the stake" (211). Delamere will reiterate this point a few paragraphs later when he claims that lynching turns "the whole white population into a mob of primitive savages"—an argument that Carteret himself will endorse when he declaims to the white mob attacking the African American hospital: "this is murder, it is madness, it is a disgrace to our city, to our state, to our civilization" (212; 305). Chesnutt has his most genteel white southern characters represent the lynch mob as a sign of all that is antithetical to civilization—a critique that renders absurd the notion that racist violence can generate any sort of meaningful sectional reunion, let alone an appealing prospect for the entire nation.

Chesnutt hardly devotes the same amount of attention to the degeneracy of the white imperialist that he does to the white lyncher, but his deft sketch of the Panama hat–wearing, vaguely Conradian General Belmont offers us a provocative glimpse of how empire may prove detrimental to rather than productive of a unified polity.[66] While Carteret and McBane seem to understand in a general sense the connection between Jim Crow and Anglo-Saxon imperialism, it is Belmont who links regional white supremacy and U.S. foreign policy. Invoking his service as a former "minister . . . under a Democratic Administration, to a small Central American state," Belmont argues that U.S. knowledge of "inferior" Latin American nations might be put to profitable use on a lower spatial scale:

> Down in the American tropics . . . they have a way of doing things. I was in Nicaragua, ten years ago, when Paterno's revolution drove out Igorroto's government. It was as easy as falling off a log. Paterno had the arms and the best men. Igorroto was not looking for trouble, and the guns were at his breast before he knew it. We have the guns. The negroes are not expecting trouble, and are easy to manage compared with the fiery mixture that flourishes in the tropics. (249)

Chesnutt engages in some creative license here; no such coup occurred in Nicaragua in the late 1880s, and Wilmington resident Alfred Moore Waddell, one of the main inspirations for General Belmont, had no experience south of the U.S. border.[67] Yet as Frederick Wegener has argued, Nicaragua is an appropriate example for Chesnutt, not only because of the long, tangled history of U.S. involvement in the nation, but also because, at the turn of the century, the McKinley administration viewed the Central American nation as a likely site for an isthmus canal.

In 1901, the same year *Marrow* was published, the First U.S. Isthmian Canal Commission recommended that such a waterway should be built in Nicaragua. Indeed, Chesnutt's invocation of Nicaragua seems more a comment on contemporary U.S. imperialism than an attempt to chronicle particular events in Central American history. Belmont is thus less interested in the specificity of intra-Nicaraguan violence than in what it can teach him about how to manage the darker races. He draws an implicit comparison between the "Negroes" with whom he and his fellow white supremacists must contend and the "fiery" Negroes of Nicaragua, suggesting that Paterno confronted a similar challenge from insurgents of color. And this parallel reverberates in other geographic spaces as well. In an intriguing twist, Chesnutt further emphasizes that Belmont finds in imperial practice a model for white southern racism by naming the deposed Nicaraguan leader Igorroto, a moniker that recalls the Igorot tribe then combating U.S. forces in the Philippines.[68] Belmont is aligned with the paternal (Paterno) leader of the coup while hemispheric people of color are linked to U.S. opponents thousands of miles away. Chesnutt blurs Central America and the Pacific Rim, Latino and Filipino, U.S. and hemispheric Americans, to reveal the disturbing entanglement of white southern racism and U.S. foreign policy. In this era of fluid and intersecting geographic formations, white racist violence in the South seems not so much antithetical to, as constitutive of, Washington policy toward people of color the world over.[69]

While no Wellington resident other than Belmont seems to understand the extent to which white supremacy in the South and U.S. expansionism inform one another, the ever-genteel Major Carteret does find his colleague's citation of Latin American violence somewhat unsettling. The Major is no less eager than Belmont to conquer the town, but the idea that a Nicaraguan coup might provide the model for a white supremacist "revolution" in a North Carolina city seems to him farfetched, if not outrageous. Carteret suggests as much when he worries openly about the bloodshed to which this sort of plan might lead: "I should not advocate murder. . . . We are animated by high and holy principles. We wish to right a wrong, to remedy an abuse, to save our state from anarchy and our race from humiliation" (250). Belmont tries to pacify him by claiming that "in Central and South America none are hurt except those who get in the way," a point that seems to refer implicitly to U.S. military aggression in the area, but Carteret's objection doesn't concern violence exclusively; it speaks to the geographic, political, and racial implications of treating a white southern insurrection as a Latin American coup—of suggesting, in other words, that the U.S. South shares certain qualities with an anarchic Latin American nation where "high and holy principles" have no purchase. One senses here

Carteret's repressed awareness that in attempting a white coup, he and his colleagues were not so much confirming their superiority to degenerate blacks as revealing themselves to be similar to the Latin Americans from whom they have borrowed their strategy.

Belmont manages to calm his colleague, and the Central American method carries the day. The African Americans of Wellington suffer a white revolution that employs strategies derived from U.S. experience south of the border. Yet Carteret's anxieties over being tainted by the Nicaraguan "way of doing things" are still significant for the reader, not only because the Major, like old Mr. Delamere, fears anything that smacks of the low and the profane, but also because any invocation of a "Central American or a South American state" necessarily recalls the fact that these fellow American polities have by and large accepted the idea of race-mixing. Belmont can look to Nicaragua for a model of "raced" revolution, but one suspects that both he and Carteret know that the Central American nation—like most Latin American communities, but unlike the U.S. South—is a place where "questions of color [are] not regarded as vitally important" (75). Belmont attempts to save Wellington "from anarchy" in a manner that inadvertently refers to the very interracial relations so dreaded by virtually all of the town's white citizens. The lessons of imperial violence cannot hide the fact that, to borrow from John Matthews, "hybridity . . . is the white South's unacknowledged history, not just its dreaded future."[70]

Yet Chesnutt is not content to demonstrate how white racist violence at home and abroad obstructs rather than promotes the future unity of the nation. His is not an obsession with white degeneracy alone. Rather, he wants to find in the interracial relationships that so alarm white supremacists a potential source of national strength and cohesion. Thus his argument about white degeneration exists in dynamic relation to a more hopeful thesis that affirms the possibilities for interracial familial and community connection. *Marrow* may offer what seems a relentless account of white racist terror, but Chesnutt still manages to find in his account of Wellington families, black and white, the slim possibility of an amalgamated future. The complex histories of the Merkells, the Carterets, and the Millers bear this out. After his wife's death, affluent white southerner Samuel Merkell legally marries his black housekeeper Julia Brown—an option that exists because of the Union military occupation. Julia dies soon after childbirth and her husband, ashamed of his union with a black woman, keeps the relationship private until he too passes, leaving behind a will that bequeaths a significant portion of property to his black daughter, Janet. The marriage certificate and will remain hidden for years until Olivia (the daughter of Merkell's first marriage, now married to Carteret) discovers them. Distraught over what legal recognition of her father's relationship with Julia Brown might suggest, Olivia burns both documents. She and Major Carteret will thus have no obligation to recognize Janet or her husband, Dr. Miller, but can continue avoiding them in the usual racist fashion. If Major Carteret helps promote white supremacy through his newspaper, he and his wife pursue a more private, but no less hateful version of the same creed with respect to their African American kin.

What allows Chesnutt to tease from this miserable situation the dream of an alternative interracial future is the generosity and benevolence of the Millers, his black bourgeois heroes. As Bryan Wagner has argued, the Millers represent the antithesis to white degeneration and decline.[71] Born of humble circumstances, but now well educated and successful, both Janet and William Miller have relinquished a comfortable expatriate life in Europe to return to their native town, build a hospital, and care for the sick. The Doctor can appear elitist on occasion—consider his response to the working-class African Americans on the train (60–62)—but in general both he and Janet embody an egalitarian civic-mindedness that stands in marked counterpoint to the divisiveness practiced by the Carterets and the other influential white supremacists of the novel. For Chesnutt's exemplary black bourgeois couple, the creation of a new Wellington, and, indeed, a new south and a new nation seems to demand recognition that "among all the varieties of mankind the similarities are vastly more important . . . than the differences" (49). Taking their own mixed-race backgrounds as something of a template, the Millers suggest openness to interracial community reminiscent of Chesnutt's comments on amalgamation in "The Future American." Theirs is a social vision that renders the many examples of black and white connection in the town less a historical burden than a harbinger of a modern future.

While the Carterets have no appreciation for the Millers for the majority of the novel, viewing their black kin as an affront, if not a danger, to their whiteness, Chesnutt cleverly redirects this trajectory toward the end of the narrative, and has the ever-uneasy Olivia find in her own familial anxieties a reason to rethink the racial and the imperial. Horrified by the fact that she has destroyed her father's marriage certificate and his will—that she has in fact committed a crime—Olivia confronts evidence of her own version of white decline and realizes, however briefly, that she is part of a corrupt society, one based first on the enslavement and now the regulated exploitation and murder of human beings. In her words, "Slavery had been . . . a great crime against humanity" (266). Olivia may not resemble the most degenerate of southern whites—the Tom Carterets, the Captain McBanes, the lynch mob—but she recognizes nonetheless that she exists in a compromised "moral pocket" that bears little relationship to the glorious white identity of which her husband speaks (267).

Olivia's disturbing thoughts don't last, they are perhaps too painful to sustain, but in the short term they provoke a nightmare in which the white desire for power leads not to a grand future, but rather to disaster and death. In this nocturnal scene, Olivia dreams that she and her son Dodie are sailing across the ocean toward "a golden island." "Her son . . . was a fairy prince, and yonder lay his kingdom, to which he was being borne, lying there at her feet, in this beautiful boat, across the sunlit sea" (268). In many respects, this dream seems typical, almost clichéd, a mother's fairy-tale fantasy for her beloved son. Yet Chesnutt was an author who in his book *The Conjure Woman* had used seemingly innocuous stories to make complex political points; and Olivia's dream while hardly an Uncle Julius folktale, constitutes another example of his strategy. Olivia's vision recalls her husband's grand plans for their son, and also suggests the rapacious fantasies of contemporary U.S. imperialism—fantasies in which U.S. men voyaged toward islands they felt destined to rule, whether in the Caribbean or the Pacific. The very words "golden island" would for some turn-of-the-century U.S. readers have suggested the Chinese island of Kin-shan, an exotic site on the Yangtze river where the U.S. Navy had begun regular patrols in the aftermath of the Boxer Rebellion (1900). Eliza Scidmore and other travel writers published articles on these islands and Western expansion while Chesnutt was working on *Marrow*.[72] To acknowledge that "the Chinaman" who boards Dr. Miller's train early in the novel would hardly have been the only figure to identify the geopolitical resonance of the phrase "golden island" is to remember that by the fin de siècle many Americans shared fantasies of overseas empire (59).

Yet if Olivia's dream of traveling with her princely son toward his kingdom constitutes an allegory of empire, it is an allegory with dire implications indeed. In a terrifying moment, their boat capsizes and Olivia and Dodie find themselves in the water. Had Olivia's dream ended here with her son drowning and the golden island nowhere in sight, one would be tempted to interpret the episode as a comment on empire alone. Yet Chesnutt, intent as always to link white expansionist fantasies to southern interracial realities, turns Olivia's unconscious in a different direction. Struggling to keep Dodie afloat, Olivia sees her mixed-race half-sister Janet rowing next to them and, hopeful of rescue, reaches out only to find herself "clutching at the empty air" (268). The imperial plot of U.S. travel turns resolutely regional. Janet gives Olivia "one mute, reproachful glance" before she rows on, leaving the exhausted mother unable to save her son from slipping beneath the waves (269). In this terrifying nightmare, Chesnutt encapsulates a critique of both Jim Crow and empire that adumbrates the climactic end of the novel. Janet's potentially life-saving function in the dream corresponds to that of both her and her husband, Dr. Miller, in waking life. While Major Carteret rejects Dr. Miller's help when Dodie is ill in the early pages of the novel, claiming that the black physician will further upset his wife, the Carterets adopt a considerably different tack in the narrative's closing moments. Dodie falls sick in the aftermath of the riot, but no white doctor, indeed no white American, can save him. Only Dr. Miller can help the boy, and the physician does so after Olivia has implored Janet to direct her husband to the task. A black family member ensures the survival of the Carteret family. The message is potent: rather than dream of ruling golden islands and brilliant empires, of imagining a world dominated by whites, the Carterets should devote themselves to recognizing and appreciating their black relations. Their future may depend on abandoning the violent fictions of white supremacy both at home and abroad.

This lesson leaves little immediate hope for the African Americans of Wellington. Dr. Miller's rescue of Dodie occurs as his own son lies dead and the African American community lies in shambles. Indeed, if the novel seems intent on teaching white bourgeois southerners and, more important, white bourgeois northerners the value of acknowledging their African American kin and African American fellow citizens, this lesson comes at a bitter price for those potential objects of white recognition. Un-teaching whiteness is painful process indeed for the African American instructor. Yet if many twenty-first-century readers find frustrating Dr. Miller's willingness to help young Dodie Carteret even as he refrains from armed defense of black people and property, it is worth remembering that Chesnutt was attempting a difficult task with this novel: that of reviving a moribund white Republican interest in black southerners during a time of rampant Anglo-Saxonism and white imperialism. The African American writer no doubt recognized that the GOP would not return to the radical democratic ideals of the mid-nineteenth century—what he described as "grand achievements and glorious traditions" in his 1892 speech "Why I am a Republican"—but he still seems to have hoped that his novel of southern white and black kin discovering a shared future would make a favorable impression upon white northerners increasingly hostile toward blacks.[73] To emphasize the existing amalgamation of the South was for Chesnutt not only to remind white southerners of their close black kin, but also to remind white northerners that they too needed African Americans as they embarked on an ill-advised mission to seize golden islands around the world. African Americans did not have the leverage needed to stop U.S. imperialism abroad, but they could perhaps slowly impress upon whites that unity was a concept capable of crossing more than sectional lines.

Both "The Future American" and *The Marrow of Tradition* argue against the white supremacists of the era that African Americans are not a hindrance or a threat, but rather those who might end up saving the nation from the dangers of perilous waters. Chesnutt figures mixed-race relationships and mixed-race subjects as a sign of how a frank acknowledgment of amalgamation might offer all Americans a chance to pull from the "smouldering . . . ruins" of racist violence at home and abroad some prospect for true democracy (310). White rioters may take over the town, the nation, and perhaps even the world, but the theme of interracial connection always manages to lay claim to pride of place in Chesnutt's imagination. In his own complicated black and white origins, Chesnutt finds the dream of a future democratic payoff for an expansionist nation.

It comes as no surprise that Dixon's geography of reunion proved far more appealing than that of Chesnutt. Dixon was after all promoting a more Dixie-sensitive version of the dominant imperial rhetoric of the day. The white supremacist novelist would go on to publish two more volumes in his "anti-Reconstruction trilogy" and then reap the rewards of even greater fame when his friend D. W. Griffith drew upon these novels to create the appropriately titled film *The Birth of a Nation* (1915). Thanks to Dixon's extraordinarily popular texts and their cinematic incarnation, the idea that the white South somehow represented the future of a unified, coherent, and expanding nation seemed increasingly true as the United States retained de facto control over Cuba, the Philippines, and other conquered territories well into the new century. Both men may have desired a type of reunion; but it was Dixon who understood that at the beginning of the modern era, the fashion for empire signified a desire to revive the (fictive) golden age of cohesive white nationhood, not to relive the racial debates associated with a tragic civil war. If the South were to anchor a geography of reunion, it would be a geography of white rapacity.

Yet if *Marrow* proved unpopular with most readers, selling only slightly more than three thousand copies and generally failing to provoke the union of blacks and white northerners that Chesnutt sought, it did demonstrate one singularly important fact: the desire of African Americans and other people of color to imagine how the nation's rise to global power might provide them with a new way of reconstructing their lives as U.S. citizens. Even as white Americans repeatedly invoked white supremacist ideology to authorize a cohesive national investment in conquest and global power, their black counterparts worked no less assiduously to invoke alternate conceptions of solidarity and community that reconfigured U.S. empire as a phenomenon inadvertently threatening to the status quo. These radical visions of color and geography were quixotic, to be sure, but over the course of the next sixty-odd years they proved beneficial to new social movements that forced the nation's white elite to reconsider the place of the South in a century named American.

2

UP FROM EMPIRE

*James Weldon Johnson, Latin America,
and the Jim Crow South*

At one point in James Weldon Johnson's *Autobiography of an Ex-Colored Man* (1912), the protagonist overhears an argument between a white Union army veteran and a white Texan.[1] Overtly about the Civil War, the debate also comments on another type of division, one not of national but of hemispheric dimensions. The Union veteran, invoking the contemporary condition of Latin America, proclaims: "Can you imagine . . . what would have been the condition of things eventually if there had been no war, and the South had been allowed to follow its course? Instead of one great, prosperous country with nothing before it but the conquest of peace, a score of petty republics, as in Central and South America, wasting their energies in war with each other or in revolutions" (339–40). His interlocutor responds by rejecting not only the veteran's investment in national integrity, but also the need for nations altogether. "Well," replied the Texan, "anything—no country at all—is better than having niggers over you" (340). If the Texan states that "anything . . . is better" than black power, the Union veteran suggests that anything is better than allowing the United States to degenerate into a collection of what O. Henry would dub "banana republics."[2] For the soldier of the Grand Army of the Republic (GAR), the idea of slipping into the Latin American way of life outweighs the danger of black insurgency reiterated by the Texan.

To be sure, the veteran seems interested in the deplorable state of Latin America only as an example of what Union victory spared the United States; he does not comment on turn-of-the-century U.S. policy in the region and refers to U.S. imperialism only through the euphemistic phrase "the conquest of peace." Yet the 1912 publication date of Johnson's novel invites us to read the old soldier's words in light of the "big stick" diplomacy that characterized U.S. relations with its southern neighbors. Between 1898 and 1914, the United States intervened militarily in Cuba, Puerto Rico, the Dominican Republic, Honduras, Mexico, and Nicaragua even as U.S. banks and businesses assumed control of national economies in these and other Latin American polities.[3] When we place the Union veteran's statement in the context of contemporary U.S. imperialism south of the border, the implications of his extravagant historical analogy grow palpable: the U.S. government stands in much the same relation to an unruly South and Central America at the close of the nineteenth century as it did to a disordered and insurgent "Dixie" forty years before.[4] The problem of a rebellious U.S. South had demanded a violent Yankee response; the current disorder of the hemispheric South seems to require another type of northern intervention.

The titular narrator of *The Autobiography of an Ex-Colored Man* does not comment on the larger meaning of this historical analogy, but James Weldon Johnson devoted serious thought to the relationship of the national and the hemispheric North/South divides in his richly varied public writings. And he did so in a manner that often seems to echo the Union veteran's argument. Eager to link the federal administration of the domestic South with U.S. intervention abroad, Johnson had few problems supporting the new U.S. imperialism so long as the party of Lincoln articulated that expansionist vision. His diplomatic work suggests as much. A staunch Republican, author of the campaign song "You're Alright Teddy," Johnson transformed himself from a Broadway songwriter into a gunboat diplomat, winning the post of U.S. consul to Puerto Cabello, Venezuela, in 1906. His subsequent assignment as consul to Corinto, Nicaragua (1909) would make manifest his role in the new U.S. empire. In 1912, Johnson would defend U.S. interests in Nicaragua during the civil conflict between President Adolfo Diaz and rebel leader Luis Mena, a contest that pitted a conservative dictator against a peasant insurgent. Eager to preserve Diaz's pro-U.S. regime, Johnson not only convinced the rebels to refrain from invading Corinto, he also facilitated the deployment of U.S. military forces. In July 1912, several thousand Marines landed in Nicaragua and soon routed the insurgents; government executioners dispatched Mena, and U.S. financiers quietly took control of the central Nicaraguan bank. Johnson's rhetorical skill and logistical intelligence played a vital role in suppressing the peasant rebellion and setting the stage for a military and fiscal U.S. presence in Nicaragua that would last well into the twentieth century. With respect to U.S. expansion in the Americas, Johnson seemed to accept the principle underlying Theodore Roosevelt's Corollary to the Monroe Doctrine (1904)—the idea that the United States had the right to intervene in the affairs of other American nations when hemispheric stability was at stake.[5]

Johnson wasn't alone among African Americans in supporting the new U.S. empire. As Kevin Gaines has recently reminded us, such prominent African Americans as Edward Cooper, Pauline Hopkins, and Booker T. Washington supported U.S. imperialism in the late 1890s; and some black intellectuals would continue to defend U.S. policy into the new century.[6] Why would such personages support U.S. expansionism? Certainly looming large among the variety of factors inspiring black support—patriotic ideals, a belief in the idea of the civilizing mission, personal ambition—was a desire for some prophylactic connection to the white power elite. As we have seen in the previous chapter, with the elimination of vestigial Reconstruction came an increase in black disenfranchisement and white racist violence throughout much of the nation, but particularly in the South. In 1906, the year Johnson began working for the consular service, sixty-two black men and women were lynched in the region and one of the worst white racist riots of the era erupted in Atlanta.[7] These episodes of lethal white violence vivified the more quotidian forms of white racism endured by African Americans in the U.S. South. A willingness to identify with and support the Republican party, the party of Emancipation and Reconstruction, seemed to offer some protection, however minor, from the threats of regional white supremacy. And the African American investment in the Republican vision of federal policy and power extended to the new imperialism of the era.[8] In the eyes of some African Americans, the new empire held forth the prospect of close affiliation with Washington during a terrible time. Not only did serving the new Republican empire entitle some African American soldiers to receive military training and carry guns—a fact that sparked no end of confrontations throughout the southeast—it also confirmed the black bourgeoisie's sense of metropolitan superiority to both the underdeveloped U.S. South and the seemingly uncivilized spaces of U.S. expansion. During a time of pronounced and savage white supremacy, in other words, U.S. imperialism offered some members of the black bourgeoisie a sense of "northernness" and a concomitant feeling of civilized belonging.

That the fantasy of an imperial reconstruction of the African American demanded considerable ethical compromise on the part of contemporary black intellectuals goes without saying. The vexed relationship between dreams of enfranchisement and nightmares of complicity proved a heavy burden for even the most sensitive and articulate of these figures. That Johnson—talented, ambitious, and well aware that

African American success often depended on white patronage—would do the empire's work should hardly come as a surprise. Yet even as he endorsed U.S. imperialism and defended U.S. interests in Nicaragua, he also expressed considerable anxiety over the nation's new expansionist policies and their potential consequences for African Americans. Evidence of concern over this issue appears early in his literary career. Johnson's poem "The Colored Sergeant" (1898) rebuts Theodore Roosevelt's charge that black soldiers performed poorly on San Juan Hill, while his libretto to the unproduced opera "Toloso" (1899) satirizes the U.S. annexation of Pacific islands. Johnson would continue to criticize U.S. expansion well into the new century. He would attack Roosevelt again in the lyrics to the song "The Presidente and the Yellow Peril": "We'll nail the 'big stick' to the wall / and round it will drape / No streamers red white and blue / But ordinary crepe"; and he would complain to Booker T. Washington that Jim Crow racism made the United States unpopular among the dark-skinned populations of the Caribbean and South America—a position which would inform his forceful speech "Why Latin Americans Dislike the United States" (1913). Long before he indicted the U.S. occupation of Haiti in his essays for the *Nation* (1920), Johnson addressed the problem of empire.

Such a delicate, indeed, uncomfortable, balancing act would be for some intellectuals a largely private affair, but in Johnson's case, literary ambition and racial politics inspired an unusual commentary on his conflicted relationship to empire: not an essay, lecture, or polemic, but the novel with which we began. A narrative that chronicles the mainly domestic adventures of an African American musician who eventually passes for white, *The Autobiography of an Ex-Colored Man* seems to have little if anything to do with the new U.S. expansionism that emerged, large and rapacious, with the sinking of the *U.S.S. Maine*. While critics have read the novel in light of myriad issues—publication history, the unreliable narrator, African American music, the representation of male sexuality, and, of course, the vexed question of racial passing—few have considered how *The Autobiography* might speak to the contemporary question of empire.[9] Such an occlusion will come as no surprise to those readers familiar with scholarship on African American literature and culture. With few exceptions, most critics tend to read black texts in exclusively national terms, the odd reference to African roots notwithstanding. Yet as Brent Edwards and Michelle Stephens have recently reminded us, the diasporic range of black literary culture demands more of a transnational approach—one sensitive to both the hemispheric and transatlantic orientations of African America.[10] The case of Johnson's *Autobiography* well illustrates this point, for the black polymath interwove his diplomatic responsibilities and his literary efforts. Johnson wrote much of the novel during his diplomatic assignment to Puerto Cabello, Venezuela, and received news of its publication while working with the Marines in Nicaragua. At the same time that he defended and promoted U.S. empire, in other words, Johnson generated an account of a man torn between black and white, between racial solidarity and bourgeois opportunism, between domestic struggle and imperial reward. *The Autobiography* engages subtly, but significantly, with a constellation of themes that denote the range and complexity of fin-de-siècle U.S. expansion. By examining issues that include the politics of the Cuban independence movement, the globalization of black popular music, and Wall Street's exploitation of Latin America, Johnson queries the idea that U.S. expansion will offer African Americans an opportunity to claim their citizenship and civil rights. That he weaves his commentary on empire into a tale of acquisitiveness and weakness suggests the degree to which imperial temptations emerge in the novel only to be critiqued.

In what follows, I argue that Johnson critically imagines the racial passer and the imperialist of color as linked figures: both abandon the potential glories of racial struggle for the thin possibility of recognition by the white status quo, both attempt to remake themselves at the expense of black people throughout the Americas. The picaresque titular character of *The Autobiography* escapes the tyranny of the Jim Crow South not through trickery or resistance, but by exploiting foreign people of color. Each time he ventures southward, the ex-colored man ends up in a difficult, if not perilous, situation that is eased or resolved through his manipulation of Latin Americans. A virtual (Latin American) South provides him with the comforts he cannot locate in the domestic southland or anywhere in the United States. Indeed, the ex-colored man's ability to jettison the terrifying problems of the regional for the colonialist compensations of the hemispheric enables him to live as a racial passer. U.S. imperialism thus not only seduces African Americans into believing that colonialism will offer them all they have been denied at home; empire also deprives them of a sense of hemispheric racial and political identity through much the same strategy. Little wonder, then, that Johnson's turn to an anti-imperialist politics coincided with his transformation of the NAACP through grassroots organizational work in the South. By the mid-teens Johnson had recognized that empire must be combated in a tandem fashion, at home and in the world.

History Travels with the Seas

A native of Jacksonville, Florida, Johnson experienced the geographic proximity of Latin American society and culture from childhood onward. Learning Spanish from his father, he befriended Cuban American cigar factory owners and workers. Most important, his family hosted a visiting Cuban student, Ricardo Ponce. Ponce and Johnson became great friends, attending both high school and college together. As Johnson writes in his memoir *Along This Way*, there grew "between us a strong bond of companionship; and what was, perhaps, more binding, the bond of [the Spanish] language" (63). One cannot overestimate the importance of this Cuban connection to Johnson's conceptions of race, space, and community. The Latin presence within "Dixie" would offer the black intellectual a third term with which to better negotiate his relationship to the U.S. region for much of his life. For him, the black/ white divide could never completely encapsulate the U.S. South. At the same time, Johnson's early sensitivity to his region's hemispheric connections would also inform his vision of Latin America. He would draw upon and respond to this formative exposure to Cuban American culture repeatedly in his future experiences in Venezuela and Nicaragua. His adult understanding of U.S. policy in the Americas would emerge from his youthful exposure to a hybridized, if still violently white supremacist, domestic southland.

Johnson was hardly unusual in linking what Deborah Cohn has called "the two souths."[11] As Cohn, Edouard Glissant, George Handley, Kirsten Gruesz, and other scholars have recently argued, blacks and whites of the U.S. southeast had for centuries maintained a variety of connections to Latin America.[12] In his recent book *Faulkner, Mississippi*, Glissant reminds us that such disparate phenomena as cherry wood furniture, piquant cuisine, vibrant dance, and the literary figure of the black female servant link the cultures of the U.S. South to the Caribbean and parts of Central and South America. For Glissant that connection stems from a shared history of colonialism, slavery, racism, and poverty. As he puts it with respect to the legacy of New World plantation culture, "The same architecture, furniture, and rows of slave shacks, the same instruments of torture are found everywhere in the old slave order. . . . History travels with the seas."[13] The nineteenth- and early twentieth-century record of this relationship presents us with ample evidence of the myriad crossings and exchanges that constitute a sea-borne history: the celebration of Cuban poetry in antebellum New Orleans' newspapers, William Walker's ill-fated attempt to reproduce U.S. southern culture in Mexico and Nicaragua, black Cubans' migration to the U.S. South after the abolition of slavery, the manipulative presence of Alabaman Samuel Zemurray's United Fruit Company throughout Central and South America. No less than the Mexico-southwest U.S. contact zone, the southeast border exists as a site of dynamic encounters between black, white, and Latin, between master and slave, between capital and labor.[14]

As his memoir affirms, at an early age Johnson experienced firsthand the value of his Latin American connections. At one point in the narrative, Johnson and his Cuban friend Ponce manage to retain their seats in the first-class compartment of a segregated train because the conductor overhears them speaking Spanish and misidentifies Johnson as a Latin American visitor. As Johnson puts it, "as soon as the conductor heard us speaking a foreign language, his attitude changed" (65). In another train scene from *Along This Way,* Johnson receives a warm welcome from a group of white men after they realize he can help them understand Cuban society in the wake of the Spanish-American War. They even pause to admire and examine his authentic Panama hat—an object that seems to validate his supposed Latin American origin (88). Johnson punctuates his narration of these autobiographical episodes with a tag line that captures perfectly the fluctuating meaning of black identity in the turn-of-the-century United States: "In such situations any kind of Negro will do; provided he is not one who is an American citizen." Johnson makes clear that "Negroes" who seem Latin American "will do" far better than any others in the Jim Crow South. He would later make this point more explicitly in his essay "The Absurdity of American Prejudice" (1922): "there are many instances of prejudice being laid aside when it was thought or known that the colored person concerned was a Cuban, or a South American" (48).

Johnson would have recognized that exoticism alone did not explain the success of his Latin passing. Adopting a Latin American identity momentarily liberated the black U.S. citizen from the oppressiveness of the U.S. South not only because that alternate black identity was alien or exotic, but also because the hemispheric South represented an alluring space of economic and political opportunity.[15] Whatever their feelings about the mixed-race populations south of the border, U.S. southern capitalists viewed Latin America as a new market for the region's burgeoning textile industry—not to mention as a potential source of cheap labor.[16]

Yet every manipulation of identity demands something of the subject in question, and Johnson's Latino masquerade is no exception. While we might interpret Johnson's Latino act in the U.S. South in terms of a nascent and necessarily complex solidarity with Latin Americans against white U.S. racism and imperialism, an equally valid reading of this performance suggests the power plays of U.S. empire. By passing for Latino in order to improve momentarily his position in a segregated society, Johnson engages in his own version of the imperial aggression so tantalizing to white Americans, north and south. Even as Johnson experienced a brief thrill of liberation by dazzling provincial southern whites with his Latin American savoir-faire, that moment of freedom from Jim

Crow stood in tension with a U.S. expansionist regime eager to appropriate things Latin for far less commendable reasons. We see but a hint of this appetitive impulse in the white train passengers' desire for information about Cuba; "the preacher asked me about conditions in Cuba . . . concerning which I had a good deal of information" (89). Johnson's willingness to appropriate a Latin American identity for his own domestic purposes points ahead to his future interest in pursuing imperial ambitions south of the border. His Latino act in the Jim Crow South at once challenges and supports the white hegemony of an expansionist United States.

Johnson would stage a very different type of Latino performance years later when serving as U.S. consul in Corinto, Nicaragua, during an attempted coup d'état. If he had played the exotic Latin outsider in the U.S. South, he would play the faux native informant for the U.S. military in the Latin American context. In a contemporary letter to his wife, Grace Nail Johnson, he describes the relationship between his appropriation of "Latinness" and his new connection to a powerful white U.S. admiral:

> I shall have to tell you in order to make you know how fine Admiral Southerland's treatment of me has been. I don't mean any more patting on the back as a very nice *colored* man [emphasis in original]; but recognizing me in the fullest degree as a man and officer. I am called into every consultation with him and his staff. He takes no important step or action without asking my opinion and advice. In dealing with communications from the rebels he has even asked I always sit near him. . . . I feel sure that I have measured up to his estimate of me.
>
> Another thing with reference to the Admiral—the day after arriving here he issued a general order to all the American forces occupying Corinto, and in that order he commanded that the consul was to receive the same naval honors as those accorded to officers of the fleet; so whenever I pass, the men on duty come to 'present arms' and I salute. A little thing, but it means a great deal. He never sends me back from the flag ship except in his 'barge', which is, in fact, a luxurious little steam yacht. But, as I intimated in the first part of my letter, I've been through enough to merit these little honors.[17]

Johnson claims to have good reason to dwell so long on these "little honors" elsewhere in the letter. He was at this point in his diplomatic career striving for a better post, preferably one in France, and the approval of an influential admiral held great value for him. Yet even if we acknowledge these career aspirations, we must still ponder the meaning of a letter that links Johnson's knowledge of Nicaragua with his newfound status among the white U.S. military brass. On the face of it, the many gestures of respect offered by the admiral demonstrate that Johnson had indeed escaped the stereotype of the "very nice *colored* man" in his capacity as U.S. consul. Yet as the letter suggests, he has received the recognition due "a man and officer" only because he has taken on the role of Latin America expert—of knowledgeable "local"—for the U.S. admiral and his staff. Fluent in Spanish, familiar with Nicaragua, knowledgeable about the rebels, Johnson has the counterinsurgency expertise needed by the U.S. military; as he boasts to his wife in the letter, "I *know* this revolution from A to Z." By giving the representatives of the U.S. state an insider's perspective on Nicaragua and its political turmoil, Johnson is able to indulge in a fantasy of enfranchisement. His special relationship to the Latin world has enabled to him to shift from subaltern black subject to a white admiral's valued confidant.[18]

Yet the letter by no means presents us with an unqualified celebration of this exchange. When Johnson claims "he's been through enough to merit these little honors," he connects his arduous, not to say ethically questionable, work on behalf of U.S. empire to the special recognition he receives from the white naval officer. He further suggests his unease with the appropriation of a Latin identity by segueing from a discussion of his role in suppressing the rebellion of Luis Mena's peasant forces to a comment on his newly published narrative of racial passing, *The Autobiography of an Ex-Colored Man*. He queries his wife about the reviews the book has received—"so the *Crisis* has not yet reviewed my book," he remarks—and discusses the novel's chances in the literary marketplace. These questions evince Johnson's ambition; thrilled at his new success on the diplomatic front, he demands news of further achievement in the world of letters. Yet the problem of the color line cuts across these two fields of endeavor, linking his pleasure over the admiral's attention to his desire to be recognized by W. E. B. Du Bois's new periodical. Johnson's exploitation of Latino identity in the imperial context cannot help but recall the vexed issue of racial passing that informs his narrative. When we read the line "whenever *I pass*, the men on duty come to 'present arms' and I salute" (emphasis added), it is difficult indeed not to consider that Johnson senses a certain disturbing connection between his work on behalf of U.S. empire and the machinations of his literary protagonist. Inasmuch as Johnson's new "white" privileges are predicated on the value of his Latin connections to the military, he too is a "passer." And the contingent nature of this masquerade unsettles him. Whatever Johnson's hope that U.S. expansion will allow him to exist in a space where he can assume all the prerogatives of U.S. citizenship, both the letter and the passing novel to which it refers register the impossibility of this dream. *The Autobiography* stands, as we shall see, as an African American diplomat's uneasy commentary on his position between a white imperial elite, a black U.S. population, and Latin America; with its tale of an African American man's anxiety over an abandoned racial identity, this classic literary work tells a related story of an African American man's concern over the acquisition of imperial privilege.

Going South

Early in *The Autobiography,* Johnson connects the struggles of Caribbean peoples and African Americans in a manner that belies any notion that the latter group might exploit foreign people of color in support of U.S. policy. While attending his grammar school graduation in a Connecticut town, the novel's protagonist listens, rapt, to his African American friend "Shiny" deliver Wendell Phillips's 1861 lecture "Toussaint L'Ouverture"—an abolitionist hagiography of the Haitian leader that celebrates his opposition to European colonialism and New World white racism. The "magical" experience of listening to Shiny read this encomium before a mainly white audience causes the young man to undergo something of a racial epiphany. "I could talk of nothing else with my mother except my ambitions to be a great man, a great colored man, to reflect credit on the race and gain fame for myself" (291–92). In these lines, the child shifts radically from the racial identity he registers just a few pages earlier in the novel. At that point he was horrified to learn of his blackness: "Mother, am I white? Are you white?" he asks tearfully after being labeled black by his teacher (280). But listening to Shiny's rendition of "Toussaint" has inspired the youth to accept a new racial identity with pride. Shiny's passionate articulation of the great Haitian's accomplishments gives the main character a new perspective on the race question throughout the Americas.[19] Nothing could seem further from the Union veteran's dismissive treatment of Latin American republics with which we began.

The youth's conception of Toussaint L'Ouverture reminds us that black U.S. citizens have often invoked the famed Haitian revolutionary as a model of black social and political action. Yet Johnson's protagonist responds to the example of Toussaint in a distinctly personal manner. Ignorant of racial realities, sheltered and sensitive, the young man views the great Haitian as a guide to reclaiming a familial legacy and finding his own triumphant way in the world. Rather than inspire him to struggle against white oppression in the United States, the example of the Caribbean leader leads the hero to seek out his potentially successful connection to southern society. The ex-colored man prefaces his experience listening to Shiny recite "Toussaint L'Ouverture" with an account of how conversations with his mother had made him curious about U.S.

southern culture: "What she told me interested and even fascinated me, and, what may seem strange, kindled in me a strong desire to see the South" (290). Johnson's protagonist has ample reason to be curious. After all, the young man has only recently learned that that he is "the child of . . . unsanctioned love" between his Georgia-born mother and a wealthy and nameless southern white man (290). While the bitterly racist customs and laws of the region demand that they resettle in the North when the white southern father weds "a young lady of a . . . great Southern family," the young man still feels an understandable, if impossible, desire to recover his place of origin (290).

By imaginatively traveling south of the U.S. border with the help of Shiny's performance of "Toussaint," the youth thinks he has found his way back to his natal zone; the invocation of a hemispheric southern hero will help Johnson's protagonist come to terms, however temporarily, with his own deeply problematic U.S. southern legacy. Or so it seems. For we soon discover that when the protagonist eventually makes his journey, he experiences little more than the ugly facts of racism. His trip into the U.S. South represents less an imaginative rewriting of southern genealogies and geographies than a frightening incarceration in the prison-house of his past. On his train trip south to attend college in Atlanta, the young man reflects unfavorably on the unkempt fields and poverty-ridden housing he sees along the route. His arrival in Atlanta confirms his growing distaste for the region. The city offends him aesthetically—too "big," too "dull"—and somatically: his lodging and food prove barely tolerable (294–96). To compound matters, his bankroll, the money with which he planned to pay tuition fees, is stolen during his first night in town. The South provides our protagonist with no vaunted opportunity to bond with black people, let alone aspire to the status of a latter-day Toussaint L'Ouverture. Rather than constituting a site of redefined origins, of a new black regional identity, the South suggests a life of poor diet, bad accommodations, ugly scenery, and confining, not to say racially divided, living spaces. The ex-colored man leaves the city squashed into the dirty space of a porter's laundry closet; his filthy entombment allegorizes the horrors of a region that seems as stultifying as it is segregated (300).

The Cuban Question

Given his experience in the South, one would expect the ex-colored man to have reversed direction and in time-honored African American fashion found his way back to the allegedly liberated spaces of the North. Yet Johnson sends his hero further south; the man flees Atlanta to find himself in a Jacksonville Cuban American community strongly identified with the Cuban independence movement. The sign of L'Ouverture returns here dressed in Cuban revolutionary garb—an inadvertent reminder that the image of the Toussaint-affirming Wendell Philips graced the office wall of Cuban patriot José Martí. This very different southern community embraces the protagonist from the first. His Cuban American landlord finds him work as a tobacco stripper in a cigar factory and teaches him Spanish, thus offering our displaced character a chance to assume a new linguistic and social identity: "I was able in less than a year to speak like a native," the ex-colored man soon boasts (303). Before long, his language skills and general competence enable him to move from the lowly job of tobacco stripper to the esteemed position of factory lector—a role in which he reads from and comments on Hispanophone novels, newspapers, and magazines for the benefit of the Cuban émigrés toiling around him (303). The protagonist's ability to "go Cuban" within the confines of the U.S. South speaks powerfully to the complex elasticity of both the region and the nation. The presence of an anti-imperialist Cuban American community in northern Florida suggests the commendable heterogeneity of the U.S. South despite its stringent Jim Crow codes. Yet the existence of this Cuban pocket in "Dixie" also testifies to the ability of the southeastern United States to absorb and exploit persons from proximate nations, regardless of their politics. Pluralism may presage the future transformation of social relations in the U.S. South even as it denotes how the white elite can hijack identities and cultures in the service of future expansion south of the border.[20]

This is not to deny the subversive politics of the Cuban American community in *The Autobiography,* particularly with respect to questions of race. The Cuban American world of cigar manufacture seems to stand in direct counterpoint to the racial segregation the ex-colored man experiences elsewhere in the U.S. South for one important reason: its fierce identification with the radical political and social ideals of the anticolonialist Cuban independence movement. In the Cuban world of cigar manufacture, "the color line is not drawn" (301); race does not seem to be perceived as a problem; blacks and whites work side by side as equals. To be sure, racism did exist in the Cuban American cigar factory, as it existed in Cuban America and in Cuba itself; the persistence in Cuban society of the raza de color, a rule that differentiated between whites and all people of color, rendered Cuban racial politics disturbingly similar to the binary racialism of the turn-of-the-century United States.[21] Yet as Johnson may have known given his longstanding relationship with Cuban Americans, during the independence movement at the turn of the century, issues of race and racism were suppressed in favor of a new supposedly colorblind Cuban nationalism.[22]

Whether underground in Cuba or displaced in the United States, members of the anti-imperialist independence movement strove to live up to the inspirational words of José Martí. "There can be no racial animosity, because there are no races," Martí preached to his fellow Cubans in "Our America," adding, "The soul, equal and eternal, emanates from the bodies of various shapes and colors. Whoever foments and spreads antagonism and hate between the races, sins against humanity."[23] A hint of Martí's utopian racial vision for the independence movement materializes in *The Autobiography* when Johnson has the ex-colored man's Cuban landlord recite the names of both black and white military leaders central to the cause: "the Gomezes, both the white one and the black one . . . Maceo and Bandera" (303).[24] This list interweaves black with white heroes gesturing, if only briefly, toward the liberated racial ideal of the cause. By invoking the interracial nature of the Cuban independence movement in the Jacksonville context, Johnson links the egalitarian race relations of the cigar factory to an anti-imperial social movement. The fight against empire south of the border has an important, if inchoate, relationship to the African American struggle against segregation in the United States. From Toussaint to Maceo, Caribbean independence movements seem capable of giving African Americans new forms with which to contest life under Jim Crow, forms that affirm national struggle even as they suggest new transnational alliances of color. The Cuban American radicals of Jacksonville are from this perspective a thorn in the side of the monster—Martí's gothic appellation for the large and terrifying nation to the north.[25]

Given the inspiring example of the Cuban Americans, one cannot help but note that the remaining pages of the Jacksonville chapter offer no further commentary on the utopian dimensions of the Cuban fight against Spanish colonialism. The ex-colored man never again mentions the idea of an egalitarian racial dynamic or the Cuban independence movement, despite the fact that his job as factory lector would have required him to comment publicly on these and other pressing political issues.[26] The ex-colored man understands his job as lector in far more possessive and individualistic terms; he values the salary and the freedom from manual labor. As he will later explain while working once again as a cigar roller in New York, "making cigars became more and more irksome to me; perhaps my more congenial work as a 'reader' had unfitted me for work at the table" (319). In effect, he treats his job at the politically charged space of the cigar factory as little more than a well-paying gig. The radical politics of Cuban America mean little to him.

This turn away from the Cuban Americans is typical of Johnson's insecure and chameleon-like protagonist; like many picaresque characters, he abandons identities and friendships as swiftly as he acquires them. At the same time, however, his meandering ways take on a very different meaning from that which we might identify in the narrative movements of a Moll Flanders or a Dean Moriarty. The often emancipatory meaning of travel in African American letters—in slave narratives, great migration stories, and ethnic rediscovery tales—invites us to read the protagonist's abrupt swerve away from a politically idealistic community in a rather negative light. After all, when he abandons the Cuban Americans after losing his job as lector, he does not strive to find his place in the mythic black South as he had envisioned ever since his epiphanic response to the performative invocation of Toussaint L'Ouverture. Instead, he criticizes the black lumpenproleteriat, condescends to the black working class, and identifies smugly with the black bourgeoisie (305–8). The very impulse to reify the black social hierarchy of Jacksonville stands in marked opposition to the Cuban American utopian spirit. Even as the Cuban Americans fight imperialism and reimagine race relations, Johnson has his nameless protagonist abandon their company in order to find a place in the most exclusive social scene in black Jacksonville. The open embrace of the Cuban Americans becomes the closed circle of the black middle class.

Johnson seems to suggest through this narrative movement that the exchange of communities does not so much testify to the protagonist's racial solidarity as reveal the extent of his elitism. What complicates any interpretation of the protagonist's shift from Cuban American to black bourgeois Jacksonville is Johnson's own membership in the latter community, as well as his own delicate relationship with Latin American politics and New Negro ambitions.[27] The latter issue warrants our attention. If the ex-colored man drew social and economic sustenance from his well-paid position as lector in the Cuban American cigar-making community, it seems clear that Johnson generated social capital from his role as U.S. consul in the turbulent societies of Venezuela and Nicaragua. As Johnson's biographer Eugene Levy has pointed out, "a position as a consular official, unlike that of a songwriter, was of unquestioned respectability."[28] Johnson's courtship of and marriage to Grace Nail, the daughter of affluent New York businessman John Nail, may have benefited from his emerging status as a U.S. State Department official. Johnson met Grace Nail in 1901 and married her in 1910 when his future prospects in the State Department seemed bright. To put it another way, Johnson's success as a black bourgeois resulted in part from his willingness to exploit Latin America in the name of U.S. empire—to represent U.S. interests, serve admirals, and suppress unwanted coups. Johnson never suggests anything of the sort in his work, yet we may speculate that the decision to contrast his protagonist's Cuban American experience with his ascendancy of the black social hierarchy—not the least of which is an impending marriage to a genteel black woman—reveals some recognition of the relationship between exploiting Latin America and becoming a black bourgeois success. If Johnson couldn't address this disturbing conjunction of state violence and black ambition directly, he could gesture toward the problem in his fictional autobiography.

The Empire Rag

Such arguments must remain at the level of speculation. What is clear is that Johnson devoted important sections of *The Autobiography* to examining the relationship of U.S. globalism to black success and, more specifically, black cultural achievement. Johnson couldn't focus openly on the connection between the black bourgeoisie and national expansion, but he could take up the issue of black achievement and U.S. empire via a veiled commentary on the accomplished musical career he had abandoned for the consul assignment in Venezuela. A lyricist who in partnership with his composer brother Rosamond achieved considerable success, Johnson saw in the burgeoning U.S. empire a chance to reimagine the relationship of black U.S. music to the nation and the world. He often asserted that a globally hegemonic black culture would generate acceptance of blacks not only abroad, but, more important, at home. *The Autobiography* makes the appeal of this imperial conception of black culture manifest shortly before the ex-colored man loses his job as lector at the factory. Surveying some of the more prominent contemporary forms of black popular culture—the cakewalk, the Uncle Remus stories, and the Jubilee songs—the ex-colored man soon focuses on ragtime as a sign of U.S. global power that accrues to black as well as white Americans. "No one who has traveled can question the *world-conquering* influence of ragtime," boasts the ex-colored man (emphasis mine, 309). His notably imperialist celebration of ragtime comes on the heels of a dismissal of Native American cultural achievement when compared to African Americans. For the ex-colored man, "all of the Indians between Alaska and Patagonia haven't done as much" as African Americans (310).[29] The anti-imperial lesson of the Cuban American political movement seems to have been lost on him; the worldwide success of a black popular music suggests to him not the capacity for African Americans to develop new interracial and international connections—with Cubans, with "Indians"—but rather the African American ability to play an important role in the burgeoning U.S. empire. An era of U.S. hegemony will at once reflect and promote the globalization of black U.S. music.[30]

His protagonist's infatuation with an expansionist image of black music reflects Johnson's point of view, which he would reiterate into the early 1920s. Consider the black writer's description of black musical achievement in "American Music" (1916): "While [white] American composers have been making fair and mediocre copies of German, Italian, and French compositions, American Negro music in its triumphant march has swept the world" (287). In this reading, black music has more in common with U.S. imperial achievement than does white music; of all Americans, only black musicians can outdo the Europeans and win global fame for U.S. culture. Likewise, Johnson argues in the preface to *The Book of American Negro Poetry* (1922), that ragtime "is the one artistic production by which America is known the world over. It has been all-conquering. Everywhere it is hailed as 'American music'" (x). As with the ex-colored man's term "world-conquering," Johnson's choice of "all-conquering" registers the link between ragtime and U.S. imperialism—a connection the writer makes more explicit elsewhere in the preface: "[Ragtime] has become the popular medium for our national expression musically. And who can say that it does not express the blare and jangle and the surge, too, of our national spirit?" (xv). Johnson's use of aggressive ("blare") and expansionist ("surge") nouns in this description captures the sense in which he imagines ragtime to embody a new alliance between an imperial United States and a rising black U.S. culture.

Now, to be sure, Johnson was hardly the only U.S. citizen, black or white, to imagine that ragtime might play a constitutive role in a new expansionist version of the national-popular. From the early days of blackface minstrelsy, black music has facilitated the formation of a U.S. public culture.[31] What did change during the fin de siècle was the increasing acceptance of a "raced" national-popular culture by various portions of the state and its allied institutions. During the rise of the new U.S. imperialism, black music came to play an even more visible role in official military and mainstream nationalist cultures than ever before. Ragtime's appearance in the late 1890s—whether in Tom Turpin's "Harlem Rag" (1897) or in Joplin's "Maple Leaf Rag" (1898)—coincided with the Spanish-American War, a fact not lost on the writers of such contemporary songs as "Get off of Cuba's Toes," "Panama Rag," and "Philippine Rag." Charles Nelan's cartoon "The New Member of the Orchestra" emphasizes this point by naming the two U.S. contributions to the orchestra's repertoire, "Manila Quick Step" and "A Hot Time at Santiago" (Figure 6). Ragtime would play an even more important role in the era's premier form of musical jingoism: brass band music. John Philip Sousa's Afro-Latino number "El Capitan" would be played on the deck of Admiral Dewey's flagship in Manila Harbor; the brass band maestro would subsequently market ragtime to the Europeans and

THE NEW MEMBER OF THE ORCHESTRA.

Figure 6. The New Member of the Orchestra
Credit: Charles Nelan, *New York Herald*

publish his own Hawaiian—that is to say, colonialist—ragtime number, "Hu-la, Hu-la Cakewalk," in 1901. His expansionist appropriation of ragtime would be emulated by the U.S. Marine Corps Band in their version of "Maple Leaf Rag" in 1906 and by Arthur Pryor's "Triumph of Old Glory," a patriotic rag for his military band, in 1907. When Johnson describes ragtime in terms of triumphant marches and "the blare and jangle of national spirit," he reminds us that fin-de-siècle black music traveled to global fame with the help of the U.S. military. The seductive appeal of this notion loomed large: if U.S. empire and black music could work together for national glory, then one could believe in the enfranchisement of African Americans during a time of growing U.S. power.

Global North and U.S. South

For all its representation of black music as world-conquering, however, *The Autobiography* stands apart from Johnson's frequent affirmations of a global black culture. Focused on the travels and travails of its ragtime-playing protagonist, the novel constitutes the one major text in which Johnson troubles the expansionist image of black music that he found so appealing. The global allure of black popular sounds leads the titular character to expect financial and professional rewards that never materialize. Upon leaving Jacksonville, the ex-colored man learns how to play ragtime in a New York gambling house. Before long he has fallen under the sway of a white millionaire patron who takes him to Europe as a personal musician and companion. The shift in the novel's geography from the north–south axis of the coastal United States (Connecticut, Atlanta, Jacksonville, New York) to a decidedly North Atlantic orientation (New York, London, Paris, Amsterdam, Berlin) might suggest that our anti-hero has left both the hemispheric and the U.S. South behind: that, in effect, the novel has shifted to a new emphasis on the global North. Yet the net result of the European tour suggests otherwise. The South—both a problem and an opportunity—shadows the protagonist during his northern travels.

Johnson first makes this evident by having the ex-colored man see his biologic white southern father and white southern half-sister at the Paris Opera, a traumatic experience that sends the musician running from the hall (328–29). But this southern orientation emerges as even more important in the German portion of the ex-colored man's grand tour, when his internationalist claims of black musical triumph are challenged and his relationship to his native region redefined. During a performance in Berlin, the protagonist's demonstration of ragtime, the "new American music," ends disastrously:

> Before there was time for anybody to express an opinion on what had I done, a big, bespectacled, bushy-headed man rushed over, and, shoving me out of the chair, exclaimed: "Get up, Get up!" He seated himself at the piano, and, taking the theme of my ragtime, played it through first in straight chords; then varied and developed it through every known musical form. I sat amazed. I had been turning classic music into ragtime, a comparatively easy task; and this man had taken ragtime and made it classic. (332)

When he shoves the ex-colored man off the piano bench and begins classicizing ragtime, this clichéd version of a classically trained German musician ("bespectacled, bushy-headed") offers an allegory of how black music could easily be pushed from the world stage. The scene reveals ragtime less as world-conquering than as a cultural form that must still contend with challenges from more established cultural and political contenders, the Europeans. Whatever the success of ragtime as a popular music, indeed, whatever the success of the United States as an imperial power, the Europeans still seem to rule the global roost.[32]

One would expect the ex-colored man to react angrily to such boorish behavior and defend the music he represents abroad. Yet he does not take offense at the German's actions. Instead, our ever-materialistic protagonist understands this moment of displacement as an imperial wakeup call rendered in cultural terms. In Jacksonville, the protagonist learned how to exploit the Cuban American scene in order to bankroll his accession to black bourgeois society; in Berlin, the capital of the most musically renowned nation in Europe, he receives an oblique hint at how he might exploit black southern music to foster his attempt at becoming a serious composer. Rather than anger him, the German musician inspires the ex-colored man to think of how he might expropriate black U.S. folk music for the purpose of writing serious musical compositions. "I could think of nothing else. I made up my mind to go back into the very heart of the South, to live among the people, and drink in my inspiration firsthand. I gloated over the immense amount of material I had to work with, not only modern rag-time, but also the old slave songs—material which no one had yet touched" (471). The protagonist claims that the encounter with the boorish German had helped him recognize "the way of carrying out the ambition [he] had formed when a boy," yet the desire to steal gloatingly the folk rhythms and melodies of the black rural people for his own professional ambitions hardly corresponds to his earlier desire to bring "honour and glory to the Negro race." He no longer seeks inspiration from the likes of Toussaint L'Ouverture; instead he seeks to colonize the black musical cultures of the Deep South for his own personal gain. Visiting the global North has not so much informed the ex-colored man of the imbalance between white and black, North and South, as offered him a salutary reminder of what his experience in Jacksonville had already begun to teach him: that the South is ripe with economic and professional opportunity. His willingness to exploit even the slave songs—those testaments to suffering and resistance—suggests his mercenary vision. When the black man informs his white patron that he will not be accompanying him to such global southern locales as Egypt and Japan, he does not so much deny himself the colonial pleasures of those lands as assert his right to grab his own colonialist rewards in a more familiar southern space.

This lesson not only corrects the dream of U.S. global conquest through ragtime; it reverses it as well. Instead of a black southern cultural product colonizing the world—instead of ragtime marching triumphantly across the globe—the black South becomes the site of colonization itself. Imagining the world of culture and the culture of the world in black imperial terms has not linked the protagonist closer to his mother's people in a glorious manner; instead it has separated him from them. Black culture and black people now constitute the object, not the subject, of the ex-colored man's global vision. Johnson thus describes the ex-colored man's behavior in the rural South in aggressively ethnographic terms—"gathering material for work, jotting down in my note-book themes and melodies . . . trying to catch the spirit of the Negro in his relatively primitive state" (345). Our hero's willingness to continue identifying with the urban black bourgeoisie during this primitivist undertaking only suggests how the lesson in cultural expropriation received in Berlin helps him negotiate the linked hierarchies—geographic (Europe / U.S.), racial (white / black), class (black bourgeoisie / black folk)—that inform his imperial dreams.

The ex-colored man tells us that he worked hard at his ethnographic task, yet he leaves the South without any of the cultural riches he has come to retrieve. The protagonist's trip to the hinterland exposes him not only to the oratorical passion and musical power of the black folk, but also to the vicious white scourge which haunts that culturally abundant landscape: lynching. Toward the end of his time in Georgia, he watches local whites burn a black man alive—a sight so terrible that it serves to reorient his relationship to the region yet again. While the confrontation with the German musician had inspired the protagonist to return to the U.S. South, the lynching destroys this dream. He finds himself at an impasse with respect to the region of his birth; he no longer wants to go forth as an emissary of black southern music but he cannot pursue a colonial relationship with such a terrifying, if musically rich, part of the country. His crisis forces him to step back and for the first time ponder his relationship both to the South and to the larger polity that tacitly endorses the region's notorious racist violence. Whatever his former pride in being an African American who can represent the imperial drive of a "raced" United States, the brute horror of lynching alienates him from both race and nation:

> A great wave of humiliation and shame swept over me. Shame that I belonged to a race that could be so dealt with; and shame for my country, that it, the greatest example of democracy to the world, should be the only

civilized, if not the only state on earth, where a human being would be burned alive. (352)

The aural power of ragtime no longer sutures this African American to an expansionist United States; the glorious "blare" and "surge" of black popular music has given way to the terrible screams of the black victims of white mob murder.

Given the two challenges the ex-colored man endures during the latter part of the novel—the German's shove, the terrible scene of lynching—it should come as no surprise that he feels compelled to reassess his sense of self. The impasse results in a moment of crisis wherein the protagonist realizes he can no longer bear a black U.S. identity and decides to become a racial passer or, as he puts it: "I would change my name, raise a mustache, and let the world take me for what it would . . . it was not necessary for me to go about with a label of inferiority pasted across my forehead" (353). The ex-colored man's choice to pass seems on the face of it a direct reaction to the lynching he has just witnessed. Yet perhaps we should see this action as his response to a long-term inability to negotiate a successful relationship to his mother's South—the region he associates with his blackness. Characterized by theft, discomfort, rejection, and terror, the ex-colored man's increasingly tense engagements with the culture and the society of the region have all failed. His only successful experience in the U.S. South depended on the kindness and openness of the Cuban Americans and their independence movement, a group from which he separated himself. The dream of a return to the black southern natal place—the dream which first took shape during his graduation—has grown increasingly impossible.

The ex-colored man's sense of national belonging evaporates as well. He does not suggest that he will replace his lost southern connection with a renewed tie to Connecticut, the site of his schooling and happiest years. He does not celebrate New England as he had earlier. Instead, he describes his decision to pass as an action analogous to that of immigration: "I argued that to forsake one's race to better one's condition was no less worthy an action than to forsake one's country for the same purpose" (353). The ex-colored man's account of his arrival in New York only reinforces his standing as someone with no preexisting connection to the United States, black or white, southern or northern: "When I reached New York, I was completely lost. I could not have felt more a stranger had I been suddenly dropped into Constantinople. I knew not where to turn or how to strike out" (353). Disregarding completely his earlier connection to the city, the ex-colored man constructs New York as an alien world—a place as strange as that most exotic of metropoles, Constantinople. His usual talents seem to have abandoned him; he is isolated, jobless, and bereft of resources. Passing for white hasn't linked him more tightly to a secure sense of U.S. citizenship; it has instead placed him beyond a sense of U.S. belonging as completely as it has placed him beyond a sense of black southern connection.

Certainly, the ex-colored man mourns the loss of national connection far less than he does his loss of black identity. And with good reason. However much the ex-colored man might appear a failed cosmopolite, as Ross Posnock has argued, this marginal man also proves successful at reconstructing himself as an imperialist.[33] Contrary to his protests that passing has nothing to do with ambition, the ex-colored man is indeed looking "for a larger field of action and opportunity" (353), not so much for the cosmopolitan as for the financial rewards. His odd and dislocated relationship to white and black New York stands in inverse proportion to his capacity to function as an imperial subject. He suggests as much when he explains that the initial loneliness he experienced in New York evaporated after he developed a relationship with a New York investment house pursuing South American possibilities:

> I kept my eyes open, watching for a chance to better my condition. It finally came in the form of a position with a house which was at the time establishing a South American department. My knowledge of Spanish was, of course, the principal cause of my good luck; and it did more for me: it placed me where the other clerks were practically put out of competition with me. I was not slow in taking advantage of the opportunity to make myself indispensable to the firm. (354–55)

Of course, given the preceding emphasis on the ex-colored man's extranational position, one might say that he is already "placed" "where the other clerks" in this department cannot compete with him. Like the investment house itself, situated in New York, but eager to exploit financial opportunities south of the border, the ex-colored man recognizes the rich potential of being at once inside and outside the nation. To be sure, he emphasizes how it is his knowledge of Spanish, not his sense of alienation as a racial passer that renders him "indispensable to the firm." Yet as we have already seen in the Cuban American sequence of the novel— not to mention Johnson's experience as U.S. consul during the Nicaraguan coup—knowing Spanish, demonstrating knowledge of Latin American society, can serve as a profitable form of identity manipulation; it can allow the African American, or at least the light-skinned African American, to somehow escape the prison house of the one-drop rule. Within the contemporary imperial context, the ex-colored man's racial passing and his sociolinguistic connection to South America inform one another to his seeming financial and social advantage. If the

ex-colored man was once at least tangentially related to the radical politics of the Cuban independence movement—a movement opposed to
both Spanish and U.S. empires—he now represents the very forces of
imperial greed and colonial rapacity his Cuban landlord decried.

The ex-colored man has indeed found the "endless territory" he desired as a young southern boy (274); the dream of an infinite sprawl that
originates in a Georgia garden materializes in the ever-expanding hemispheric spaces of the U.S. empire. The challenge of the Cuban Americans, the imperial failure of ragtime, the terrors of lynching: all of these
manifestations of what we might call the southern Real are replaced by
a South that exists only in terms of investments and financial statements.[34] South America has become, in effect, a virtual South—the only
sort of South this character can exploit without having to take a stand
on the problem of the color line, the only sort of South that can bolster
his life as a racial passer.

To pass for white in the end is not only to betray the protagonist's
African American roots and the ongoing black struggle for justice; it is
also to trade on his hemispheric southern connection as a means of en-
suring that his racial passing succeeds within the United States. His new
identity depends on the exploitation of Latin America, and that exploitation in turn suggests the transnational costs of black U.S. collaboration with the white imperial elite. If the protagonist has sold his
birthright for a mess of pottage, perhaps we should see that birthright
not simply as a connection to black U.S. society, but in larger terms as a
tie to a more hemispheric community of color, one that transcends national and linguistic boundaries. The ex-colored man is no longer African
American in the fullest and most contentious sense of the term.[35]

Coda

Less than a year after *The Autobiography* was published, Johnson resigned his consular post in Corinto owing to the new Wilson administration's refusal to promote him or, indeed, any African American.
Johnson's work on behalf of the U.S. empire in Latin America had failed
to win over an administration that promoted an even more overt white
supremacist ideology than that of its Republican predecessor. Johnson
would use his anger over a frustrated diplomatic career to fuel a new
political career in the NAACP, but he would also draw on his fury to begin crafting a more explicit critique of the relationship between white
southern racism and U.S. imperialism.[36] Within weeks of leaving his position at the State Department, the black intellectual delivered a speech
entitled "Why Latin America Dislikes the United States." In this speech,
Johnson redefines traditional notions of conquest by pointing out that

Latin Americans have more to fear from the hemispheric spread of U.S. white supremacy than they do from U.S. designs on their land. For Johnson, imperialism is a matter not so much of territorial control, but of racial discourse. Citing the Latin American media's obsession with the high incidence of lynching in the United States, Johnson argues that many brown-skinned Latin Americans worry about the dangerous capacity of white U.S. racism to infect other parts of the hemisphere. Even those Latin American intellectuals such as Manuel Ugarte, the Argentine known for passionate anti-imperialist polemics, fear "not that southern republics will lose their independence to the United States, but that they will fall under the bane of American prejudice, a process which he has without doubt, observed going on slowly but surely in Cuba, Puerto Rico, and Panama."[37] In his response to Wilson and, indeed, all U.S. hemispheric imperialists, Johnson rejects the fiction of a civilizing mission and argues instead that U.S. expansion has led to nothing less than the deterioration of culture and society throughout the Americas. He suggests a perspective directly opposed to that of the fictional Union soldier with which we began. If the GAR man had suggested that the United States was superior to the Latin republics because it has solved its own southern problem, Johnson argues to the contrary that not only did the problem of the U.S. South persist but that it was being exported to the very countries the United States intended to uplift. Johnson would reiterate this point seven years later when he indicted the U.S. occupation of Haiti: "the mere idea of white Mississippians going down to civilize Haitians and teach them law and order would be laughable except for the fact that the attempt is actually being made to put the idea into execution."[38] The United States did not constitute some ordered hemispheric North to a chaotic hemispheric South, but instead suggested the degree to which one region could render an entire nation prejudiced, unjust, and violently oppressive. By reading the U.S. empire through a southern regional lens, Johnson managed to articulate publicly a critique he had woven into the subtext of his passing novel. The "dixiefication" of the White House undermines the Roosevelt Corollary Johnson had once found so appealing.

3

"TAKE YOUR GEOGRAPHY AND TRACE IT"

W. E. B. Du Bois and the Reconstruction of the South

Here in this South is the gateway to the colored millions of the
West Indies, Central and South America. Here is the straight
path to Africa, the Indies, China, and the South Seas. Here is the
path to the greater, freer, truer world.

W. E. B. Du Bois, "Behold the Land"

Few modern U.S. intellectuals had a greater claim to a global purview
than W. E. B. Du Bois, the African American polymath whose rich and
complex life ranged from Atlanta to Accra, the Berkshires to Berlin. Du
Bois made his internationalism particularly evident in his wide-ranging
work on race and racism. Such texts as *Darkwater* (1919) and *Color and
Democracy* (1945) demonstrate that Du Bois devoted considerable time
and energy to examining the domestic problem of the color line in tandem with its global counterpart. *Darkwater*, for example, links the 1917
riot in St. Louis to international imperialism by arguing that "Streams
of gold lost from the world's workers . . . put new power into the thun-
derbolts of East St. Louis"; while *Color and Democracy* opens by pointing
out that the 1944 conference to create the United Nations Security Council occurred at Dumbarton Oaks, a former slave plantation in Washington, D.C. where "problems of race and color . . . lingered."[1] Du Bois,
without question, was fiercely dedicated to the African American struggle for radical democracy in the United States. But crucially, he rarely
understood the question of black rights as an exclusively national question. For this black intellectual, color almost always exceeded the normative bounds of the American polity.

To examine the figure of the domestic South in the work of such a global thinker might seem counterintuitive. After all, if Du Bois insisted on examining issues of race and justice in a national and international framework, then surely a focus on region denies the expansive geography of his political imagination. Much of the best recent work on Du Bois suggests as much. Critics including Dohra Ahmad, Paul Gilroy, Amy Kaplan, Bill Mullen, Ross Posnock, John Carlos Rowe, Kenneth Warren, and Alys Weinbaum have reexamined the Du Bois oeuvre with a particular emphasis on issues of race, space, and power.[2] Those scholars have celebrated the international Du Bois, an intellectual sensitive to matters of nation and world, cosmopolitanism and imperialism, Africa and Asia; yet in the process they have tended to minimize the question of the local and the regional.[3] That is, even as a few of these figures— Amy Kaplan and Alys Weinbaum, for example—devote some attention to Du Bois's commentary on the black belt, they distance their work on this geographic formation from any broader analysis of his representation of the South. For the new Du Boisians, what is at stake in the writer's massive corpus is neither his finely wrought representation of a Georgia county in *The Souls of Black Folk* (1903) nor his astute commentary on Mer Rouge, Louisiana, in "The Shape of Fear" (1926) but rather his extraordinary capacity to subvert and reimagine our largest geographies.

This general discounting of the role of the regional in Du Bois ignores the black intellectual's own biography and interests. Du Bois spent almost thirty years of his adult life in the South—mainly in Georgia and Tennessee—and well understood that, as Thadious Davis has put it, this portion of the United States, "though fraught with pain and difficulty, provides a major grounding of identity" for African Americans.[4] More remarkably, Du Bois also emphasized that the region notorious for domestic racial crisis held extraordinary significance for the global struggle against white empire.[5] His internationalism, in other words, didn't so much oppose as stand in dynamic relation to his regionalism. Du Bois recognized that the white supremacist practices of the South had played a crucial role in national racism, and through the rising global power of the United States, attained a newly visible role on the world stage. The sad spectacle of the Jim Crow South could hardly be ignored during an era in which the United States was emerging as a global hegemon. Yet if Du Bois invoked the regional question to stress that, as he argued in a 1927 debate with white supremacist Lothrop Stoddard, the world noticed brutal lynchings in Mississippi, he also believed that the South had another potential global meaning, one based not on its capacity to reveal the depredations of white Americans to "hundreds of darker millions," but on its extraordinary power to illustrate the strength and resistance of oppressed colored subjects.[6] Eager to instantiate his belief in African America as the vanguard of the colored world, Du Bois found in the black communities of the South a political-cum-mythic touch-stone for the colored contest with imperialism. For Du Bois, the South seemed at once geopolitically relevant and spiritually resonant, an exceptional region where politics and prophecy spoke in equal measure.[7] The racist violence endemic to the region might generate a certain international significance, but for Du Bois the South proved even more meaningful because its black citizens had demonstrated their ability to extract from terrible suffering a fierce call for global justice.[8]

One can find early evidence for this thesis when Du Bois imagines "the sorrow songs" as "the articulate message of the slave to the world" in *The Souls of Black Folk* (123); or elsewhere, in *The Quest of the Silver Fleece*, when he states that the world craves the clothing that only black-grown cotton can provide.[9] Yet it is only in the latter half of his career that one finds Du Bois fully reimagining normative geography to claim the black South as an integral part of the insurgent colored world; or, as he puts it in the speech "Behold the Land" (1947), to identify the South as "the straight path to Africa, the Indies, China, and the South Seas."[10] In what follows, I examine the novel *Dark Princess* (1928) and the history *Black Reconstruction* (1935), two texts that demonstrate Du Bois's belief that any attempt to understand and combat the problem of global racism demands that one recognize how the U.S. South is at once part of a white imperial nation and part of Africa and Asia. Positing the southland as a threshold space, "the gateway to the colored millions," *Dark Princess* and *Black Reconstruction* reveal that Du Bois was during the 1920s and 1930s crafting his own version of what Kenneth Frampton calls "critical regionalism": an attempt to "mediate the impact" of global capitalism "with elements derived *indirectly* from the peculiarities of a particular place" (emphasis in the original).[11] Dismissing the modern metropole as a site of consumerism and degradation, affirming the virtues of rural work and culture, Du Bois found in southern life the potential for international resistance to modern capital and empire.[12]

If Du Bois's brand of critical regionalism sometimes grows overly pastoral—if he, in other words, sometimes slips into a bit of African American agrarianism—his affective investment in the southland proved integral to his capacity to imagine a new black internationalism, one sensitive to the complex interplay between city and country, metropole and province, home and away. Du Bois may have occasionally over-indulged his georgic tastes, but he valued the culture African Americans created in the South and found in black rural life and work inspiration for the great struggle against white empire. It was on southern ground, Du Bois argued, that black Americans pursued lives that, for all their pain, were not reducible to capitalism but instead manifested an insurgent ethos shared with millions of other poor people of color around the globe. It was in this bloody and contested place that the blossoming of the cotton field and the pathos of the sorrow song provided a rationale for redrawing the maps of power. For all his pastoral excesses, Du Bois still managed to redefine the U.S. South as nothing less than a portal to an anti-imperial world.

Du Bois in the 1920s

The post–World War I era witnessed searching and widespread reassessments of region and regionalism on the part of many artists and intellectuals. European Americans and African Americans alike responded to their nation's unprecedented involvement in a European conflict not only by embracing isolation, but also by rediscovering the virtues of the local and the grassroots. Indeed, as Robert Dorman has argued, an era we often think of as typified by a "revolt against the village" was in many ways exemplified by an equally important "revolt of the provinces."[13] For white liberal philosophers like John Dewey that regional turn meant claiming that "locality is the only universal";[14] for immigrant geographers like Carl Sauer an interest in the local demanded a new culturalist definition of region;[15] for elements of the white avant-garde like Mabel Dodge Luhan, the exotic terrain of Taos, New Mexico, beckoned; while for some white conservatives like the Agrarians the return to section meant taking a stand for the white South and the Lost Cause.

The writers of the New Negro Renaissance also participated in this contemporary writing of place, but for them urban neighborhoods like Harlem loomed as large as acknowledged regions like the Midwest or the South. Novelists such as Claude McKay (*Home to Harlem* [1928]) and Wallace Thurman (*The Blacker the Berry* [1929]) represented the black metropolis in terms that captured a rich range of African American everyday life, seamy and refined, high and low. Thanks to their efforts and related work by such white writers as Carl Van Vechten, Harlem attained a new literary status as the premier black urban region. Yet for all the hoopla surrounding the northern portion of Manhattan, important New Negro writers also focused on that older and more established African American place, the U.S. South. Even as hundreds of thousands of black southerners streamed northward, eager to make a new life for themselves in New York and Chicago, African American literati like Langston Hughes ("The Negro Speaks of Rivers" [1921]), Zora Neale Hurston ("John Redding Goes to the Sea" [1921]), and Jean Toomer (*Cane* [1923]) reimagined the very place from which the Great Migration had sprung. This new regional writing hardly downplayed the terrifying aspects of the South. Every Renaissance writer that engaged with this most important of African American places emphasized the horrors of Jim Crow. At the same time, some of the New Negro writers found among the terrors of the southland a sense of pastoral beauty and African American cultural richness that merited celebration. As white writer Waldo Frank put it when describing Toomer's experimental text, "the Southland is not a problem to be solved; it is a field of loveliness to be sung: the Georgia negro is not a downtrodden soul to be uplifted; he is material for gorgeous painting."[16] For these African American writers, we might say, the post–World War I regional turn inspired a radical redefinition of a place that had for their community typically manifested itself in tragic and terrifying terms.

Du Bois published many of the young African American literati in the *Crisis* and generally supported their work in the early 1920s. Yet if he found much to admire about the new young black writers, he also found fault with some of their chronicles of modern life. This wasn't simply a matter of a Du Boisian disdain for Harlem literature that focused on drinking, popular music, and sexuality. While Du Bois did critique such representations, he also expressed concern over the tendency of certain Jazz Age texts to accept a dominant consumerist conception of American identity rather than criticize white capital from a more diasporic or internationalist standpoint. As he put it in "Criteria for Negro Art" (1926), an essay originally delivered as a speech at the NAACP convention in Chicago, "What do we want? . . . Do we simply want to be Americans? . . . We who are dark can see America in a way that white Americans cannot. And seeing our country thus, are we satisfied with its present goals and ideals? . . . If you tonight suddenly should become full-fledged Americans; if your color faded . . . what is it that you would want? . . . the most powerful of motor cars . . . the most elaborate estate on the North Shore?"[17] That Du Bois viewed African American fascination with the crass and the commercial as a problem of both domestic and international proportions emerges elsewhere in this speech, when he invokes the examples of abrasive American tourists in Scotland and racist white visitors in Central America. In accepting the dictates of a Gatsby-like American dream, Du Bois argued, African Americans threatened to become part of the imperial problem. To criticize the more sensational work of the young writers of the Renaissance was for Du Bois to take issue with the idea that African American modernity depended on the embrace of a dehumanizing consumerism rather than on the cultivation of a critical attitude toward capitalism at home and abroad.

However, if Du Bois took African American writers to task for their

investment in a hedonistic literature of place, he also fell prey to the desire to imagine how capital might assist in the creation of an empow-
ered black geography. Even as he urged African Americans to resist the
lure of fancy motors cars and elaborate estates, he engaged in his own
1920s fantasy of redemptive capitalism, one not of consumerism at
home, but of "a fine and unusual job [of] imperialism" abroad.[18] Following his 1924 trip as the Coolidge administration's official envoy to
the inauguration of Liberian president-elect Charles King, Du Bois grew
passionate about a potential rubber tree plantation contract between the
Firestone Rubber Corporation and the West African republic. He urged
the Liberians to negotiate with the U.S. businessmen, sent an unsolicited
letter of advice to Harvey Firestone, and generally attempted to shape
what he hoped would be a new type of equitable arrangement between
white capital and a black polity. Du Bois's involvement in the Firestone-
Liberia arrangement was, of course, an attempt to ensure the survival
of a financially strapped African nation, not a celebration of African
American urban consumerism. Yet his hope for "a fine and unusual job
[of] imperialism" depended on a belief in capital no less unsettling than
that demonstrated by the Harlem novelists he decried. Indeed, Du
Bois's fantasy of "Black Zion" delivered by Firestone Rubber was more
significant than, for example, Claude McKay's representation of black
Manhattan, for Du Bois imagined that the Liberians would somehow
use their new corporate connections to ward off other capitalists and
employ their neocolonial relationship with the United States to block the
advances of rapacious European powers. If successful, the Liberian deal
with Firestone would reveal how a small nation of color might negotiate emerging forms of imperialism where, as Du Bois put it, "conquest
is only one method of domination. Economic onslaught with all its in-
tricacies and propaganda is often much more profitable."[19] The Liberian experiment was thus in Du Bois's view relevant not only to African
or indeed pan-African nations and peoples, but also to the colored
masses around the globe. "Liberia . . . is a little thing set upon a hill," he
wrote in 1925, "but it represents to me the world."[20]

The attempt to uplift Liberia through a new relationship to U.S. capital proved disastrous.[21] By 1926, when the final agreement for rubber
tree cultivation was signed, the Firestone Corporation, assisted by the
U.S. State Department, had strong-armed the Liberians into both borrowing five million dollars for infrastructural improvements and offering Firestone itself an absurdly profitable long-term contract to run
rubber plantations.[22] The new economic version of U.S. imperialism
proved no less devastating than the older territorial version. And Du
Bois was somewhat at fault. Instead of helping sustain an African republic and thus assist in the creation of an inspirational black polity for

all colored peoples, the eminent African American intellectual had inadvertently contributed to a new colonial crisis. He compounded matters by refusing to acknowledge fully the failings of the Liberian leaders, glossing over rampant corruption and state violence in a series of articles from the mid-1920s into the early 1930s. "Liberia is not faultless," wrote Du Bois in a postmortem on the entire affair, "She lacks training, experience, and thrift. But her chief crime is to be poor and black in a rich, white world."[23] That the Liberian elite were in fact guilty of far worse crimes such as slavery seemed less than relevant to Du Bois—an unfortunate example of how the black intellectual's longstanding belief in the need for a vanguard "Talented Tenth" could at times license what Kenneth Warren has rightly called oligarchic tendencies.[24]

Yet even as we must acknowledge that Du Bois was no less susceptible to a misguided understanding of capitalism's relation to black community than were some of the novelists of Harlem life, we also should recognize that the failure of his Liberian dream may have had other consequences for his black political geography. If the collapse of this particular black diasporic fantasy most likely contributed to a temporary diminution in Du Bois's Africanist writings and a concurrent decision to abandon temporarily the idea of Pan-African conferences, it also may have inspired him to reconsider the meaning of more proximate colored spaces.[25] This is hardly to argue that Du Bois followed the isolationist trend of the 1920s and abandoned his concern for the colored peoples of the world; his continuing investment in global anti-imperialism suggests otherwise. It is rather to contend that Du Bois's failed imperial experiment might have proven productive of a new kind of geographic thinking—one that involved not so much a rejection of the world as a new sensitivity to the relationship between the local and the global. Michelle Stephens has argued that "black notions of sovereignty . . . emerged very much in the face of and in opposition to new formations of empire following . . . WWI,"[26] and we may imagine that Du Bois found in the Firestone debacle a reason to rethink the political meaning of a more familiar black territory. That is, if the black intellectual had, as David Levering Lewis puts it, "a psychic need" to imagine a black space of global import, that need might have provoked a geographic reorientation away from Africa toward the southland.[27] Black Americans might lack "international interests," as Du Bois pointed out in a contemporary letter, but perhaps he could remap the world in a manner that somehow recovered those missing "interests" in the very act of chronicling the significance of the black natal zone. Perhaps he could, in other words, spiritually re-cross the black Atlantic to the southern United States in a manner that suggested not so much a rejection of black internationalism as an embrace of critical regionalism.[28]

"What Do You Mean by 'Southern'?"

Writing in "Worlds of Color" (1925) of the "vast gulf between the red-black South and the yellow-brown East," Du Bois pointed out that even as these cultures cannot be "pounded together artificially," they may "at no distant day come to a consciousness of aim" regarding white imperialism.[29] Three years later Du Bois published *Dark Princess,* a novel that imagined how that day might arrive in the U.S. South. *Dark Princess* chronicles the global romance of Matthew Towns, a black medical student and an exemplary representative of the Talented Tenth, and Kautilya, the Maharanee of Bwodpur, India. Through a marriage plot that unites a black southerner and an Indian, the text foreshadows the impending union of all the world's colored peoples in opposition to U.S. and European domination. Yet if this is the overt plot of the novel, the text's underlying theme is, as Arnold Rampersad has pointed out, the question "of the ability, qualifications, and real possibilities of the black race."[30] This isn't to deny Du Bois's interest in Kautilya's Indian identity or, indeed, in India itself. Like a number of prominent black intellectuals from Anna Julia Cooper to Martin Luther King, Jr., Du Bois recognized certain parallels, rough though they were, between the Indian struggle against British rule and the black American struggle against Jim Crow. Yet even as one can find references to the goddess Kali, the Ganges, and British power in the novel, *Dark Princess* is, at its core, concerned with another subject: how to map the global struggle against white empire in specifically African American terms. And it is this subject that, as we shall see, demands a new definition of the U.S. South as an internationally significant space no less extraordinary than the African American and Indian heroes it hosts.

To be sure, Du Bois recognized that such an anti-imperial fantasy of the U.S. South would likely seem absurd in light of the current Jim Crow regime, and he devoted key portions of *Dark Princess* to addressing the split between white supremacist realities and black regional possibilities. The novel's first major scene in a Berlin café makes this particularly evident. Despairing at ever being able to escape "the white leviathan," that seemingly unstoppable conglomeration of Western capital and state power, the hero Matthew Towns pines away for a specifically African American version of the southland (7):

> Oh, he was lonesome; lonesome and homesick with a dreadful home-sickness. After all, in leaving white, he had also left black America. . . . What would he not give to clasp a dark hand now, to hear a soft Southern roll of speech, to kiss a brown cheek? To see warm, brown, crinkly hair and laughing eyes. God—was he lonesome. So utterly, terribly lonesome. And then—he saw the Princess! (7–8).[31]

Lamenting the loss of his black natal zone, Matthew finds solace in the Princess, whose "golden brown skin" stands out within the German "world of pale yellowish and pinkish parchment" that surrounds both her and Matthew.[32] Her "glow" of radiant color has reparative capacities. The "brown cheek" of an aristocrat from the tropics stands in for the familiar brown cheek from Virginia; an Indian woman becomes Matthew's South away from home.

That Matthew longs for an implicitly feminine black South is hinted at in his references to softness and gentleness, but his turn to the Indian princess serves further to manifest how he understands both his loss and the possibility of reparation in explicitly gendered terms. Such an association of a natal space with the feminine is hardly surprising; from the idea of Mother Russia to the American icon of Lady Liberty, imagined communities have often been identified with some vision of the feminine or the maternal or both. Yet the Princess's capacity to figure Matthew's distant home is equivocal. The soothing vision of her "brown cheek" overlaps with the jarring voice of a white American who reminds Matthew that his feminized black South continues to endure the predatory attentions of a white supremacist society. "Look, there's that darky again," exclaims the white American racist. "Bet you a ten-spot I get her number before she leaves this café . . . I know niggers, and I don't mean perhaps" (9). Matthew may recognize the Princess as a comforting sign of his beloved black Virginia, but the white tourist "knows" her in racist and sexist terms. Even in Germany, a reassuring suggestion of the black belt must also conjure up its alter ego, the Jim Crow South.

Kautilya ignores the white American and leaves the café, but, undeterred, the aggressive racist approaches her again on the street, only to find himself knocked down by an enraged Matthew. Given the preceding invocation of a "southern roll of speech" and "a brown cheek," we may assume that Du Bois's hero defends the exotic woman's honor in the name of southern black women. His is a chivalric gesture that takes as its objective local, not global politics, the German setting notwithstanding. Yet if Matthew, the displaced black southerner, finds in a European café an opportunity to fight a regional battle, the Indian Princess locates a broader meaning in his physical confrontation with the white racist—a meaning that resonates far beyond the specificity of a particular Berlin establishment or a U.S. southern county. As she puts it a few pages later, referring to Matthew's act of heroism, "I had a curious sense of some greater inner meaning to your act—some world movement" (17). In taking a strange Indian Princess as a synecdoche for his black southern motherland, Matthew has sparked a transnational and interracial connection that will have enormous political ramifications. Within days of their first encounter, the Princess will recruit Matthew for the Great Council of Darker Peoples she leads, a primarily Asian and North African conglomerate of politicians and intellectuals who seek to end white domination throughout the world.

Yet if the Princess educates Matthew about the global struggle of colored peoples, Matthew offers her an equally important lesson about the African American dimensions of this contest, a lesson that demands some commentary on the southern question. He informs the Princess of his rural origins and long experience with white racism in the South, but also lays stress on the fluidity of this region as a space and an identity. After he states that "one Southern professor" at the University of Manhattan "gave me the devil of a time," the Princess interrupts with a question about geography: "Southern . . . What do you mean by 'Southern'?" only to receive a response that reveals quite a bit about Matthew and, as we shall see, Du Bois's attitude toward color and region: "I mean from the former slave States—although the phrase isn't just fair. Some of our most professional Southerners are Northern-born" (11). To explain the meaning of African American identity to his new Indian friend, Matthew must register the competing meanings of the South as a geographic and a political formation. "Southern" can mean white racists irrespective of location or, we might imagine, people who hail from "the former slave states," people who possess the "soft Southern roll of speech," and the "warm, brown, crinkly hair and laughing eyes" for which Matthew pines. In registering the home truth that white Northerners are profoundly implicated in Jim Crow, Matthew unwittingly raises the possibility of detaching the normative space of the region from any assumed relationship with white racism. The answer to "What do you mean by southern?" might seem to be "Jim Crow," but Du Bois refuses to foreclose the possibility that the South might have other meanings as well.

This isn't to deny Du Bois's recognition of white southern racism. Matthew emphasizes the terrors of the Jim Crow regime repeatedly throughout *Dark Princess,* most visibly perhaps in his mother's recollections of abuse or in the sequence when a Pullman porter is lynched by a group of Klansmen. Yet just as Du Bois was willing to cite and endorse white liberal Edwin Mims's claim that there were "two divisions of the South" in a March, 1927, issue of the *Crisis,* so too was the black intellectual willing to explore in his novel the idea that one could reclaim from the terrors of white supremacy an alternate space of black global potential.[33] The Indian Princess takes the lead in this regard. Kautilya's primary role in rehabilitating the South stems from no firsthand experience with the region, but from her persistent belief that any site of racial oppression can be reclaimed and transformed. As the most important member of an interracial global "committee" that seeks to address the situation of "darker peoples" "who suffer under the arrogance and tyranny of the white world," she realizes that the word "southern" has the potential to name something larger and more oppositional than a beleaguered black community (16). For Kautilya, as we shall see, the U.S. South is as much a part of an insurgent tropical world as it is a part of a white supremacist nation.

What makes her task difficult, and Matthew's introduction to the committee rather strained, is the fact that her group of passionate anti-imperialists is itself rather hierarchical. Composed of Indians, Chinese, Japanese, Egyptians, indeed, all peoples of color except members of the African diaspora, this group of cultured and in some case royal emissaries believe that they are superior to the white and black masses. Elite to the core, the various members of what we might call a global version of the Talented Tenth completely reject the notion that the world's workers should arise and reconstruct the world. Yet their mandarin attitude, however cultured, hardly receives the Princess's approval. To the contrary, Kautilya invokes her recent trip to the Soviet Union to rebut her colleagues' snobbishness with respect to a particular group of black diasporic people, African Americans. (Africans receive almost no attention in the novel.) The Princess explains to the committee members that during her time in the Communist nation she had the opportunity to read a report on African America. "If the report is true," she informs them, African Americans "are a nation today, a modern nation worthy to stand beside any nation here" (22). Kautilya's claim that black America constitutes "a modern nation" is repeated elsewhere in the chapter, and recalls what would become the single most important aspect of Communist policy with respect to black Americans during the 1920s and early 1930s (16). As Alys Weinbaum and Bill Mullen have each reminded us, the Fourth Congress of the Communist International (1922) endorsed the idea that "Negro Americans" had the right to pursue national self-determination. During the Sixth Party Congress (1928), the Comintern reaffirmed the thesis that African America was more than "a national minority"—the Soviet equivalent of "a mere amorphous handful"—but was instead "a nation within a nation."[34] While Du Bois never explicitly embraced the Communist position, choosing instead to promote his own equally controversial notion of voluntary African American segregation during the early 1930s, he was undoubtedly familiar with the "nation within a nation" idea during the writing of *Dark Princess* and uses it to add *gravitas* to the Princess's appeal.[35]

Yet even as we note the influence of Communist discourse on Kautilya's argument, it is important to recognize that her assertion of African American nationhood proves unpersuasive. The Princess's fellow committee members reject the Communist notion of a black "nation within a nation" and remain committed to an elitism that precludes any valuation of the black masses and their potential. Indeed, it is only after Matthew redefines the nationhood thesis in specifically southern pastoral terms that the assembled Asians and North Africans prove willing to rethink their objections. Angered by an Egyptian's assumption that "the canaille" could never produce anything of value, Matthew abandons international political rhetoric for regional musical performance and gives the Princess and her associates an impromptu version of "Go Down, Moses" (25): "His voice full, untrained but mellow, quivered down the first plaintive bar: 'When Israel was in Egypt land—'" (25–26). However distant from his contested natal zone, Matthew uses the iteration of this sorrow song as what Gilles Deleuze and Félix Guattari call a refrain—a musical means of ordering chaotic territory that, as the French philosophers argue, "always carries earth with it."[36] Matthew's musical performance both reterritorializes a German room as an African American space and demonstrates what the Princess had failed to prove through her citation of the Comintern report: the existence of an oppressed African American community worthy of Middle Eastern and Asian support.[37] Singing "as his people sang in Virginia, twenty years ago," Matthew dramatizes the African American claim to land, to territory—a precondition to being taken seriously as an imagined community by his Asian and Arab auditors and a first step toward redefining this part of the United States as a black polity with crucial ties to the rest of the colored world.

The Imperial City

"Go Down, Moses" is, as the Chinese member of Kautilya's committee puts it, "an American slave song." But it is also a country song—"the Voice of Angels upon the Hills of God," as Du Bois points out in a contemporary reminiscence of his time in Tennessee—that recalls "the sorrow of riven souls suddenly articulate . . . and the defiance of deathless hope."[38] These lines from "What Is Civilization?" (1925) well suggest how Du Bois located in black rural life and culture a vital source of anti-racism and remind us of how different his regionalism was from that of his contemporaries, the Vanderbilt Agrarians. Du Bois's emphasis on the value of the rural south may recall *I'll Take My Stand* (1930), but the black intellectual's inheritance of the Jeffersonian legacy hardly conforms to that of Donald Davidson, John Crowe Ransom, Allen Tate, and their colleagues. As Davidson would make evident in his brief review of *Dark Princess*, Du Bois's "extreme propagandist" critique of "white civilization" stood far apart from the Agrarian challenge to the modern and the urban.[39] The African American writer would affirm the point in *Black Reconstruction* when he indicted the work of Vanderbilt historian Walter Fleming, the Agrarians' mentor and the dedicatee of *I'll Take My Stand*. For Du Bois, rural black Southern culture offers important lessons not only because it opposes urban capital and urban modernity, but also because it indicts white racism and white empire: colonial modernity by another name.

That said, Du Bois does devote a fair amount of time in *Dark Princess* to contrasting the power of black rural life with the degeneration of African American metropolitan existence—a theme that affects his representation of black labor. The novel signals its profound investment in labor from the beginning of its second section, "The Pullman Porter," until its last sublime affirmation of pastoral black Virginia, but it also suggests that the customary forms and contexts of worker organization will not suffice to link the domestic and global problems of the color line. Shortly after meeting with the Princess and her committee, Matthew returns to the United States and takes a job as a Pullman porter, the most militant of any group of black workers during the 1920s. This association with the Pullman porters helps Matthew meet Perigua, the Marcus Garvey–like leader of a black organization to whom the Princess has sent a message about global colored insurgency. Matthew's homecoming, in other words, connects him with two of the most powerful examples of black working-class activism in modern U.S. history: the Brotherhood of Sleeping Car Porters, the first major black union, and the United Negro Improvement Association, arguably the most important example of black nationalism in twentieth-century America. Yet Du Bois does not pursue this fantastic possibility for African American working-class solidarity; in other words, he fails to offer a national version of the transnational colored insurgency affirmed by the Committee in the novel's opening pages. What might have served as a narrative opportunity to imagine an inspiring collaboration of A. Philip Randolph's union and Marcus Garvey's nationalist organization becomes instead an occasion for loss and grief. The porters' association cannot protect black workers from being treated miserably and on one occasion killed. For all their narrative interest and documentary detail, neither labor association affords Matthew an opportunity to uplift either himself or black America. Instead of enabling him to live up to his heroic potential, Matthew's involvement with Perigua lands him in jail.

To some extent, Du Bois's dystopic representation of both the Pullman porters and Perigua's UNIA-like organization may reflect personal animosity. During the 1920s, Randolph criticized Du Bois for his elitism in the pages of the *Chicago Defender* while Garvey attacked the NAACP leader in a more personal fashion, arguing that Du Bois's light skin made him less than fully African American. Du Bois and his associates at the *Crisis* and the NAACP responded in kind, labeling Garvey a vulgar and dark-skinned foreigner. Yet even as biographical and historical factors can explain Matthew's miserable experience with the porters and Perigua, with northern and urban working-class activism, the novel's constant attention to issues of geography raise another possibility: that the failure of the porters' association signals less Du Bois's elitism and disinterest in black nationalism than the author's critical regionalism of a distinctly pastoral kind. Du Bois criticizes both black activist rebellions for their urban modernity, their alienation from a rural experience that could connect them to the world's colored peasantry.

Nowhere is Du Bois's critique of urban identity more visible than in the Chicago section of the novel, where Matthew, freed from jail through the machinations of Sara, an ambitious African American woman, and Sammy, her politician boss, finds himself seduced by the decadent pleasures of urban life and the unctuous attractions of machine politics. The South Side of Chicago, Sammy's fiefdom, is no less African American than the southern black belt from which many of these city dwellers hail. Yet for Du Bois, the obsession with cash and commodities that informs urban life renders what should be an epicenter of black working-class insurgency little more than a site of black immorality. Du Bois recalls here the critique of metropolitan capital he offered in "Criteria of Negro Art" (1926). Sammy and Sara, the two figures central to Matthew's tenure in Chicago, are both obsessed with money and influence. Matthew's willingness not only to become the power couple's political candidate but also to marry Sara as a campaign stratagem, renders him part of the problem. And this is, importantly, a dilemma of domestic and international scope. Matthew claims to one of the Princess's Japanese associates visiting him in Chicago that African Americans "have nothing in common with other peoples. We are fighting our own battle here in America with more or less success. We are not looking for help beyond our borders, and we need all our strength at home" (150). One senses here Du Bois's critical representation of those African Americans who had in the post–World War I era rejected internationalism as irrelevant to their daily lives. For in Du Bois's view, Matthew's exclusive focus on domestic politics suggests not so much a form of black activism as a tragic willingness to accept a modern American way that was as dominated by capital as it was by whiteness. It comes as no surprise that Sammy and Sara are willing to negotiate with white businessmen to "colonize" the nation's rivers, for the two black politicos are no less imperialist than the white urban interests to which they minister (152).

Digging for the Bottom

When Kautilya rescues Matthew just before he is about to sell what remains of his soul to urban power, black and white, she inspires him to recover his political values through an earthy task indeed: the excavation of the new Chicago subway. "To dig, that's it," she writes Matthew enthusiastically. "To get down to reality. . . . We start to dig, remaking the world" (256). If Matthew's willingness to shame himself with dirt suggests a certain Christian lesson about humility and personal growth, for Kautilya it also bespeaks a need to get to the gritty bottom of workers' reality—to plumb the depths of labor's experience in order to gain the perspective needed to reconstruct the world. When Matthew decides to dig for a new identity among the urban proletariat, his Indian love chooses to return to Virginia, to a black U.S. South that seems to recall for her "the black South" of the Indian subcontinent (228). Worried that she has forsaken everything for a quixotic dream of uplifting the masses, Kautilya despairs over her future and that of the world until she returns to Matthew's small Virginia cabin and the strong woman who lives there, "tall, big, and brown" (268). For the Indian princess, this humble cabin and its rustic surroundings soon evolve from a "temporary refuge" where she can ponder her next step to a permanent "founding-stone" where she can not only experience the lessons of proletarian life, but also plan with Matthew a revolution against white capital and empire (278). Toward that end, she emphasizes to Matthew in a letter that his southern natal space is far less geographically and politically isolated than he imagines:

> This world is really much nearer to our world than I had thought. . . .
> Think, Matthew, take your geography and trace it: from Hampton Roads
> to Guiana is a world of colored folk, and a world, men tell me, physically
> beautiful beyond conception; socially enslaved, industrially ruined, spir-
> itually dead; but ready for the breath of Life and Resurrection. South is
> Latin America, east is Africa, and east of east lies my own Asia. (278)

By urging Matthew to take his geography "and trace it," Kautilya suggests the importance of redrawing existing cartographies in a manner that better promotes interracial solidarity against empire. To think of the U.S. South as separate from Latin America, Africa, and Asia is to capitulate cartographically to white empire; resistance demands new maps and new futures. Or, as she puts it, in remapping the world, "we sense a new age."

Du Bois does not allow this radical reconception of a global U.S. South to stand unchallenged. Even as the black intellectual sought to redefine this black place as a pastoral site of colored resistance, he was all too aware of its terrible past and present. Matthew thus writes back hurriedly to warn Kautilya that her new geography will not hold. The South is a "horror" (279); only the modern metropole will provide them with a proper staging ground for revolution and change. "No, no, Kautilya of the World, no, no!" he protests to his cosmopolitan correspondent:

> This land is literally accursed with the blood and pain of three hundred years of slavery. . . . Ask mother. Ask her to tell you how many years she has fought and clawed for the honor of her own body. . . . Only in the center of the world can our work be done. We must stand, you and I, even if apart, where beats down the fiercest blaze of Western civilization, and pushing back this hell, raise a black world upon it. (279)

Emphasizing the vulnerability of the black woman and the black home, Matthew insists that Kautilya has not traced her geography accurately. Remote and rural, this Virginia county at once countenances racist violence and lies too far from the "fiercest blaze of Western civilization" for any African American rebellion to matter in meaningful political terms. The South's lack of modernity renders the prospect of contesting control of the region at once frightening and meaningless. Instead, radicals of color should foment a black rebellion in the urban centers of modern capitalism. "If . . . in Chicago we can kill the thing that America stands for," he writes Kautilya, "we emancipate the world" (284–85).[40] Matthew thus envisions an insurrection that recalls the Haymarket bombing— "great strokes of force—clubs, guns, dynamite in the hand of fanatics"—and dreams of a black revolution that will demolish white power at its nodal point (284).

But Du Bois undercuts his hero's macho affirmation of black metropolitan insurrection with Kautilya's more modest, not to say domestic, vision of human resilience and generativity—a vision that emphasizes the capacity of female bodies to both commemorate injustice (e.g., the scars Matthew's mother bears [279]) and physically and intellectually produce change.[41] While fully aware that she and Matthew's mother are tremendously vulnerable to local white racists, Kautilya rejects the "fire and sword" of traditional revolution for the green fecundity of natural renewal (285). She expresses her rural pacifism through a number of pastoral images, none more distinctly southern than her appropriation of cotton: "The cotton lies dark green, dim crimson . . . my own hand has carried the cotton basket, and now I sit and know that everywhere seed that is hidden, dark, inert, dead, will one day be alive, and here, here!" (282). Kautilya reminds us of her pregnancy; the agricultural growth of the plant parallels the uterine growth of her child. Yet, as Alys

Weinbaum has argued, in suggesting that a fertile revolution lies waiting in the seeds of cotton, Du Bois also directs us to the radical global
gathering that this unborn child will inspire.[42] Du Bois had engaged
with the international implications of the cotton crop several times before in his work. In *The Souls of Black Folk,* he emphasizes that the sweat
of African American labor ensures that "the Cotton Kingdom still lives;
the world still bows beneath her sceptre. Even the markets that once de-
fied the parvenu have crept one by one across the seas, and then slowly
and reluctantly, but surely, have started toward the Black Belt"; adding,
"the Negro forms to-day one of the chief figures in a great world-in-
dustry" (66). And in *The Quest of the Silver Fleece,* Du Bois links the pro-
ductivity of black cotton farmers explicitly to an interracial global
sphere: "From the peasant toiling in Russia, the lady lolling in London,
the chieftain burning up in Africa, and the Esquimaux freezing in
Alaska . . . went up the cry, 'Clothes, clothes!' . . . All that dark earth
heaved in mighty travail with the bursting bolls of the cotton while
black attendant earth spirits swarmed above" (54). Yet if these references
highlight connections between the black rural workers of the U.S. South
and the many peoples of the world, Kautilya's suggestion that an oppressive symbol of the plantation system might be appropriated for an
international insurrection of color brings these implications to fruition.
The pastoral mode is rendered radical; the insurgency of the masses
proves coterminous with the growth of the cotton over which they toil.
Much as the rural peoples are dark and inert, dead to their political potential, so too will they erupt into life and beget a new age.

Indeed, Kautilya's political riff on the southern pastoral tradition suggests the degree to which she imagines the entire U.S. South as vulnerable to appropriation from within. While the Indian princess does agree
with Matthew that anti-imperialist intellectuals must situate their struggle in the most powerful nation of all, the United States, she also insists
that rebels of color cannot take a stand in the metropole itself. As she
argues,

> To be in the center of power is not enough. You must be free and able to
> act. You are not free in Chicago or New York. But here in Virginia you are
> at the edge of a black world. The black belt of the Congo, the Nile, and the
> Ganges reaches by way of Guiana, Haiti, and Jamaica, like a red arrow, up
> into the heart of white America. Thus I see a mighty synthesis: you can
> work in Africa and Asia right here in America if you work in the Black
> Belt. (286)

Du Bois returns here to the figure of the black belt that plays such a
prominent role in his most famous work, *The Souls of Black Folk.* Yet if the
black belt in *Souls* names a largely domestic geography long dominated

by white racists, here it suggest the transnational flow of color from the rivers of the developing world into the heart of the United States, a transnational flow that offers black people just enough space to rebel against white America from within. The black belt of which Kautilya writes may be in "this ruthless, terrible, intriguing Thing," white America, but its connection to an international colored sphere renders it strong enough to resist the depredations of local white racism (286). Indeed, insofar as the black belt brings Africa and Asia to white capitalist America, it provides anti-imperialists with a unique Archimedean point from which "to lift earth and seas and stars" (286). If the black belt provides activists of color with the room needed to operate, its place within and without the U.S. ensures that their rebellion will resonate throughout the world.

Kautilya's appropriation of the U.S. South as a place of global revolutionary significance does not suggest the sort of color bias some of her fellow committee members had suggested earlier in the novel. Instead, the Indian princess's turn to the South and its potential suggests her faith in "the unlovely masses of men," black, yellow, brown, and white. For Kautilya, the inclusion of white labor in a revolution of the entire proletariat must follow the emergence of colored peoples in a process of "gradual emancipation, self-rule, and world-wide abolition of the color line, and of poverty and war" (297). And this colored liberation depends, in time-honored Du Boisian fashion, on intellectuals capable of leading people forward. Thus, the denouement of the novel includes a gathering of global representatives of colored peoples in Matthew's humble Virginia home. The once seemingly provincial backwater now hosts emissaries from Japan, China, Persia, Arabia, Afghanistan, the Sudan, South America, the West Indies, and "Black America" (297). The event is indeed auspicious. Upon arriving in rural Virginia Matthew realizes that Kautilya has invited him not only for a meeting of the council but also for a wedding and a meeting with his child. When Kautilya informs Matthew that she has given birth to Madhu, the novel's messianic figure, she affirms the capacity of the body to produce a bridge over the gulf between "the black-red South" and "the yellow-brown East," to find in amalgamation a connection between disparate races and far-flung spaces. And Madhu's mediatory role in the novel's closing pages cannot help but recall the similar function of the South as a mythic geographic conduit between African Americans and the colored masses, the United States and the world. Virginia, the black belt, the South: these overlapping geographic formations provided Du Bois with a way of grounding his dreams of a pan-colored union in a recognizably African American space. That he would continue to explore this idea in his next major work, *Black Reconstruction*, doesn't so much suggest that his African fantasies had disappeared as emphasize how the counter-intuitive notion of a *global* U.S. South retained a persistent hold on his imagination.

Remapping *Black Reconstruction*

In *Black Reconstruction,* begun in 1931 and published in 1935, Du Bois reframed the idea of a globalized U.S. South in diachronic terms.[43] Dispensing with narrative fiction to return to his customary role as an activist-scholar, Du Bois created in this radical text a new historical narrative, one that explained "the part in which black folk played in the attempt to reconstruct democracy in America." In opposition to John Burgess, William Dunning, Walter Fleming, and other influential white historians of the era, Du Bois challenged the idea that Reconstruction was in its fleeting attempt to establish equal rights for blacks a monstrous aberration. He emphasized not only that Reconstruction was too short-lived, but also, and more important, that African Americans themselves were historical agents—escaping the peculiar institution with regularity, serving as the "underlying cause" of the massive conflagration, turning on white plantation owners with the arrival of northern troops, and insisting on their right to citizenship (15). And for Du Bois, this agency persisted despite the oppression perpetrated by late nineteenth- and twentieth-century white southerners *and* northerners eager to reap capitalist rewards from the exploitation of black labor.

To be sure, *Dark Princess* and *Black Reconstruction* are very different texts. *Dark Princess* is a rapturous and meditative novel; *Black Reconstruction* is a well-researched historiography. *Dark Princess* addresses the reading public; *Black Reconstruction* takes as its audience scholars and political activists. Yet for all their divergent qualities, these two works overlap in significant ways, suggesting perhaps that Du Bois's interest in combining different genres in one volume (e.g., *Darkwater*) also may have obtained in two major publications separated chronologically and formally.[44] *Dark Princess* and *Black Reconstruction* both showcase the singular place of the black South in the global anti-imperialist project. In each work, Du Bois represents the black rural worker's experience in the South as "the founding stone" (*Dark Princess*) or "foundation stone" (*Black Reconstruction*) of the ongoing struggle between white empire and colored labor in the modern world. That this is a historical conceit goes without saying; black rural workers in both texts lay claim to a primary role in both the creation of and the challenge to white empire. Yet as the shared emphasis on foundations should suggest, it is as well a spatial notion, one that links a domestic region to the developing world. The black southern experience is not only "the very first chapter of that great story of industry, wage and wealth, government, life," as Kautilya puts it in *Dark Princess;* it is also a story of "the black man . . . on whom the South had built an oligarchy similar to . . . colonial imperialism" (237). Du Bois needed to find in the nightmarish sprawl of the African American experience some landmark, some site, from which to draw a new map, and in *Black Reconstruction* as in *Dark Princess,* he locates that place in the very southland African Americans have insisted against all odds on making their own. Much as fugitive slaves used "the physical geography of America with its paths north, by swamp, river, and mountain range" to make a new life for themselves, so too does Du Bois use the regional formation of the southeast to blaze a path toward a new understanding of nation and world (13).

One senses as much in some of the key passages in which Du Bois leads the reader from the regional to the national to the global. Thus in one introductory paragraph focused largely on the antebellum era, he moves fluidly from delineating a vertical hierarchy in which black slaves occupy "the bottom" to an expansive internationalism in which their experience now takes on potentially new political meanings:

> The black workers . . . bent at the bottom of a growing pyramid of commerce and industry . . . became the cause of . . . new dreams of power and visions of empire.
>   First of all, their work called for widening stretches of new, rich black soil—in Florida, Louisiana, in Mexico. . . . This land, added to cheap labor, and labor easily regulated and distributed, made profits so high that a whole system of culture arose in the South. . . . Black labor became the foundation stone not only of the Southern social structure, but of Northern manufacture and commerce, of the English factory system, of European commerce, of buying and selling on a world-wide scale. (5)

In recovering the suppressed history of black labor in the South, Du Bois links those exploited workers to spaces—England, Europe—that seem to exceed the putatively national limits of his revisionist project and hence indicate the shadow that the peculiar institution continued to cast across the entire world. Like such later scholars as Eric Williams, Oliver Cromwell Cox, and Paul Gilroy, Du Bois insists that slavery is part of global modernity. Yet this expansive strategy has another dimension as well. Through his emphasis on the global significance of the black southern condition, Du Bois also highlights the potential power of the black worker. Du Bois emphasizes the terrible wrongs inflicted on black labor in the antebellum and postbellum South, but he also suggests that bearing this burden has rendered black labor an agent in the construction of the modern world: "the cause of new dreams of power" and "the founding stone" of global empire. International capitalism grew from both the profits and the ideology of the South's peculiar institution, but at the same time capital could not help but render black slaves an integral part of the developmental process. To make broad claims about the international significance of exploited black labor in the U.S. South is at the same time to begin to build the case for the agency black labor possessed. Matthew's hard-working mother provides a touchstone for Kautilya's global anti-imperialist movement in *Dark Princess;* her slave ancestors serve a similar function for Du Bois's anti-imperialist argument in *Black Reconstruction.*

Such a thesis will recall Marx's claims about the international power of labor—one more example of how Du Bois, while not yet a Communist, continued to maintain a steady interest in the idea of a powerful proletariat long after his trip to the Soviet Union.[45] Indeed, even when Du Bois admits that the "redemption" of the white South and the creation of the Jim Crow regime seem to have destroyed black political hopes, one senses on his part an insistence that black workers still play a singularly important role in national and global imperialism: "The United States [government], reinforced by the increased political power of the South based on disenfranchisement of black voters, took its place to reinforce the capitalistic dictatorship of the United States . . . which backed the new industrial capitalism and degraded colored labor the world over" (630–31). Du Bois contends that the disenfranchisement of black voters has helped the United States establish itself as an imperial powerhouse, thus adumbrating C. Vann Woodward's similar argument about the relationship between the notorious Mississippi plan and U.S. expansion in *The Origins of the New South* (1951). Yet for Du Bois the exclusion of the black southern voter from the postbellum regional and national political process does not simply illustrate the increasing influence of white southern racism in an imperial age; it also suggests the degree to which a concern with free African Americans haunts the nation's status as a rising global power. As Du Bois puts it elsewhere in the volume, "there was the black man looming like a dark ghost on the horizon" (240). If "the United States . . . became the cornerstone of that new imperialism which is subjecting the labor of yellow, brown and black peoples to the dictation of capitalism organized on a world basis," the nation's singular status still depended in slippery and potentially disastrous ways on black southerners (631). As the United States grows ever more central to colonial modernity, so too do black southerners by default grow more significant, dark ghosts inhabiting the new global hegemon and its capitalist allies around the world.

This is of course the message of *Dark Princess* that first Kautilya and then eventually Matthew learns. The black rural proletariat of the South signifies freedom far in excess of its education, economic resources, and political opportunities. The "forty-acre farm" tilled by Matthew's mother hardly delimits the range of her agency or, indeed, the historical meaning of the unfinished Reconstruction that provided the family with the land some fifty years before (11). But what ties *Black Reconstruction* more closely still to its novelistic predecessor is its covert appreciation of the agricultural work accomplished by black rural labor and its more explicit denunciation of the modern city. While *Black Reconstruction* does not wax lyrical about the pastoral black South—Du Bois's relentless critique of slavery and Jim Crow does not allow for that—it does emphasize that African Americans grew the cotton that "clothed the masses of a ragged world" during the nineteenth century, and that it is colored labor that spawns "the world's raw material and luxury" in the present (4, 15). As in *Dark Princess*, cotton, that iconic sign of the South, serves Du Bois as a means of invoking the enormous energy and historical potential of African America. This focus on the extraordinary capacities of the cotton worker underwrites Du Bois's sense of the black South as a historically oppressed, but still extraordinary region resistant to metropolitan imperialism.

Nowhere in *Black Reconstruction* does this contrast between the corrupt city and the prophetic black South emerge more powerfully than in the penultimate moments of the chapter "The Coming of the Lord." After discussing Emancipation in fairly sober historiographic terms, Du Bois turns to one of the more purple passages for which *Black Reconstruction* is often faulted. "Suppose on some gray day, as you plod down Wall Street," Du Bois writes, "you should see God sitting on the Treasury steps, in His Glory . . . ? Suppose on Michigan Avenue, between the lakes and hills of stone, and in the midst of hastening automobiles and jostling crowds, suddenly you see living and walking toward you, the Christ" (123–24). Du Bois labels all of this "foolish talk" but the bitter contrast between God and the Treasury or Christ and "the lakes and hills of stone" suggests that we have once again returned to the critique of the city central to *Dark Princess*'s radical agrarianism. Much like Sammy and Sara, the anonymous urban walkers in New York and Chicago know nothing of the spiritual world.

Du Bois invokes the contemporary city here not to dwell on its failures, but rather to dramatize all the more the amazing effusion of black hope that erupts from the South after 1865. He represents this "joy in the South" by turning once again to his leitmotif of the sorrow songs,

A great song arose, the loveliest things borne this side of the seas. It was a new song. It did not come from Africa, though the dark throb and beat of that Ancient of days was in it and through it. It did not come from white America—never from so pale and thin a thing, however deep these vulgar and surrounding tones had driven. Not in the Indies nor the hot South, the cold East or the heavy West made that music. It was a new song and its deep and plaintive beauty, its great cadences and wild appeal wailed, throbbed and thundered on the world's ears with a message seldom voiced by man. (124–25)

Note the care with which Du Bois maps this "message seldom voiced by man." While he clearly claims that the "great song" has meaning for all people, its origins are particular to the natal geography of African American labor. He emphasizes that the spirituals are from neither Africa nor white America, neither the Indies nor the other great spaces of the globe. This music is from black America, and black America in this volume, as in *Dark Princess*, is located in the southland. In a sense this passage constitutes Du Bois's recapitulation of Matthew's gesture before the anti-imperialist committee in *Dark Princess*. If the black hero turned to "Go Down, Moses" to dramatize for his skeptical colored interlocutors the black claim on community, Du Bois makes much the same move here. In their demand for radical democracy for all workers of color, the sorrow songs at once hearken back to a specifically black and southern point of origin and, at the same time, manage to call out to "the world's ears." In *Black Reconstruction* black country music not only highlights the many failings of a corrupt city but also demonstrates to the world the agency and drive of black people, their capacity to fight "the battle of all the oppressed and despised humanity of every race and color" from the more remote rural corners of the nation (708).

For Du Bois, the "sorrow songs" manage to keep this cry alive, calling out to oppressed labor on four continents, claiming listeners even after the U.S. South itself began undergoing its own process of modernization. And, as Du Bois argues toward the end of *Black Reconstruction*, these musical testaments to loss and change are still needed, not only in the sprawling agrarian areas, but also in the cities of the north. The battle over the national and international meanings of the South extends well beyond the cotton field and the textile mill into the lecture halls and publishing houses of the northern metropole. *Dark Princess* includes a debate between Kautilya's faith in the black southern worker and Matthew's claim that the revolution must occur in the northern capitalist city. *Black Reconstruction* suggests a similar contest between a southern-based affirmation of black song and a metropolitan denunciation of white racist history.

Thus in the famous concluding sequence of the latter volume, Du Bois cites white historian John Burgess declaiming that "The white men of the South need now have no further fear that the Republican party . . . will ever again give themselves over to the vain imagination of the political equality of man" and then "cuts" in an almost cinematic manner to various imperialist scenes throughout the world:

> Immediately in Africa, a black back runs red with the blood of a lash; in India, a brown girl is raped; in China; a coolie starves; in Alabama, seven darkies are more than lynched; while in London, the white limbs of a prostitute are hung with jewels and silk, the brains of little children are smeared across the hills. (728)

Du Bois ends his magnum opus on a nightmarish note with this gothic panorama of the world. Nothing could seem farther from the glorious finale of his preceding novel. *Dark Princess* concludes with "a golden child" of black and Indian parentage being born as a messianic sign of a better future; *Black Reconstruction* terminates with the murder of countless children of color. Yet even as we acknowledge the bleakness of Du Bois's final gesture, we should also note that this litany of white imperial violence at once begs the question "how shall we end the list and where?" and provides something of answer as well (573). When Du Bois includes the line "in Alabama, seven darkies are more than lynched" in this list of white racist atrocities, he asks us to consider the place of the Scottsboro Boys and the campaign to free them as an (anti)imperialist event.[46] These black accused suggest not only another disturbing example of white injustice, but also a sign of how the black southern question resounds far beyond its local geography. Those Alabama farm workers now stand as reminders to the world of the unfinished project of democracy in the land of the free. The seven African Americans recall the fact that if black southerners had provided the foundation for the global capitalist system of which the United States is a leading light, they also provided the main example of its failings, particularly during an era in which, as Du Bois puts it elsewhere in the text, "grotesque Profits and Poverty, Plenty and Starvation, Empire and Democracy, [stare] at each other across World Depression" (635). No less than *Dark Princess*, *Black Reconstruction* urges us to take our geography and trace it to a southern origin: the recovery of a neglected past and the envisioning of a brighter future depend on a capacity to remap the world with this particular place in mind. This radical history is Du Bois's sorrow song: a tragic yet rapturous call for the United States to return to "the basic principles of Reconstruction in the United States during 1867–76. Land, Light, and Leading for slaves"—a call for turning the domestic South into the birthplace of a "greater, freer, truer world" (541).

4

"MEMBERS OF THE WHOLE WORLD"
Carson McCullers's Military Fictions

Few Southern writers are truly cosmopolitan.

CARSON McCULLERS, "The Flowering Dream: Notes on Writing"

Critics often celebrate Carson McCullers as a regional author whose sensitive portrayal of freaks and grotesques, loners and outcasts, seems to epitomize the violence and injustice associated with the South.[1] McCullers herself thought that the gothic mode well suited writers from the region that Jake Blount of *The Heart Is a Lonely Hunter* (1940) dubs "the most uncivilized area on the face of this globe."[2] As she argued in 1940, the gothic, a brutal form of "moral realism," enabled southern artists to "transpose the painful substance of life around them as accurately as possible."[3] Yet if McCullers believed that the South warranted its own "Gothic school" of literary expression, she also understood that such a school might connect a local literature to national and international themes (252). Her characters do not hail exclusively from the usual southern locations, but also from other oppressed or impoverished sites familiar with "the painful substance of life": Nazi Germany (the Jewish refugee violinist in "Aliens" [1935]), Greece (Antonopoulos in *The Heart Is a Lonely Hunter*), and the Philippines (Anacleto in *Reflections in a Golden Eye* [1940]). In an era of economic depression and international fascism, the domestic South was not so much separate from as linked to a terrible world.[4] For this southern gothic writer, the nation's most notorious region should be understood in a broader geographic frame.

We can track McCullers's internationalism in her representations of immigrant experience, yet her most resonant global meditations stem from her literary engagement with a part of the state apparatus more than familiar with violence, the U.S. Army. While many 1940s intellec-

tuals and pundits took up the military question in some form—the omnipresence of war demanded as much—McCullers proved more at-
tuned than most to the geopolitical significance of an expanded U.S.
armed forces and their global deployment. Novels like *Reflections* and
The Member of the Wedding (1946) and essays like "We Carried Our Ban-
ners—We Were Pacifists, Too" (1941) and "Our Heads Are Bowed"
(1945) comment on the function and role of the U.S. military for a rising
nation—and do so in a manner that reflects McCullers's longstanding
interaction with members of the armed forces and their families. The
writer spent much of her youth taking music lessons from Mary Tucker,
an officer's wife at Fort Benning, a formative exposure to the military
that presaged a marriage to James Reeves McCullers, a professional soldier from the same base.[5] That these personal experiences with the U.S.
Army were then followed by the U.S. entry into World War II (1941) and
Reeves's participation in a series of major offensives ensured all the
more McCullers's sensitivity to the military and its capacity to link region, nation, and world. From her early years of piano lessons at Fort
Benning to the last days of the war, McCullers recognized how the U.S.
military could transgress and transform "frontiers, both of the earth and
of the spirit" (*Mortgaged Heart*, 213).

To read McCullers in light of the war and the world, the space of the
military and the militarization of space, is to recognize with Patricia
Yaeger that this southern writer "struggles to make" her "own version
of history."[6] Yaeger's recent work on McCullers and the modern black
struggle for civil rights, like other contemporary scholarship on the
writer by Rachel Adams, Thadious M. Davis, Elizabeth Freeman, Charles
Hannon, and McKay Jenkins, has enriched our understanding of this un-
derstudied figure, demonstrating that a writer once disparaged as a
Harper's Bazaar "Faulknerite," a second-rate talent, has much to teach us
about aesthetics and politics during a particularly fraught period in our
national history.[7] I follow Yaeger and a number of other McCullers
scholars in focusing on *The Member of the Wedding*, the popular and critically acclaimed novel that chronicles the summer angst of twelve-year
old Frankie Addams, a white southern girl who feels disconnected from
anyone or anything that matters. Yet unlike those of most critics, old and
new, my starting point in reading the novel is neither adolescent confusion nor gender politics, but rather *Member*'s rich commentary on the
military and the world. Originating, as McCullers once suggested, from
her own anger over the departure of Mary Tucker and her family from
Fort Benning, *Member* takes as its primal scene the young writer's vexed
relationship to an ever-mobile U.S. military, a claim vivified by Frankie's
desire to explore the world either by becoming a soldier or by joining
the wedding of her soldier brother and his wife.[8] The army and the war

do more than provide a provocative backdrop to this adolescent tale; they inform McCullers's characterization of Frankie Addams and play key roles in the arc of the plot. McCullers's capacity to craft her own literary version of local and global history depends in no small way on her representation of the military that cast such a long shadow across her adolescence and adulthood.

In weaving the subject of the expanding wartime military together with the theme of female adolescence, McCullers created a fiction that engages critically with the rise of the United States as a world power. Putting aside such mature female national exemplars as Lady Liberty or Rosie the Riveter, *Member* allegorizes the nation as a white southern girl eager "to light out" for the global territory and leave her small town behind. Frankie may suggest a young (female) America framed by the southern question, a sort of tomboy Huck Finn, but McCullers makes clear that this tale of adolescence by no means affirms the nation's newfound global clout. The novel dwells at length on the impact of militarization on the southern home front and the world not to celebrate but to criticize Frankie's cosmopolitan dreams. As McCullers suggests in a contemporary essay on the effects of the war, young America must come to terms with its new power and new responsibilities as it changes from isolated nation to global power: "America is youthful, but it can not always be young. Like an adolescent . . . America feels now the shock of transition" (*Mortgaged Heart*, 213). If *Member* is a classic rite-of-passage novel, it takes as its subject the growing pangs of both a white southern girl and a rising nation.

That the novel accomplishes this balancing act in large part through the figure of Berenice, a black housekeeper and surrogate mother figure for Frankie, is McCullers's most impressive achievement. Leslie Fiedler has argued that the Georgian writer's decision to pair a female Huck Finn with a female Jim places *Member* in the tradition of white and black buddy narratives that runs from *The Leatherstocking Tales* to *The Lone Ranger.*[9] What Fiedler and his inheritors have not recognized is that Berenice's function in the narrative extends beyond her shaping of Frankie's racial perspective to a related role: the delimiting and correction of the white girl's imperialistic conception of moving into the world. For all her lack of formal schooling and limited travel, Berenice serves as something of an African American critic of U.S. hegemony, a homespun radical who undercuts Frankie's seemingly innocent desire to be a "member of the whole world" by alerting us to the more disturbing aspects of white American incursions into the international sphere. Berenice demonstrates that McCullers was sensitive not only to the modern black struggle for equal rights, as Yaeger has shown, but also to the way in which the domestic racial crisis necessarily informed the exercise of U.S. global power. If the South represents a place of bloody injustice, the national military it hosts proves just as frightening, just as representative of the nation's desire to push aggressively into other people's lands and markets, usually in what we now call the global South. Rather than making Frankie a member of the world, the U.S. military places her and other white Americans in much the same violent relationship to other nations that they have long maintained toward their African American fellow citizens. For McCullers, to leave the South for the world may signify less a move toward freedom than a journey back to terror.

The Alien Army Base

We shouldn't find it surprising that a fledgling southern artist drew on her experiences with army families and soldiers at the start of what became an acclaimed literary career, for the region also turned to the military to accomplish its own transformation during this period, changing from "the Nation's No. 1 economic problem," as President Roosevelt put it in 1938, to an emerging sunbelt economic miracle some ten years later. As Bruce Schulman and other historians have pointed out, the *new* new South was very much a militarized region.[10] The southland would undergo modernization not only through the introduction of New Deal agricultural policies and the mechanization of rural life but also through the federal government's investment in new military bases and new munitions factories. While the South as a whole wouldn't undergo these changes until the 1940s, portions of the area enjoyed something of a preview thanks to the federal works projects of the 1930s. During the four years McCullers spent visiting the Tuckers at Fort Benning (1930–34), for example, the federal government spent close to ten million dollars on the base, expanding facilities and erecting new buildings. What had been a rather small installation, famous mainly for its Infantry School, soon became a major base, complete with a nationally known stadium. The work needed to refurbish and expand Fort Benning went by and large to local men, providing the greater Columbus community with a new source of capital at a time when a failing cotton industry had lowered income and eliminated jobs. If McCullers's exposure to the army base contributed to her development as a major writer, her town's proximity to Fort Benning assisted in the recovery and development of the local economy during an era of dwindling agricultural fortunes and widespread economic depression.[11]

A member of a white upper middle-class family, McCullers did not require the financial boon offered by the military base to her hometown.[12] Her family enjoyed a comfortable existence in a respectable and well-maintained part of Columbus. Yet monetary wealth hardly precludes other kinds of needs, and for McCullers, Fort Benning offered a means of imaginatively overcoming her alienation from the small-town South. Like so many writers and artists from the region, McCullers felt estranged from normative southern society. These feelings stemmed in part from her mother's insistence that she was special, too good for the common herd, but they also emerged from McCullers's own awareness that she did not and, indeed, could not conform to local bourgeois standards.[13] The budding writer's tomboy persona, gangly body, and uncertain health separated her from the vast majority of her more conventional peers, many of whom mocked and derided her.[14] While the young McCullers was hardly bereft of friends as child, she was more than familiar with the lonely status of the freak, a favorite word of hers, who existed on the social margins.[15] In a small town of limited social opportunities, the future writer often found herself alone.

To McCullers's credit, her isolation inspired not only greater feats of artistry, but also expressions of solidarity with persons deemed peculiar or valueless by the vast majority of the local white bourgeoisie: recent immigrants, the physically challenged, poor whites, and, most important for our purposes, African Americans. From her childhood horror that a white taxi driver wouldn't accept Lucille, the family's black housekeeper, as a passenger, to her adult claim that she "is fully integrated," McCullers steadfastly maintained a sense of connection to her native region's most vilified community.[16] Indeed, of all the major white writers to emerge from the South during the 1930s, virtually no one seemed to identify more than McCullers did with the marginalized black population. The capacity to find in her own estrangement a link to Africans Americans so informed her life and work that Richard Wright would in his review of *The Heart Is a Lonely Hunter* commend the "astonishing humanity that enables a white writer, for the first time in Southern fiction, to handle Negro characters with as much ease and justice as those of her own race."[17] McCullers experienced a sense of anomie in her hometown, but she also understood the painful situation of those who found themselves still more marginalized.

And yet even as we recognize McCullers's sensitivity to the black question, it is important to acknowledge that her natal alienation did not steer her toward a life as a white activist, toward becoming a Lillian Smith or a Virginia Durr, but instead inspired her to seek out alternatives to the Jim Crow South. This proved a difficult undertaking, to say the least. A veritable "Sahara of the Bozart," Columbus lacked the museums, concert halls, and literary venues where a young artist might find a space distinct from the stifling conformity of the local white bourgeoisie. In the absence of such alternatives, the adolescent McCullers found her way to

the one institution that seemed to stand apart from the tedium of the local, the neighboring army base. Fort Benning was at once strange, powerful, and connected to the world beyond the small-town South; the
young McCullers appears to have viewed the base as an oasis from an
oppressive environment that alienated creative white girls, poor whites,
and African Americans. McCullers's first connection with the military
world emerged from her piano lessons with Mary Tucker and her general inclusion in Tucker family life at Fort Benning. "Never shy or self-
conscious with the Tucker family," writes biographer Virginia Carr,
"Carson embraced them as her *we of me*" (26). The Tuckers were hardly
"artsy," let alone nonconformist. Colonel Albert Tucker commanded the
renowned Infantry School at the fort and included among his friends
such future military eminences as General George C. Marshall. But for a
young frustrated artist such as McCullers, the Tuckers' familiarity with
highbrow music, with distant bases, some of them in Central America
(e.g., Panama) and the Pacific (e.g., Hawaii), and with the entire cultural
and geographic world beyond the South, appears to have rendered them
and indeed the entire base alluringly unusual. In McCullers's view, Fort
Benning was "alien territory" and, while initially frightening, appealed
to her as a seemingly cosmopolitan space that had the power to license
her eccentricity and artistic behavior (qtd. in Carr, 91). When mocked for
riding a horse in an outrageous outfit (black ascot and flowing gown) by
her neighbors in Columbus, for example, she simply responded, "that's
the way we ride at the fort"—a comment that well suggests how a military connection, no matter how tenuous, provided her with something
of a cover for behavior that exceeded bourgeois propriety (qtd. in Carr,
27). Cynthia Enloe, bell hooks, and other feminist scholars have argued
that the U.S. armed forces have historically either been uninterested
in or hostile toward women, but for McCullers, the military seemed
strangely empowering.[18]

The announcement that the Tuckers had been ordered to Fort Howard, Maryland, in 1934 proved devastating to McCullers. The Tuckers
would leave western Georgia for new places and new experiences while
she remained mired there, bereft of even a connection to Fort Benning.
That McCullers missed not only Mary Tucker and her family, but also
the military installation where they once had lived emerged in her almost immediate discovery of a new base friend, Civilian Conservation
Corps employee Edwin Peacock. Peacock, a fellow classical music afi-
cionado, suggested the same cosmopolitan qualities that McCullers
found so appealing about the Tuckers, characteristics that denoted a life,
a world, that ranged far beyond Columbus and its environs. The burgeoning friendship with Peacock survived McCullers's year in Manhattan in 1934–35, and led, upon her return, to a new military relationship

with James Reeves McCullers, a cultured soldier of leftist sympathies stationed at Fort Benning. While the Tuckers had provided McCullers with music and a sense of familial connection, Edwin and Reeves offered the young southern iconoclast camaraderie and, in the case of Reeves, romance. During the late 1930s, a marriage to Reeves provided the young southern writer with a new sense of belonging that, crucially, blossomed in the shadow of one army base, and continued to grow near another military installation when the newlyweds moved to Fayetteville, North Carolina, home of Fort Bragg. The Tuckers may have left her behind, but McCullers's military ties persisted.

However, for all its importance to her young life, for all its appeal as an exotic institution with worldly and well-traveled personnel, McCullers's image of the army base inevitably began to founder—a process in which Reeves played no small part. While one suspects the ever-observant McCullers recognized that the U.S. Army was hardly accepting of those persons who did not happen to be white, male, and heterosexual, her relationship with a professional soldier of Marxist leanings no doubt helped bring this realization to the fore. Reeves had decided to make his career in the army—a decision popular with many white southern men of the era—yet he resented military hierarchy and found its social structure oppressive. The army was segregationist to the core and enforced distinctions between officers and enlisted men in a manner that mimicked class divisions in civilian life. Black soldiers were assigned to separate barracks; lower-ranking white soldiers were segregated from their superiors in local movie theaters.[19] Reeves's sympathy for the plight of the downtrodden would influence McCullers's writing of *The Heart Is a Lonely Hunter,* her most overtly leftist novel, but his antipathy to army rigidity would play an equally significant role in shaping her next novel, an indictment of base life first entitled "Army Camp" and then published as *Reflections in a Golden Eye.*

A savage portrait of U.S. Army officers and their wives in the South, *Reflections* mercilessly skewers the military. In this closed society, homosexuality is repressed, adultery runs rampant, women are abused, animals beaten, and Jim Crow racism informs everyday affairs as a matter of course. Life at the installation is nothing less than nightmarish. Focusing on the betrayed officer wife, Alison Langdon, and her beloved Filipino servant Anacleto, the oppressed heroes of this vicious world, the novella reveals McCullers's new awareness that whatever her adolescent cathexis to the "alien territory" of the base, the U.S. Army now seemed an institution marked by extraordinary intolerance. Relentless in its enforcement of "rigid patterns" of hierarchy and exclusion, the U.S. military didn't so much reflect as exacerbate the many tyrannies of the Jim Crow South.[20] As Catherine Lutz has put it, by "controlling the soldier, the army controls others."[21] Little wonder, then, that McCullers has Alison and Anacleto struggle to survive on base by conjuring up an oasis of cultural delights and dreaming of escape to New York and Quebec. Instead of recalling the military refuge of her youth, the fort in *Reflections* is a horrifying site of hatred and violence from which its protagonists are desperate to flee.

Mrs. George Patton, wife of the general and first lady of Fort Benning, recoiled in horror at the 1940 *Harper's Bazaar* publication of *Reflections*. Recognizing a harsh portrait of her beloved base, the military wife canceled her subscription to the magazine and urged her friends to do the same (Carr, 91). Yet even as Mrs. Patton rejected the novella as horribly misrepresentative of Fort Benning, at least one significant portion of the U.S. public, while hardly typical *Harper's* readers, may have found McCullers's gothic indictment of the southern army base frighteningly accurate. In the spring of 1941, thousands of African American men reported to army installations throughout the South and found themselves confronted by an extraordinarily hostile white military. While the very names and buildings of the southern bases long had publicized the military's respect for the Lost Cause—for example, Fort Benning was named for a local Confederate general and used a former plantation home as its HQ—the violent racist behavior of white soldiers exposed the army's continuing commitment to white supremacy.[22] The army and the other branches of the service were more than willing to use African American labor to build roads, cook food, and deal with sanitation, but they resisted the notion that black men might be given the respect traditionally accorded men in uniform.

Racist incidents occurred at a number of bases during the early 1940s, but among the most notorious was the lynching of African American Private Felix Hall at Fort Benning.[23] Sometime in early April of 1941, Hall was found hung from a tree in a remote wooded area of the base. While racist violence directed at African Americans at Fort Benning had gone unnoticed for some time, the Hall case attracted attention because the army sought to suppress the scandal of a white military lynching by labeling the lethal attack first a suicide (ignoring the fact that Hall's hands were tied) and then a sex murder. Despite the attempted military cover-up, African American servicemen and their advocates succeeded in publicizing the case and other instances of white supremacist violence at the fort. In one letter, for example, an anonymous African American soldier informed NAACP leader Walter White of the horrendous conditions at the Fort Benning hospital (Figure 7). Much of the resulting coverage by the NAACP, the *Nation*, the Communist Party–USA, and other organizations and periodicals focused precisely on the race question the army attempted to suppress, scoring important political points by drawing parallels between the fascistic behavior of the Nazis and the crimes of the nation's ostensibly democratic forces. Citing the letter of one black G.I. stationed at Fort Benning, the *Ohio State News* wrote, "Charges of inhuman conditions in a United States Army camp, equaling or dropping below those supposedly existing in a German concentration camp, were revealed . . . when a Columbus (OH) youth, now in training in a southern fort, told members of his family of the hardships and un-American treatment being imposed upon colored soldiers there."[24] Fort Benning appears in the newspaper story as less a site from which Americans, black and white, issue forth to defend freedom and democracy, than an "un-American" place redolent of fascist states abroad. As McCullers pointed out in a contemporary essay, "To fight for the betterment of Democracy . . . with Democratic means" was one thing; to commit racist crimes in the name of a fight against international fascism was quite another" ("We Carried," 224).

The horrific news from Fort Benning and other military installations no doubt confirmed for McCullers that the army base that had once seemed so appealingly alien now seemed monstrously oppressive.[25] Fort Benning wasn't so much an exotic elsewhere as an uncanny space that both mirrored a proximate Jim Crow regime and recalled the horrors of Nazi Germany. Yet like such radical African American intellectuals of the era as W. E. B. Du Bois, Chester Himes, and Mary McLeod Bethune, McCullers also recognized and emphasized a more unsettling truth. White racism and white racist violence were by no means limited to the South or to a "dixiefied" U.S. military, but were instead integral to the white state's desire for power, at home and abroad. The lynching of Felix Hall may have reminded Americans of atrocities perpetrated by fascist Germany and Japan, but it also suggested the U.S. military's crimes of empire, whether among Filipinos such as Anacleto in *Reflections*, the Latin Americans central to McCullers's narrative critique of the Good Neighbor Policy, "Correspondence" (1941), or myriad other peoples whose hearts, minds, and markets, if not lands, constituted the objects of U.S. empire in the 1940s. That the southern U.S. military installations were already part of an incipient "empire of bases" suggests all the more that the racist violence endemic to western Georgia had important institutional and ideological ties to U.S.-controlled portions of Cuba, Panama, and the Philippines.[26]

Lighting Out for the World

The climax of U.S. hegemony in the 1940s coincided with the height of McCullers's cultural celebrity. Her literary career took off a short six months before the United States entered the war, and the first half of the

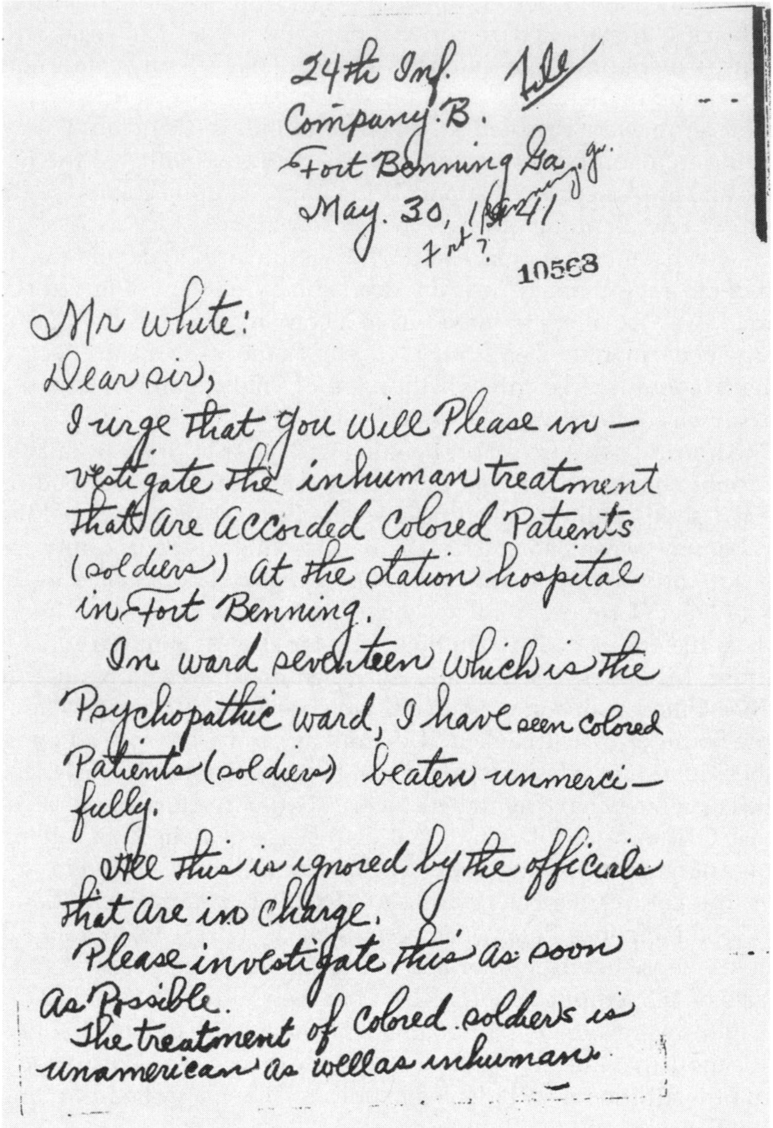

24th Inf.
Company B.
Fort Benning Ga.
May. 30, 1941
105E8

Mr White:
Dear sir,

I urge that you will Please investigate the inhuman treatment that are accorded Colored Patients (soldiers) at the station hospital in Fort Benning.

In ward seventeen which is the Psychopathic ward, I have seen colored Patients (soldiers) beaten unmercifully.

All this is ignored by the officials that are in charge.

Please investigate this as soon as Possible.

The treatment of Colored soldiers is unamerican as well as inhuman.

Figure 7. Anonymous Letter to Walter White, NAACP
Credit: NAACP General Collection, Library of Congress

decade would witness the publication of her most popular and critically acclaimed works. *The Heart Is a Lonely Hunter, Reflections in a Golden Eye, The Ballad of the Sad Café,* and *The Member of the Wedding* all appeared just before, during, or immediately after the U.S. involvement in the global conflict. By the end of the war, McCullers was recognized as one of the nation's best new writers by *Quick Magazine* and received the Mademoiselle Merit Award as one of the ten most deserving women in America. The correspondence between the nation's and McCullers's rising fortunes was a coincidence, but a coincidence with consequences; over the course of the 1940s the increasingly well-known young writer began taking seriously the responsibilities thrust upon her as a public intellectual during a turbulent era in regional, national, and world history. In part, this meant that McCullers contributed articles on the challenges of the home front to such magazines as *Harper's Bazaar, Vogue,* and *Mademoiselle;* she was nothing if not a recognized presence in women's magazine culture. But her newfound identity as a public intellectual also inspired her to incorporate into her essays and fictions thoughtful meditations on how the war might accrue new power to the United States and other Western nations. Drawing on her frequent conversations with such well-known "red" littérateurs as Louis Untermeyer, Muriel Rukeseyer, W. H. Auden, and Richard Wright—the last two her housemates in Brooklyn—McCullers attempted the difficult task of supporting the Allies while criticizing their perpetuation of capitalism and colonialism.[27] McCullers wasn't upset only by "the pain and suffering of hundreds of thousands of tortured, deprived humans" during the war, as Virginia Carr has argued; the writer was also disturbed by what she saw as the West's aggression and avarice. However much she longed for an Allied victory and a quick conclusion to the conflict, McCullers sought to address her nation's continuing investment in global power.

The war looms large in *The Member of the Wedding,* a novel that foregrounds its twelve-year-old protagonist's fascination with the newly mobilized soldiers and their opportunities for travel.[28] A resident of a small southern town adjacent to a large army base, fictionalized versions of Columbus and Fort Benning, Frankie Addams sees "the brown river" of soldiers move through her town on weekend evenings and envies their capacity for travel (302–3). For Frankie, home is little more than a point of transit between far more exotic origins and destinations: They "came from all over the whole country and were soon going all over the world. . . . She imagined the many cities that these soldiers came from, and thought of the countries where they would go—while she was stuck in this town forever" (303). The presence of the U.S. military sparks her desire for places beyond her town and region.[29]

The Member of the Wedding continually emphasizes Frankie's unful-

filled desire to escape the South for exotic, glamorous, and metropolitan destinations: "she ought to leave the town and go to some place far
away" (275); "everyday she wanted more and more to leave the town:
to light out for South America or Hollywood or New York City" (277).
Troubled by a massive growth spurt, a motherless household, a strong
and idiosyncratic personality, and a general sense of teenage anomie,
Frankie can no longer bear her current locale. As the narrator puts it,
"the town began to hurt Frankie" (275). What upsets Frankie most, what
generates her feeling of injury, is a general sense that she, like the young
McCullers, is disconnected from anyone or anything that matters. De-
void of friends her own age, left in the company of Berenice and John
Henry, her six-year-old cousin, Frankie despairs over the lack of a relationship to what she considers normative society. To belong to a community of black women and white children is to belong "to no club" and
be "a member of nothing in the world" (257). If Berenice and John Henry
constitute her "we of me," Frankie despairs, she is indeed "unjoined"
(257).

It is important to recognize that Frankie's devaluation of her domestic community amounts to a rejection both of childhood *and* of blackness
(291). Like so many white middle-class southerners of the era, she sees
in the mixed-race company of her childhood a sign of all that holds her
back from real, which is to say adult and white, experience.[30] McCullers
treats these expressions of teenage angst with compassion and respect,
but the white southern girl's anomie isn't allowed to exist in a political
vacuum. *Member,* as Patricia Yaeger puts it, "exceeds its putative source—
the pimply sorrows of a young girl's trying adolescence," and it does so
in large part by highlighting the trials and terrors of African American
southerners (168). As McCullers knew from her experience growing up
under a Jim Crow regime, the people in the small southern town who
suffered most from exclusion and marginalization were hardly bourgeois white girls, however sensitive and unusual they might be, but
African Americans. Frankie's envious invocation of Berenice's overlapping black communities—"when Berenice said *we,* she meant Honey
and Big Mama, her lodge, or her church"—hardly mitigates the horrors
of black life in the Jim Crow South (291). *Member* gives ample evidence
of these nightmares, offering the reader such disturbing tales as the
story of Lon Baker, "a colored boy" whose "throat was slashed with a
razor blade" (334); the narrative of Honey Brown, Berenice's half-brother,
a brilliant young man whose series of dead-end jobs and prison sen-
tences manifests his identity as a "sick, loose person," most likely gay,
who has been rejected by an army as homophobic as it is racist (287);
and Berenice's account of her failed or tragic marriages, a gothic saga
that moves from the untimely death of her first and most beloved hus-

band, Ludie Freeman, to the vicious attack she endured from her fourth spouse who blinded her in one eye (279). All of the grotesque touches typical of this stultifying southern burg—freak-shows (271), random violence (303), knife-throwing (286)—diminish before the "grieving and low" "blues tune" of local black life (293).

Yet if the novel suggests that this small Georgia town "hurts" many of its residents, from eccentric white girls to the vast majority of the black population, the world beyond the South hardly offers a viable alternative. *Member* proves as sensitive to the violence of a militarized world as it does to the oppressive conditions of Frankie's natal zone. As the narrator reminds us through an early reference to Patton's tanks racing across France (274) and a late nod to the liberation of Paris (350), the world beyond Frankie's hometown is undone by total war. Instead of suggesting a complex, but comprehensible, space, the modern world appears "huge and cracked and loose" (274), "faster and looser and bigger than ever it had been before" (287), a mess of unreliable coordinates and inaccurate maps that precipitate a crisis of cognitive mapping.[31] Frankie's attempt to focus on specific battles only compounds her confusion: "She saw the battles and the soldiers. But there were too many different battles, and she could not see in her mind the millions and millions of soldiers all at once" (274). The news of the war swamps her with an experience of the numerical sublime; the innumerable foreign places and infinite array of military conflicts are at once fascinating and horrible in their exotic multiplicity:

> The pictures of the war sprang out and clashed together in her mind. She saw bright flowered islands and a land by a northern sea with the gray waves on the shore. Bombed eyes and the shuttle of soldiers' feet. Tanks and a plane, wing broken, burning and downward-falling in a desert sky. The world was cracked by the loud battles and turning a thousand miles a minute. The names of places spin in Frankie's mind: China, Peachville, New Zealand, Paris, Cincinnati, Rome. (287)

When Frankie does manage to specify discrete places and persons, the results only intensify her sense that the world is a vast and chaotic madhouse: "The single Japs with slanted eyes on a jungle island gliding among green vines. Europe and people hung in trees and the battleships on the blue oceans. Four-motor planes and burning cities and a soldier in a steel helmet, laughing" (274). Frankie envies the soldiers' mobility, but focusing on the war-torn world they inhabit doesn't so much enable her to gain perspective on the world's changing spaces as send her careening out of control. Fantasies of travel end up forcing her to confront the increasingly terrifying aspects of a world at war.[32]

Worse still, as the phrase "people hung in trees" suggests, the horrors of global military conflict cannot help but recall the racist terrors of Frankie's native region.[33] As we have already seen with the Felix Hall case at Fort Benning, the 1940s witnessed a resurgence of lynching in the South and McCullers's early drafts of *Member* suggest an awareness of such crimes. In an excised portion of the novel, an alternative version of the line "people hung in trees" makes clear the connection between genocide and Jim Crow: "Jews in Europe and lynching burning colored people strung from trees."[34] The connection between fascist mass-murder abroad and white mass-murder in the South could not be more explicit. Though in the published version of the novel, the "lynched burning colored people" have become generic humans "hung in trees," the terrible vision of "strange fruit," as Billie Holiday sang of black victims in the era, still haunts Frankie's litany of 1940s horrors.[35] The violence of the white racist South reflects and refracts the terrors of global warfare (the "Japs" in the jungle) and naval bombardment (the "battleships on the blue oceans"). In this time of violence, sanctioned and illicit, locations blur in troubling ways indeed. The scales of region, nation, and world do not so much "nestle," to borrow geographer Neil Smith's description of conventional scalar relations, as collapse into one another.[36] Boundaries grow unstable, fluid—a prospect that even as it appeals to Frankie also terrifies her.[37]

Frankie, to be sure, cannot admit to the links between "people hung in trees" in her native South and the violence of the war-torn globe, for she is determined to locate in the world all that her region lacks. Indeed, such is her desire to travel that she seizes upon the U.S. military itself, the source of Felix Hall's lynchers and the contributor to violence abroad, as the means by which she will escape the South. Whatever the U.S. military's involvement in the grotesque chaos of the South and the world, its capacity for movement still holds out the promise of a cosmopolitan reward. Viewing the U.S. armed forces as something of a rough-and-ready travel agency, Frankie indulges in various unlikely fantasies of military belonging: she will enlist in the Army; she will fight with the Marines; she will give blood to soldiers of different races via the Red Cross (275). Yet she knows at some level that both her age and her gender render these aspirations little more than outrageous dreams. Her only recourse is to imagine another way of joining the military and thus joining the world—one that involves enlisting not in the state's war effort, but in a very personal affair, her brother's upcoming wedding. As Frankie puts it to John Henry at the end of part one, "After the wedding . . . I'm going off with the two of them to whatever place they will ever go. . . . We'll go to every place together" (294). She cannot "join the war" to embark on a global adventure, but perhaps she can gain entrée to the world by joining a soldier and his wife. For all the horrors of the Jim Crow South and the war, Frankie finds in this wedding the bright prospect of gaining all that her current life seems to deny her.

The Whiteness of the Wedding

Frankie believes that "because of the wedding . . . the world . . . seemed altogether possible and near" for two linked reasons: first, the notion that the wedding denotes a mature community of worldly adults; and second, the idea that her brother's military status—he is stationed in Alaska—ensures that his marriage will entail exotic travel linked in some vague but nonthreatening way to the war (316). By connecting marriage with mobility, Frankie displaces the maturation process onto global geography. For her, we might say, adulthood is another country. Yet for most white Americans of the era and certainly for the contemporary nation-state, any attempt to invoke a wartime "we of me," a wartime claim on full citizenship, must also cite notions of white racial belonging. The wedding's capacity to render Frankie both an adult and a world traveler—indeed, to render the two identities somewhat synonymous—stems from the novel's association of the nuptial ritual with whiteness, that all-important southern and U.S. category of identity that seems to stand apart from black housekeepers, hot kitchens, and a circumscribed domestic sphere. This isn't to discount what Elizabeth Freeman has rightly argued is the heterosexual mandate underwriting the official power of the wedding in the novel and its culture.[38] Rather, it is to contend that at the moment of the American Century, the nation's fixation on compulsory heterosexuality was no more powerful than—and certainly not distinct from—the nation's obsession with whiteness.[39] Normative conceptions of U.S. identity, which is to say accepted patriotic images of U.S. identity, relied upon both sex and race. As Mason Stokes puts it, in American marriage ideology, "whiteness and heterosexuality become normative copartners, both invested in buttressing and feeding off of the cultural normativity of the other."[40] That the vagaries of procreation tend to challenge, if not demolish, the Anglo-Saxon fantasy of racial purity hardly undercuts the mutually codependent relationship of whiteness and heterosexuality in U.S. culture.[41]

The U.S. Department of Defense promoted a white conception of heterosexual patriotism during the 1940s, one well suited to its explicitly racist prosecution of a "war without mercy" against the Japanese, not to mention its steady maintenance of a Jim Crow military.[42] George Lipsitz notes, for example, that the U.S. government distributed "pin-up photos of blonde and snow-white Betty Grable as a symbol of white womanhood and companionate marriage to soldiers during World War

II," thus testifying to how "patriotism has often been constructed in the United States as a matter of a gendered and racialized obligation."[43] Racialized forms of obligation took on even greater force when linked to the contemporary U.S. South, a region where the potential threat of a black ancestor rendered matters of color a key subtext for many ostensibly white weddings. Consider that when *The Member of the Wedding* was first published in the January 1946 issue of *Harper's Bazaar,* the magazine juxtaposed the page in which Berenice describes Frankie's brother Jarvis and his fiancée Janice visiting the family home shortly before the wedding with a full-page ad for "Plantation Whiskey," complete with an image of a fox-hunt and copy which reads: "Life on the Old Plantation . . . when gallantry and boldness typified men of action" (Figure 8). The toasting of the engaged couple in the novel directs the reader not only to the liquor showcased on the facing page but also to the plantation culture celebrated in the advertisement image and text. *Harper's Bazaar*'s layout suggests that the wedding of Jarvis and Janice, the wedding that Frankie so desperately wants to join, testifies to plantation culture and its white supremacist ideology. Indeed, if this paratextual framing of the wedding leaves any doubt as to its racial meaning, the same page of the novel includes Berenice's explicitly racialized description of the happy couple. Giving her impression of the bride and groom to Frankie, Berenice says, "they looked natural. Your brother is a good-looking blond white boy. And the girl is kind of brunette and small and pretty. They make a nice white couple" (280). In this fantasy, to be "the member of the wedding" is to be a member of an institution as white as it is "straight"—as racially normative as it is sexually acceptable.[44]

Given that the wedding of a white southern soldier and his fiancée carried hegemonic overtones within the world of 1940s America, it comes as no surprise that Frankie locates in this ceremony a means of accruing the privilege of the racially enfranchised. Whatever her connection to African Americans, Frankie still aspires to all the prerogatives of adult whiteness, not only because of the freedom such status will afford her at home but also because of the mobility and agency it will give her abroad. For Frankie, as we shall see, claiming her right to whiteness through the wedding allows her to reconstruct a chaotic and discordant world as a space characterized by friendly cosmopolitanism. Joining the "nice white couple," seems to offer her a way of repressing thoughts of "bombed eyes" and "burning cities," of squelching the widespread images of total war omnipresent in her culture. Connected metonymically to the power of the Jim Crow military through her soldier brother, whiteness in Frankie's eyes has the normalizing capacity needed to re-order the world.

That her fascination with white power will necessarily affect Frankie's

Figure 8. In the Shadow of the Plantation
Credit: *Harper's Bazaar*, 1946

relationships with Berenice, Honey, and other African Americans goes without saying. She claims a connection to the dominant order they will always be denied. But her turn to whiteness also changes her attitude toward foreign peoples and foreign spaces. Difference seems to lose its appeal for Frankie after she claims the wedding as her own, and the transformation of her exoticist scenarios suggests as much. In the past, Frankie had found it diverting, albeit unsettling, to impersonate a foreign person of color: "wearing her Mexican hat and the high-laced boots and a cowboy rope tied round her waist, she had gone around pretending to be Mexican. . . . But when the game was over, and she was home, there would come over her a cheated discontent" (306). One senses here a predictable, if less than satisfying, attempt to appropriate the alterity of the racial and national Other as a means of imaginative escape from the normative U.S. South. Yet the qualified appeal of racial cross-dressing fades with Frankie's claim on the white wedding; her interest in travel now manifests itself in a far more muted and contained fashion. "Pretending to be Mexican" is supplanted by a fantasy of traveling with her brother and his bride to a space seemingly unmarked by racial and cultural difference—Alaska. The Alaskan territory proves attractive to Frankie less because it is where her brother happens to have been stationed, than because it seems to avoid the problems of difference so omnipresent in her Georgia town.[45] *Member* thus offers the reader countless passages detailing glaciers, ice, and snow but Inuit people barely warrant mention: "She saw the snow and frozen sea and ice glaciers. Esquimaux igloos and polar bears and beautiful northern lights" (260). If Mexico appealed to Frankie as a source of exotic brown-skinned people, Alaska proves alluring precisely because it seems to lack everything but whiteness itself.

As if to ensure that her traveler's eye will never rest on foreign persons, Frankie emphasizes the role of velocity in her future travels with "the nice white couple." In Frankie's view, her future travels with the newlyweds will entail a swift and endless tour, traversing boundaries and frontiers, breezing through cultures and societies. "Just where we will go first I don't know, and it don't matter," she tells a skeptical Berenice. "Because after we go to that place we're going on to another. We mean to keep moving the three of us. Here today and gone tomorrow. Alaska, China, Iceland, South America. Traveling on trains. Letting her rip on motorcycles. Flying around all over the world in aeroplanes. Here today and gone tomorrow. All over the world" (355). Destinations are unimportant to Frankie because speed has rendered insignificant a conventional understanding of geography. She can shuttle across the Pacific Rim from Alaska to China, hop over to Iceland, and then zip down to South America with nary a thought to the hard facts of distance and location. The sheer momentum of her imagined travels—"we mean to keep moving the three of us"—renders customary distinctions between geographic formations almost quaint. At this pace ("here today and gone tomorrow") the differences separating communities and nations do not matter. The entire world becomes a vast undifferentiated space where (white) Americans go wherever and do whatever they please.

And with good reason: for Frankie, like so many fellow Americans before and since, believes that wherever she and her compatriots may travel, they will always be welcome. "The fantasy of American imperialism," writes Amy Kaplan, "aspires to a borderless world where it finds its own reflection everywhere."[46] No doubt influenced by media accounts of the delighted welcome accorded U.S. soldiers in Italy and France, Frankie imagines that the wedding troika will receive an enthusiastic embrace from all the world's peoples, irrespective of their particular attitudes toward the United States. "We will just walk up to people and know them right away," she boasts. "We will be walking down a dark road and see a lighted house and knock on the door and strangers will rush to meet us and say: 'Come in! Come in!' . . . We will have thousands of friends, thousands and thousands and thousands of friends. We will belong to so many clubs that we can't even keep track of them all. We will be members of the whole world" (356). The dizzying array of violent wartime phenomena is redefined as a thrillingly infinite series of social possibilities. The world no longer seems a collection of competitive and warring nations but rather an endless and overlapping collection of Girl Scouts, 4–H clubs, and other associations available to all. And yet this coalition is so large, so inclusive—"the whole world," after all—that it doesn't so much suggest a desire to encounter difference as reveal Frankie's implicit understanding that white American power has the capacity to make the other the same: to collapse all imagined communities into one big group of united (and indistinct) nations.

Frankie's fantasies should remind us that many contemporary Americans seized upon the nation's growing power to imagine a new relationship to the world.[47] From Henry Luce's *The American Century* (1941) to Henry Wallace's riposte *Century of the Common Man* (1943), from Wendell Wilkie's *One World* (1943) to Mary McLeod Bethune's "Americans All: Which Way, America???" (1947), the era saw no shortage of diverse commentaries on the nation's new geopolitical standing. Not surprisingly, given her investment in a white global order, Frankie's fantasies recall the more conservative and popular of these texts, those that affirm the need for a powerful U.S. presence throughout the world. Her delirious account of speeding through the world echoes Henry Luce's comment in *The American Century* that in the new era of U.S. empire Americans can go "where we wish, when we wish and as we wish" unfettered by diplomatic niceties.[48] And her description of how she, Jarvis, and Janice will be benevolent "members of the whole world" recalls the spirit of Wendell Wilkie's best-selling *One World,* particularly the idea that, as Wilkie puts it, "It has been a long while since the United States had any imperialistic designs toward the outside world."[49] Excited about her impending white enfranchisement as a member of the wedding, thrilled at the prospect of escaping the South, Frankie has little interest in considering the more sober aspects of American worldliness—"people hanging from trees," "bombed eyes"—during a time of war and privation. Hers is not to wonder why American can speed through the world, interacting swiftly with adoring natives, hers is but to enjoy the power accorded a hegemonic nation and its more privileged citizens.

Yet Carson McCullers felt quite differently about U.S. global power, and the approaching end of the war only made her sentiments more palpable. In late 1944, while working on *Member,* McCullers wrote to Reeves, then serving in the European theater, to complain bitterly about how the United States and its main ally Great Britain were attempting to leverage their likely military victory into postwar imperial influence. "Why should the British Empire impose its will on other nations who want and need a democratic government[?]," demands a furious McCullers, adding: "Everywhere there is the sorry story of British (and American—Darlan, Badogglio etc.) meddling" (*Illuminations,* 105).[50] This fiercely anti-imperialist sentiment would inform another letter, sent to Reeves roughly a week later: "The international situation seems to grow worse and worse; it's so disheartening. This capitalistic division of spheres of power can only end in another war" (*Illuminations,* 109). In a comment that looks toward the cold war, McCullers bemoans the fact that while neither the United States nor Britain attempts to seize new territories, they still insist on claiming the "spheres of power" needed to maintain a new type of deterritorialized empire, one that recognizes the value of controlling markets and minds. There might be no traditional imperial plans to acquire a new Alaska or a new piece of Mexico, but the United States and its allies continue to behave as though victory over international fascism will necessarily result in neoimperial power.

Traces of McCullers's anger over "British and American meddling" emerge in *Member* when Berenice physically and linguistically opposes Frankie's global fantasies.[51] Immediately after the girl exclaims, "We will be members of the whole world" and frenetically circumnavigates the room, Berenice grabs the adolescent "so quickly that she was caught up with a jerk that made her bones crack and her teeth rattle" (356). The unusually violent nature of Berenice's action suggests a certain out-raged response to the white American dream of an available world ex-pressed by Frankie. By forcing Frankie to stop "raving wild," Berenice not only performs her duties as the maternal figure in the household, she also expresses a profound distaste for the adolescent's expansionist sentiments. For Berenice, it seems, Frankie's desire to be a "member of the whole world" is no less disturbing than the white American will to power. The United States might claim to help the world, but the vision of an American Century or, indeed, "one world" ultimately resonates in terms of a white America—a young America, to use the famous nine-teenth-century label—tearing through other communities at a break-neck pace, with little thought to the consequences of its actions.

Berenice follows her physical gesture by describing her own experi-ences with prejudice and privation in a manner that offers an emphati-cally spatial critique of white aggression. While she grants the existential point that every subject is "caught" and "wants to widen and bust free," she also insists on registering the way in which the white desire to "widen" has often taken an enormous toll on people of color "They done squeezed us off in one corner by ourself. So we caught that firstway I was telling you . . . and we caught as colored people also" (357).[52] Even as privileged southern whites such as Frankie dream of moving outward into the world, they must remember, Berenice suggests, that their African American neighbors wish to escape the segregated spaces that have resulted from longstanding white attempts to "widen and bust free." For Berenice, one community's expansion constitutes another community's annihilation. Frankie may complain about being "stuck in this town forever," but her black friends and fellow citizens are gen-uinely "stuck," trapped by a white ideology that finds all communities of color, foreign and domestic, fair game for exploitation (303).

Caught in the South

McCullers emphasizes the limited mobility of African Americans throughout the novel. While hundreds of thousands of African Ameri-cans left the South during the World War II era, lured by the promise of better jobs and less overt racism in the North and West, the black char-acters of *Member* are very much "caught" in the Jim Crow South.[53] They can hardly leave the state, let alone the region. And this isn't for lack of desire. Berenice has been to Cincinnati, has flown on an airplane (at a carnival), and generally expresses interest in seeing more of the nation and the world. Honey, her stepbrother, suffers a particularly acute case of wanderlust, roaming the town and its environs to the point where his mother chastises him for never sitting still. In an earlier draft, McCullers had described Honey as even more restless, traveling to New York and Canada on the one hand, and imagining a divinely ordained migration of all African Americans on the other: "a colored man who would gather [the sad dark colored race] together . . . and lead them unto San Domingo and on the long journey the white people would part before them as the waves of the Red Sea had once parted."[54] The latter example suggests a desire not so much to migrate to the great cities of the North, but rather to locate an autonomous black Zion protected by God himself. Yet in both versions of the novel, Honey's dreams of conventional and messianic black movements fail miserably—he always ends up back in his hometown. Whatever the historic realities of the Great Migration, these black citizens find themselves imprisoned by the Jim Crow South.

Sensing a connection between her alienation and Honey's disquiet, Frankie attempts to speak to the young African American at several points. She recognizes that he desperately needs to leave the town, but her sensitivity to the racism of her home region does not translate into a comparable awareness of international dynamics. In Frankie's relentlessly self-absorbed view, if Honey or for that matter any alienated subject wants to leave, he or she should view the world as place of possibilities. Frankie recognizes implicitly that, as a queer man of color, Honey probably cannot speed through the world embraced by all; after all, she knows that he has been rejected by a homophobic Jim Crow army and arrested by the police. Yet she insists that for him, hemispheric, if not global, options still exist. Speaking with the confidence of a future globetrotter, Frankie informs Honey that the rejection he suffers at home by no means excludes him from the possibility of immigrating to Latin America. Thus at one point Frankie explains the advantages of a Cuban identity to her African American interlocutor: "I've seen a whole lot of pictures of Cubans and Mexicans. They have a good time. . . . I don't think you will ever be happy in this town. I think you ought to go to Cuba. You are so light-skinned and you have a kind of Cuban expression. You could go there and change into a Cuban. You could learn to speak the foreign language and none of those Cubans would ever know you are a colored boy" (396).[55] In Frankie's understanding of U.S. relations with the world—an understanding that Johnson's ex-colored man would no doubt appreciate—even an African American man like Honey can stake claim to a foreign space, even he can assume that the Cubans will welcome him with open arms.

Honey responds with the bitter reply "that's fantastic,"—a rejection of the Cuban idea that brooks no more discussion of the international with Frankie. Yet Berenice adopts a much more thoughtful perspective on the African American relationship to the world. Even as Berenice finds herself "stuck in this town forever," tending white people's homes, she hardly refrains from commenting on geopolitics. In a wonderfully utopian scene, she imagines a "round and just and reasonable" world, a place in which "there would be no colored people and no white people to make colored people feel cheap and sorry all through their lives," a place in which there would be "no war and no hunger," "no killed Jews and no hurt colored people" (337–38). The most obvious historical referent for Berenice's vision of a peaceful postwar world is Vice President Henry Wallace's affirmation of "the people's century"; but in her emphasis on racial justice, Berenice comes closer in fact to the more radical multi-ethnic notion of a *peoples'* century promulgated by, among others, Ralph Ellison, Chester Himes, Angelo Herndon, and Mary McLeod Bethune.[56] In light of contemporary debates, Berenice's geopolitical vision particularly suggests that of Bethune, another African American woman of humble southern origins who articulated an equally bold call for a better world. As Bethune put it in 1945, "The hardships and losses of this war have developed a passion for freedom in the hearts of men and women the world over. Thirteen millions of Negroes here in America and their counterparts elsewhere in the world are dreaming, suffering, struggling, fighting, dying for freedom, justice, liberty, security, and peace."[57] While Bethune made such statements not from the humble space of a southern kitchen, but from such important international venues as the United Nations Conference on International Organization, she resembles Berenice in rejecting the giddy globalism of the mid-1940s for a radical new reconstruction of region, nation, and world.[58]

No such geopolitical visions inform Frankie's desire for imperial travel. She engages in intelligent conversation with Berenice, limning her own utopian vision of the future, but the young protagonist does not abandon her fantasy of joining the wedding and gaining the world. Berenice's critique of white expansion goes unheeded.[59] Yet if Frankie can ignore Berenice, the antsy white girl can do little about the fact that geography continues to frustrate her fantasies. The trip to the wedding at Winter Hill, the culmination of all her summer dreams, only exposes how her crisis of cognitive mapping remains unresolved. When we learn, predictably enough, that Frankie finds herself dragged from the couple's honeymoon car, humiliated and teary, this information is less significant than the knowledge of Winter Hill's intense southern quality. The narrator informs us that the bus ride to the wedding at Winter Hill forces Frankie to endure countless miles of intensely southern landscape. And this experience pushes her to acknowledge how her fantasies of the wedding's arctic ("Winter Hill") association might be nothing more than a misreading of local geography: "After a while a serious doubt came in . . . her, which even the answers of the bus-driver could not quite satisfy. They were supposed to be traveling north, but it seemed to her rather that the bus was going South instead. . . . Mile by mile the countryside became more southern" (375). Fittingly, it is only after describing the southern qualities of the trip that the narrator informs us of Frankie's abject failure to join the wedding party. Rather than serve as the first stage of her travel away from the South, the bus trip to Winter Hill has instead embedded Frankie all the more securely in the very landscape, society, and culture she had hoped to leave behind. When she runs away from home after her dismal experience at the wedding, she doesn't "jump" a train or take a bus out of town; she flees to a local bar only to be recognized by a policeman and returned to her father.

It is tempting to read McCullers's decision to have Frankie stay put as a commentary both on adolescence and on the national debate over U.S. global policy after the war. If Frankie never manages to leave her home, either by military or nuptial means, then perhaps white America itself should not hasten to embrace a new internationalism cum imperialism. Yet the end of *Member* changes this argument considerably, for McCullers pushes the theme of Frankie's worldliness beyond World War II into the era of U.S. preeminence, the all-powerful dollar, and an incipient cold war. The conclusion of the novel describes Frankie as a teenager about to begin a new life in the suburbs without John Henry, dead from meningitis, and without Berenice, now off to marry her friend T. T. Separated from her erstwhile companions, a thirteen-year-old Frankie embraces her new friend, Mary, and their gleeful plans to travel around the globe. The earlier desire to join the world via the military gives way in this final turn to a new impulse: that of traveling as a moneyed American unconcerned with warfare.

Frankie, Mary, and other white Americans have the luxury of reimagining their relationship to the world in this seemingly non-militarized manner because, as McCullers knew by 1946, a mixture of good fortune and armed might had protected the United States from the terrible hardships visited upon most communities abroad. Thanks to its military victory and its capitalist power, the postwar United States seemed the one place on earth where the threat of violence no longer loomed over everyday life. Or, as McCullers put it in her contemporary essay "Our Heads Are Bowed" (1945), "in a world of shattered cities and ruin, our land is one of the very few that has escaped the physical destruction of this war, a country of unblemished wholeness on this globe of misery and stunted want" (*Mortgaged Heart*, 227). This affluent calm appeared to include the South as well; the region Jake Blount had described as "the most uncivilized area on the face of this globe" benefited enormously from the wartime economy and became part of a prosperous postwar nation of suburbs and vacations. Indeed, if Frankie once emblematized the growing pains of a rising nation, by the end of the novel she represents the easy comfort of an imagined community that has through total war reaped considerable imperial rewards. Our youthful protagonist may not have left the South but, like her region and nation, she appears to have made a successful journey from a youth in shocked "transition," as McCullers once described a pre–World War II United States, to an established place in the world. Little wonder that *The Member of the Wedding* proved successful as a Broadway play (1950) and Hollywood film (1952). For many cultural consumers, Frankie's enfranchisement no doubt suggested a touching parable of mass embourgeoisement and social belonging redolent of contemporary claims for a new postwar settlement.

Yet to read the conclusion of *Member* solely from Frankie's giddy perspective is not only to ignore McCullers's contemporary publications on the problem of global oppression but also to occlude the continuing relevance of Berenice, her family and friends, and indeed the entirety of African America. If the power of the U.S. economy and the U.S. military inaugurated a new era of U.S. power and ease, African American activists would soon remind the nation and the world that this "country of unblemished wholeness" had more than its share of problems, many of them visible in the southland. The contradictions that obtained between the lives of affluent white Americans and of most people of color persisted, and by the late 1940s it was already clear to some Americans that the age of "raced" violence at home and terrifying militarism abroad was far from over. The question of whether the newly flush and powerful nation would address this problem, would confront the fact that, in Bethune's words, "We cannot find and bring to down-trodden nations . . . international accord while our hands are soiled with the lyncher's rope and the bull whip," haunted the peacetime era.[60] The United States might have claimed global hegemony, but the unfulfilled promise of democracy remained.

5

MISSISSIPPI ON THE PACIFIC

*William Faulkner and Richard Wright
in Postwar Asia*

World War II helped make the Jim Crow South more internationally notorious than ever before, with German and Japanese propagandists emphasizing to the world that the home of the Four Freedoms was a place
of vicious racism.[1] The cold war would see a continuation of this trend,
as the Soviet Union and its allies publicized various southern atrocities
from the mid-1940s onward. Tragically, there was no shortage of events
for the Communists to showcase. From the beatings and murders that
rendered nightmarish the return of black veterans such as South Carolinian Isaac Woodward (1946) to the legal lynching of figures such as
black Mississippian Willie McGee (1952), the white South seemed determined to undercut the oft-cited claim that the United States was the
leader of the free world. The nation's anti-Communist climate only compounded matters. Those black and white Americans willing to highlight
the moral and the strategic failings of U.S. race relations had to contend
with a cold war culture that linked forthright discussions of race and
racism to Communist subversion.[2] In some circles, to criticize the Jim
Crow regime was to run the risk of red-baiting or worse. Even when issues of color and democracy were forced to the fore, as in the case of
black labor leader A. Philip Randolph's successful campaign to desegregate the U.S. military (1948), many conservative cold warriors attempted to play down the overall significance of the problem of the
color line, arguing that it was of minor importance when compared to
the global contest between the forces of freedom and the forces of slavery. The Soviet Union might focus on racist violence in the U.S. South,

but this was for many white Americans little more than an attempt to exploit a marginal issue for propaganda purposes.

Yet if, as Penny von Eschen has argued, white racism was during the early cold war typically considered "an aberration in American life," and a domestic, not an international, problem, some Americans also recognized that the Soviet Union and its Communist allies were hardly alone in emphasizing the deplorable state of U.S. race relations.[3] Such figures as Secretary of State Dean Acheson, Ambassador Chester Bowles, and historian Arthur Schlesinger, Jr., understood that the newly decolonized nations—among them, India, Pakistan, Indonesia, and Syria—heeded reports of racist violence from the Jim Crow South as they weighed the competing overtures of the United States and the USSR. As Bowles put it in a 1952 speech at Yale University, "a year, a month, or even a week in Asia is enough to convince any perceptive American that the colored people of Asia and Africa seldom think about the U.S. without considering the limitations under which our thirteen million Negroes are living."[4] That the United States proved somewhat supportive of what remained of European colonialism while the Soviet Union openly embraced decolonization helped encourage African and Asian scrutiny of Jim Crow.[5] Indians proved particularly aware of racist violence in the United States—and sought at times to publicize the African American struggle for equal rights. The Indian press regularly represented the horrors of Jim Crow, as in the example of a 1952 cartoon from the Indian paper *Cross Roads* in which an African American man hangs lynched from a tree before a vulture "Uncle Sam" (Dudziak, 60). And Indian diplomats assisted African American activists eager to put their case before the world. In 1947, India publicly endorsed the NAACP's Petition to the United Nations.[6] The Indian interest in the African American cause suggests how the domestic problem of the color line threatened to cast a shadow across U.S. foreign policy during the late 1940s and early 1950s.

The U.S. cold warriors aware of this growing problem hardly advocated radical social change in the South as a solution to the issue; indeed, they rejected even a return to the left-liberal discourse of domestic and international racial politics so prevalent during the World War II era. (W. E. B. Du Bois and Paul Robeson, two of the most influential and celebrated advocates of an international approach to questions of color, remained personae non gratae for most of the 1950s, silenced at home and forbidden to travel abroad.) Instead, these "vital centrists" and their allies sought to defend what Secretary of State Dean Acheson dubbed the nation's "Achilles' heel" of race relations by acceding in a limited manner to African American demands for equal rights and then internationally publicizing the achievement.[7] To take the famous example of *Brown versus Board of Education* (1954), within hours of the Supreme Court's historic decision, the Voice of America (VOA) broadcast news of the legal rejection of Jim Crow to the world. Thanks to such cold war public diplomacy, the NAACP's extraordinary victory was also framed as an achievement for the U.S. status quo.[8] (That the decision contained no provision for the implementation of *Brown* was hardly emphasized to the world.) Alternately, the U.S. State Department, the U.S. Information Agency, and other state bureaucracies responsible for public diplomacy disseminated material abroad that attested to race reform (e.g., the State Department pamphlet *The Negro in American Life* [1951]) or sent on international tours African American performers whose skills and personalities seemed likely to endear the United States to foreigners (e.g., the 1952 *Porgy and Bess* performances). These overlapping strategies attempted to show foreign peoples that the U.S. government was addressing the problems of racism and segregation, and was now recognizing African Americans as full-fledged citizens.

Such claims underscored a still broader thesis: that the nation represented the greatest achievements of modernity. In this argument, the United States could recognize and solve problems such as racism and segregation because it was a uniquely advanced nation: a vanguard polity replete with the latest science and technology, a free market economy, and secularist and constitutional government, among other notable features. For postwar modernization theorists such as Daniel Lerner, Lucian Pye, Walt Rostow, and Edward Shils, the unrivaled modernity of the United States proved coterminous with its claim to represent the global force for freedom. These social scientists, all indefatigable optimists with federal ties, believed that a modernized United States would liberate underdeveloped communities from oppressive traditions and stagnant economies. Those communities included not only a few recalcitrant domestic groups, like black and white southerners, but also, more crucially, the diverse populations of the global periphery.[9] According to the modernization theorists, the United States and its Western allies had an obligation to endow "backward" nations with the stability needed to ward off the Communist threat and to produce a future in which security and happiness were possible. That the Jim Crow South, which Rostow considered "the only serious blemish on the nation's domestic report card," was undergoing new federal reform only further confirmed these intellectuals' investment in the extraordinary promise of U.S. modernity.[10] Indeed, as Nils Gilman has argued, in their most rosy-tinged scenarios, the modernization proselytizers suggested that the United States would eventually integrate the new decolonized nations into a capitalist democratic coalition—albeit as junior partners—just as it was integrating all of its own disparate racial groups into one equitable imagined community.

The advocates of modernization and their supporters were cold war liberals, figures whose fervent anti-Communism co-existed with an equally passionate investment in the modern state and its good works. To maintain their belief in the march of progress, these social scientists set aside the many diverse critiques of Western modernity that had proliferated since the early nineteenth century, choosing instead to celebrate the global virtues of capitalism and instrumental reason. Yet many of their contemporaries weren't so sanguine. The persistence of anti-modern critiques on the intellectual right (e.g., Daniel Bell, Leo Strauss) and left (e.g., Paul Goodman, Jane Jacobs, William Appleman Williams) suggests as much, but so does the vocal outcry from those groups directly affected by what was arguably the U.S. government's most visible and contentious modernization project: the desegregation of the U.S. South. As we have seen, both African Americans and white southerners were well acquainted with the federal state's various attempts at developing the region, whether through an abortive Reconstruction or through the various agricultural policies of the New Deal. This historic familiarity with federal notions of progress placed both groups in vexed relation to *Brown*. Many African Americans decried the all-too-deliberate speed with which desegregation was being implemented while white southerners grew furious at the idea that the federal state was going to force their region into what we might call "Yankee" modernity. White southern resistance to desegregation was hardly equivalent to African American anger over white liberal timidity, but in both cases dissatisfaction with the state's capacity to solve the race question rose to the fore. These two very different groups found fault with federal conceptions of modernization and reform, and their respective critiques resonated powerfully in a world in which the United States sought to represent benevolent change. If the state's capacity to uplift the backward South figured crucially in its claim to be the anti-Communist leader of the free world, then the white southern and African American anger over federal (in)action in the region provided something of an inadvertent riposte to U.S. foreign policy, one that would by the 1960s help underwrite a multifaceted reassessment of modernity itself.

Needless to say, there was a range of contemporary white southern and African American responses to U.S. modernization and its compromised promise of a better life, but two of the more important were those of William Faulkner and Richard Wright, internationally renowned writers sensitive to the politics of U.S. global power. Both writers had long-standing, if somewhat different, interests in the theory and practice of development.[11] Faulkner's response to modernization was somewhat ambivalent. On the one hand, he adored aviation and worked for the Hollywood studios—vital connections to the modern that informed his modernist fiction. On the other hand, Faulkner found the federal state's embrace of modernization during the New Deal profoundly disturbing—as Solon discovers in "Shingles for the Lord" (1941), working for the WPA means having to relinquish personal autonomy to alien forces.[12] Indeed, federal developmental policies, particularly agricultural policies, so angered Faulkner that one senses in his work of the late 1930s and beyond a new willingness to value well-established social and cultural practices in the face of the modern challenge from Washington. Thus in "The Tall Men" (1943), a town marshal informs an intrusive federal investigator that "we done invented ourselves so many alphabets and rules and recipes that we can't see anything else," and then urges him to recognize how it is "honor and pride and discipline that make a man . . . of any value."[13] This capacity to locate in hostility to state modernization a new meaning for southern tradition would take on even greater weight for Faulkner after the war, when the federal government began the slow process of compulsory desegregation in the region.

Wright's position on modernization was in certain respects opposed to that of Faulkner. Like many African Americans, Wright believed that federally mandated (and engineered) development had considerable merit. The dream of a new state reconstruction of the racist South ensured such a response—as did his short-lived belief in the Communist conception of centralized development. Yet Wright's experience with white racism in the U.S. South and the Communist party also rendered him an acute observer of modernization's failures. His first novel, *Lawd Today*, finished in 1935, but not published until 1963, represents the federal government as a source of an unneeded investigation of black postal workers in Chicago; here the federal government that offers African Americans tolerable employment also surveilles and disciplines them in a dehumanizing manner.[14] And "Long Black Song" (1938), one of Wright's early stories, critiques modern technology, linking the graphophone and the car to the "steady drone of motors" that signals the arrival of a lynch mob.[15] The sense that the modern often seemed less emancipatory than imprisoning and even atavistic, played a particularly crucial role in Wright's complex response to the question of how the United States should develop not only the domestic South but also the rapidly decolonizing communities of the newly named third-world.[16] For this survivor of the Jim Crow South, development and progress often appeared decidedly equivocal phenomena, at once compromised by their connection to racism and colonialism, and at the same time desperately needed by what he understood to be backward societies.

Figure 9. William Faulkner at a dinner for teachers in Nagano, Japan
Credit: Leon Picon, Louis Daniel Brodsky Collection of William Faulkner Materials, Southeast
Missouri State University

When Faulkner and Wright undertook separate trips to East Asia in
1955, they found themselves confronted by the question of how the
problem of the color line, so pressing in their native state of Mississippi,
informed the cold war export of Western modernity to the global periphery. They responded to this challenge by producing two very different kinds of travel texts that emphasized transracial and transnational
connections. Both *Faulkner at Nagano* (1956), Faulkner's miscellany of his
State Department–sponsored trip to Japan, and *The Color Curtain* (1956),
a journalistic report on Wright's experience at the Bandung conference
in Indonesia, intervene in debates over U.S. modernity by seeking to
imagine how (and why) white or black Americans might bond with
Asians.[17] Faulkner approached the Japanese with a desire to bond over
tradition, a stance well illustrated by his willingness to don a kimono
(Figure 9). In his view, the region's experience of military defeat and
occupation, enduring poverty, and persistent underdevelopment rendered white southerners particularly well suited to bond with the van-

quished Japanese. The fact that the Japanese, while indisputably trau-
matized by the war and subsequent occupation, were significantly different from the other decolonizing nations of East Asia, no doubt helped
Faulkner articulate this argument. For the white Mississippian, we may
speculate, the history of Japan may have appeared in certain respects
like the history of the U.S. South: both were, after all, former powers
whose previous imperial ambitions had drawn from and helped sustain
racist ideology. Both were proudly militaristic societies with long-cher-
ished traditions. To locate Dixie in Japan was at once to connect two different races and two populations whose refusal to accept the dictates of
liberal modernity rendered them alien to the United States.

Faulkner found in tradition a complicated means of imagining transnational and transracial connections; Wright located in modernity a similarly vexed means of asserting (and reason for limiting) his connection
to the largely Asian contingent in Bandung. Due in large measure to the
fact that he understood the African American as part of the compromised modernity of the United States, Wright found it difficult to link
the black southerner (and black American) to Asian peoples, however
much his own interest in the Indonesians might suggest such a connection. For him, the plight of the segregated black southerner was at once
similar to and very different from that of the postcolonial Asian—racial
injury might bind them, but modernity separated them. And yet even
as Wright knew that questions of development rendered impossible any
easy connection between black and Asian, he still promoted a black internationalist perspective that affirmed the value of some aspects of the
modern for all people of color, in the global periphery and the U.S.
metropole. That modernity often spoke in colonial accents did not render it any less important.

Although neither Faulkner nor Wright ever completely escaped the
problem of Orientalism, they still managed to dramatize in their Asian
writings how the promise of modernity gave rise to what Marshall
Berman dubs "a paradoxical unity, a unity of disunity."[18] And this
realization necessarily affected their representation of U.S. global
power during the cold war. The writers' respective attempts at imagining transnational and transracial bonds in support of the anti-Communist and anticolonialist project may have foundered, but their
imaginative responses to the challenge of East Asia had the salubrious
effect of othering the very hegemon from which they hailed. In suggesting that any attempt to rethink Pacific Rim racial politics demanded an accounting of U.S. notions of progress, Faulkner and
Wright found they had to engage with their nation's own difficulties
with modernity and democracy. To invoke the contemporary crisis of
the U.S. South in the Asian context was to remind the world that the

great champion of freedom was no less strange than the places it promised to liberate and uplift. However different these two Mississippi natives might be, they both grasped that the dream and challenge of liberation through modernity was hardly exclusive to the United States or, indeed, even the West, but rather to all peoples who sought to define progress on their own terms. The state of Mississippi might not border the Pacific, but in the heyday of U.S. hegemony, the problem of Mississippi seemed to be everywhere.

At Home in Japan

At one point in the novel *The Town* (1957), Faulkner has Charles Mallison, a white Mississippian, offer a telling observation about the place of the East Asian in the Jim Crow South. Musing on the question of those Jeffersonians who are neither black nor white, Mallison claims that the one Chinese laundryman in town hardly mattered in terms of race or politics: "Although the Chinese was definitely a colored man even if not a Negro, he was only he, single peculiar and barren; not just kinless but even kindless, half the world or anyway half the continent (we all knew about San Francisco's Chinatown) sundered from his like and therefore as threatless as a mule."[19] For Mallison, the one Chinese American in Jefferson proves more of a curiosity than a threat. Indeed, in his emphasis on the Chinese subject's singularity and isolation, Mallison offers something of a rebuttal of Ike McCaslin's prophecy from the end of "Delta Autumn" (1940), "Chinese and African and Aryan and Jew, all breed and spawn together until no man has time to say which one is which nor cares."[20] In *The Town*, after all, the "barren" Chinese seems incapable of contributing to such an amalgamated scenario; like the mule, he has no place in any reproductive scheme. In that novel, it is the omnipresent Negro, not the lone Asian, who seems important to southern racial politics.

Yet by the mid-1950s, geopolitical realities militated against such a restrictive claim. When Faulkner started writing *The Town* in the fall of 1955, China had been "lost" to the Communists; the French had suffered a major defeat at Dien Bien Phu, and, as we shall soon see when we turn to Wright, the Bandung conference had dramatized the desire of many Asian nations to pursue a policy of non-alignment. At this historical moment, East Asians were hardly perceived by most white Americans as being "as threatless as a mule"—or so distant as to seem irrelevant to U.S. everyday life. These foreign peoples might not have populated Mallison's Mississippi, but in an age of communism and anticolonialism they still constituted a major challenge to the U.S. capacity to maintain white power throughout the world. Or, as *Newsweek* put it in the title to a January 1955 cover story, "Asia: Can the West Hold Back the Tide?"[21]

Faulkner, to be sure, hardly devoted much space to Asia or Asians in his post–World War II writing. Yet the writer was aware of what we might call the Asian question and cognizant of its important relationship to desegregation. When Faulkner has his white southern character Albert remember how "the Japs were running . . . Aussies, British, French from Indo-China" "out of Malaya" toward the end of *The Mansion* (1959), one thinks not only of the war, but also of racial politics. And when Albert subsequently alludes to the decapitation of an African American soldier who, in good Jim Crow fashion, had followed the commands of a white southern lieutenant, one senses Faulkner attempting to map the forces that link "a nigger bred upon a Arkansas plantation," his white Arkansas officer, and the Japanese troops crying out "Tonigh youdigh. Maline."[22] Even as he may have at times wished, Mallison-like, for the irrelevance of an increasingly insurgent Far East, the writer also engaged the Asian question in a manner that testified to his critique of modernity. Rather than agree that the question of the Asian was for Faulkner "half a world away," then, we will examine his experience in Japan to assess how this most regional of artists attempted to imagine what we might, with deliberate anachronism, call the global South.

Faulkner's pronouncements on such vexed racial issues are, as Richard King and Noel Polk have each argued, often slippery if not inconsistent.[23] A white moderate, Faulkner did not so much synthesize two opposing points of view on the question of segregation as live a political contradiction. While he believed that Jim Crow was unjust and showed enormous courage in stating his opinion publicly, he also maintained that African Americans and the federal government should allow social change to emerge in a very deliberate and local manner from white southerners themselves. Unlike most African American activists *and* cold war modernization theorists, Faulkner found objectionable the idea that the federal state should pursue its own plan for the reform and development of the South. Thus in the essay "Letter to a Northern Editor," he urges desegregationists to "Stop now for a moment" and allow the white southerner to see "that (1) Nobody is going to force integration on him from the outside; (2) That he himself faces an obsolescence in his own land which only he can cure."[24] For Faulkner to assume a moderate position was to take on a Janus-faced role in which he pushed his white southern compatriots for change while he resisted African American and (to a much lesser extent) federal pressure to enact social reforms. That position was for the writer barely tenable, particularly in the aftermath of *Brown* when many white southerners took a stand against federal law. When Faulkner, most likely drunk, claimed in 1956 that he'd "fight for Mississippi against the United States even it meant going out into the street and shooting Negroes," he dramatized all too scandalously the challenge of maintaining any sense of middle ground when it came to this most divisive of issues.[25] Faulkner might urge African American activists to "go slow" but he had difficulty restraining himself when it came to the incendiary issue of desegregation ("Letter," 87).

To Faulkner's credit, however, a divided stance with respect to Jim Crow did not blind him to the pressing politics of color abroad. The Mississippian was well aware that the racial crisis in his own region bore certain striking parallels with the battles over colonialism in the global periphery. Indeed, as the Caribbean subplot of *Absalom, Absalom!* suggests, early in his career the writer demonstrated extraordinary sensitivity to the white South's odd status as a society at once colonized (oppressed by the northern metropole and federal state) and colonizing (exploitative of both African Americans and hemispheric Americans). In the 1950s, he grew acutely aware of how the cold war, decolonization, and other historical forces bore upon the South's peculiar relationship to a powerful nation. *Absalom*'s hemispheric meditation on the region's colonial status becomes in Faulkner's late writings a global assessment of how the "backward" region might matter to a superpower United States. That he engaged with these issues in his usual moderate—or, better, divided—fashion only reminds us how for Faulkner any turn from the South to the world had the uncanny effect of recalling for him the problems of home.

Faulkner abhorred what he described in "On Fear: The South in Labor" (1955) as "colonial expansion and exploitation based and morally condoned on the premise of inequality not because of individual incompetence but of mass race or color" (*Essays*, 103). For him Jim Crow was little different from the apartheid regime in South Africa (*Essays*, 105). He recognized as well that white Americans had new cold war incentives to view anticolonialism and decolonization in a positive light. Firmly opposed to Communism, Faulkner believed that if the United States did not recognize the legitimate aspirations of people of color in "Asia and the Middle East," the Soviet Union and China would end up with valuable new allies: "We had better take with us as many as we can of the nonwhite peoples of earth who are not completely free yet but who want and intend to be, before that other force which is opposed to individual freedom, befools and gets them."[26] Endorsing or pursuing "colonial expansion and exploitation" should offend white Americans both morally (as a form of racism) and strategically (as a major error in foreign policy).[27]

In "On Fear," Faulkner seizes upon that realization to offer a grand vision of transracial human solidarity that will affirm individuality and freedom in the face of Communist totalitarianism: "All of us who are still free had better confederate . . . with all others who still have a choice to be free—confederate not as black people nor white people nor blue or pink or green people, but as people who still are free" (*Essays*, 102).[28] These lines from "On Fear" recall a more exclusively domestic passage in *Intruder in the Dust* when Gavin Stevens suggests that southern whites ally themselves with southern blacks against a decadent and heterogeneous North: "We—he and us—should confederate; swap him the rest of the economic and cultural and political privileges which are his right, for the reversion of his capacity to wait and endure and survive . . . together we would dominate the United States."[29] The idea of a transracial confederation clearly held special meaning for the writer in the postwar era. Yet it is important to note that if the passage from "On Fear" suggests a cold war liberal Faulkner, one capable of imagining southern whites bonding with Asians, Africans, and all freedom-loving peoples, it does so in a specifically white southern manner. Not only does Faulkner employ the historically loaded verb "confederate" to describe the gathering of freedom-loving peoples—thus imbuing the project with a touch of the Lost Cause; he also attempts to evacuate the process of any racial dimensions whatsoever.[30] Color loses its importance and becomes absurd—or better, "pink or blue or green"—in the face of the Communist threat. A need to assert and defend freedom neutralizes, indeed, supplants, race as a vital geopolitical issue.

Elsewhere in "On Fear," Faulkner unsettles the idea of an anti-Communist confederation of decolonized peoples by inadvertently suggesting that the "fear" of the essay's title refers as much to his own paranoia as it does to the concerns of his recalcitrant white southern neighbors. The essay that dares to dream of a colorblind union of freedom-loving individuals also includes a reference to a potential race war pitting "the remaining handful of white people against the mass myriads of all the people on earth who are not white" (105). Faulkner thus rescales his moderate racial vision for the global arena. He indicts South Africa's apartheid system and then states "that all white southerners (all white Americans maybe) curse the day" when the first black people landed in the United States (101). Or, to take a subtler, but no less disturbing, example from the same paragraph, Faulkner defends global racial equality in a manner that suggests, however inadvertently, a desire to eliminate the threat of the colored masses. "To live anywhere in the world today and be against equality because of race and color," he argues, "is like living in Alaska and being against snow. We have already got snow. And as with the Alaskan, merely to live in armistice with it is not enough.

Like the Alaskan, we had better use it" (110). While admitting to the undeniable global presence of Asians and Africans, Faulkner also suggests that the problem of color is so troubling that it must be suppressed and transformed imaginatively into the whitest and most Nordic material imaginable. In this fantasy, race or color is for Faulkner's white auditors as snow is for the Alaskan—ubiquitous and omnipresent but immaterial. However quietly, Faulkner's simile places the racial other under erasure.[31] In such moments, Faulkner imagines a version of North America or the world where color no longer matters and the survival of the white community is no longer in doubt. "On Fear" suggests that even as democratic ideals and cold war exigencies underwrote a new Faulknerian valuation of interracial connection, this interest competed with what Noel Polk has called the writer's xenophobic worldview.[32]

Needless to say, neither Faulkner nor any cold war liberal ever managed to instantiate a deracialized confederation of freedom-loving peoples, but as the writer suggests in "On Fear," adopting "the habit of travel" did offer him new opportunities to explore the possibility of such unions with disparate peoples (101). Beginning in 1954, Faulkner agreed to represent the United States as a sort of unofficial literary ambassador in what Frances Stonor Saunders has dubbed the cultural cold war.[33] His State Department assignments took him to such predictable European destinations as France and Italy, but they also took him to places where race, history, and violence had marked the people as other to Western modernity: Brazil, Japan, the Philippines, and Venezuela. Of all these trips to nations of color, Faulkner's experience in Japan appears to have been not only the longest—he spent a month—but also the most important to his thoughts on color and politics. Rather than represent the Asiatic hordes invoked by the alarmist *Newsweek* magazine title or, indeed, recall the epithet "damn Japs" that one finds in "Shall Not Perish" (1942) and other Faulkner stories of the World War II era, the writer used his experiences to craft a vision that would link white southerners and Asians in implicit opposition to the invasive and domineering forces of modernity. This is not to claim, as Frederick Karl does, that, for Faulkner, "the Japanese experiment became buried in the Southern experience," but instead to argue that in considering how "the Southern experience" inflected his "Japanese experiment," we should recognize that Faulkner forged a version of Orientalism that redefined white regional identity in a new international mode.[34] In *Faulkner at Nagano*, the Asian no longer seems incidental or confined to the events of the WWII era, but newly bound to "Dixie" against all the pressures of state-mandated progress.

While Faulkner never explicitly dubs the Japanese honorary white southerners during his one-month trip to the land of the rising sun, his sensitivity to the fate of traditional cultures in the twentieth century underwrote a surprising transracial and transnational identification with his Asian hosts. Tradition was for Faulkner a complicated notion, a term that might name the way a landowner deals with his tenants, a certain way of hunting game, or, most famously, the vexing issue of the Lost Cause. That multifaceted view of tradition informed Faulkner's comments on Japan even as his relative ignorance of the Asian nation necessarily limited the sorts of observations he could make. *Faulkner at Nagano* includes an interview with the Japanese press on August 5, two days after his arrival, in which the writer repeatedly celebrates the cultural practices that have made Japan so remarkable, and contrasts these accomplishments with the relative poverty of American culture: "I think that your tradition is so much longer than our American tradition—you have had thousands of more years to train yourselves in culture and in intelligence, which we don't have, and any American will of course have an admiration for that."[35] His celebration of Japanese cultural tradition is to a certain extent the sort of flattery one would expect from a U.S. cultural emissary. Faulkner genuflects before Japanese history and for diplomatic reasons acknowledges the relative youth of his own nation. Yet this is hardly the only way to read his frequent comments on tradition, modernity, and change while in Japan. Celebrating the Japanese past may have suggested a certain amount of ambassadorial tact, but it also provided Faulkner with a means of commenting on the value of southern traditions in the postwar era. To acknowledge the importance of Japanese tradition vis-à-vis a young United States was to gesture, inadvertently or otherwise, toward the place of the white South in an era when elements of the U.S. government were interested in modernizing not only the global periphery, but also the seemingly backward parts of the nation. If cold war cultural diplomacy provided the ostensible reason for Faulkner's visit, the writer hardly confined himself to predictable denunciations of the Soviet Union and celebrations of the United States when speaking with the Japanese.

At least one Japanese interlocutor proved sensitive to Faulkner's interest in asserting the importance of his region. Distinguishing the writer's native land from the United States, the auditor invited the Mississippian to hold forth on questions of tradition and modernity during the seminar at Nagano University: "Mr. Faulkner, the South of your country and Japan have something in common, that is, an old tradition. . . . Now what aspect of your tradition do you find homogeneous with ours?" (85–86). Faulkner's response is telling, to say the least: "We had at one time a tradition of an aristocracy something like the Japanese samurai, and also a peasantry which was somewhat like the Japanese peasantry, that was the connection I saw between our two peoples to make us understand each other" (86). Of all the myriad parallels that he might have invoked between the U.S. South and Japan, Faulkner seizes immediately upon a loose connection between the southern cavalier and the ruling class samurai, a militaristic bond that he frames in distinctly hierarchical terms by then paralleling the peasantry (i.e., slaves and rural Japanese laborers) in both nations. That such a comparison highlights Faulkner's impulse to locate in Japan signs of white southern tradition cannot be doubted; he will make similar points about southern agriculture elsewhere in the volume. Yet to compare the southern cavalier and the Japanese samurai a year after *Brown* also was to make a political point about the right of so-called backward peoples to defend themselves against a stronger foe. The comparison suggests Faulkner's identification with the colonized and the oppressed, but it also inadvertently foreshadows the writer's disturbing comments about fighting for Mississippi against African Americans and the United States government.

For some contemporary intellectuals, Japan and the U.S. South did in fact share a common bond around such figures as the samurai and the aristocrat: the bond of feudalism. While Japan and the U.S. South were rarely if ever paralleled by U.S. scholars, both communities were often labeled feudal or backward by influential modernizers of the era. Admittedly, U.S. modernizers recognized that the once imperial Japan was hardly typical of most "decolonized" Asian nations, but they still identified the land of the rising sun as a nation out of step with normative modern progress. In their eyes, Japan was a somewhat feudal nation where, in the words of Nils Gilman, "premodern residues" had "derailed . . . liberal democracy" and produced a fascist, which is to say a perverted, modern regime (15). Or, as Richard Wright puts it in *The Color Curtain*, "There is no indication that the Japanese abandoned any of their earlier mystical notions when they embraced the disciplines of science" (218). Modernization theorists found the U.S. South equally premodern, taking as their touchstone political scientist Louis Hartz's depiction of the region as the republic's "alien child," an odd "feudal" holdover within an otherwise liberal nation.[36] These historicist arguments were invoked to legitimate the claims of U.S. modernity. In the former case, as Naoko Shibusawa has recently argued, "calling the Japanese 'feudal' justified why the United States a much younger civilization, was in a position to be Japan's teacher" (59). In the latter case, as we already have seen, labeling the South "backward" helped distance the United States from international scandal of Jim Crow racism. By ascribing to these communities the burden of premodernity, cold war liberals shored up the claim that the United States was a benevolent nation eager to remake the world in its own distinctly modern image and capable of doing so.

In the process of bonding with the Japanese over the value of tradition, then, Faulkner also implicitly articulated a critique of U.S. modernization and its challenge to the Jim Crow South. He invokes the Japanese and their traditions not only to shore up an important cold war diplomatic alliance during a charged moment in Asian-Pacific history but also to emphasize the dangers posed by U.S. power itself. At times, Faulkner's critique of U.S. imperialism emerges somewhat inchoately in affirmations of transnational agrarianism that brook no mention of modernization and federal power. In his essay "Impressions of Japan," for example, Faulkner finds himself confronted by rural phenomena uncannily reminiscent of his native southern landscape: some agricultural ("This is the same rice paddy which I know back home in Arkansas and Mississippi and Louisiana"), some botanical ("goldenrod, as evocative of dust and autumn and hay fever as ever in Mississippi"), others, most mysterious of all, linguistic: "the name [of apples] are the same names too: Jonathan and Winesap and Delicious" (*Nagano* 182–83).

Elsewhere in *Nagano,* however, Faulkner pointedly criticizes the U.S. government by returning to the primal scene of the Lost Cause. In his passionate essay "To the Youth of Japan," he draws on historical parallels to illustrate more vividly how the U.S. South and Japan share a certain tragic experience with U.S. military power. The essay opens with an extraordinary passage that testifies to past and present southern resentment of the North:

> A hundred years ago, my country, the United States, was not one economy and culture, but two of them, so opposed to each other that ninety-five years ago they went to war against each other to test which one should prevail. My side, the South, lost that war, the battles of which were fought not on neutral ground in the waste of the ocean, but in our own homes, our gardens, our farms, as if Okinawa and Guadalcanal had not been islands in the distant Pacific but the precincts of Honshu and Hokkaido. Our land, our homes were invaded by a conqueror who remained after we were defeated; we were not only devastated by the battles which we lost, the conqueror spent the next ten years after our defeat and surrender despoiling us of what little war had left. The victors in our war made no effort to rehabilitate and reestablish us in any community of men or of nations. (185)

While Faulkner goes on to say that "all this is past; our country is one now," his speech nonetheless carries with it a note of regional lament that seems very much out of keeping with his duties as a State Department speaker. Faulkner, after all, characterizes the North and its military forces as heartless conquerors that not only defeated his country-men in battle but also "despoiled" the South and made no effort to as-sist the region after the conflict had concluded. The emotion in this passage is palpable. Faulkner empathizes powerfully with the defeated Japanese in a manner that recalls his horrified comments on nuclear war in the Nobel Prize speech. In his version of history, the burning of At-lanta and the bombing of Nagasaki and Hiroshima somehow parallel one another.[37] The white southerner and the Japanese can unite across the color line against their common foe: the federal government in Washington. Thus at one point on his tour Faulkner deliberately dis-tances himself from the U.S. military and from the United States: "All of you here have known American soldiers. I am not a soldier, and I would like to talk to you not as a soldier and only incidentally as an American" (137).[38] The writer's task as cultural ambassador has become an oppor-tunity to connect with the Japanese in a manner that casts the federal government in the role of a brutal invader, forever eager to occupy ter-ritory and mandate social policies. To be sure, Faulkner never suggests that the Japanese or indeed any people should choose the Soviet Union over the United States. To do so would be anathema to him. Instead, he suggests a certain regret over the actions of the U.S. government that left white southerners and Japanese co-inhabiting a subaltern world vul-nerable to the military might of an imperial polity.[39]

Indeed, at certain moments in *Nagano*, Faulkner is even more explicit about his claim that alone among contemporary Americans white southerners know what it means to feel the burden of history: "Ameri-cans from my part of America," he states in "To the Youth of Japan," "at least can understand the feeling of Japanese young people today that the future offers him nothing but hopelessness, with nothing anymore to hold to or believe in" (185–86). The painful past of the Civil War and Reconstruction is, in Faulkner's famous words from *Requiem for a Nun* (1951), "never dead," "not even past," but living sentiments informing the worldview of contemporary white southerners.[40] Faulkner was hardly alone in suggesting that white southerners knew more of the world's pain than other U.S. citizens. Historian C. Vann Wooodward would make a related argument at several points in his postwar work, writing, for example, that "unlike the nation, the South has known de-feat and failure, long periods of frustration and poverty. . . . The South's experience with history has rather more in common with the ironic and tragic experience of other nations and the general run of mankind than have other parts of America."[41] Yet for Faulkner to make this claim as a white southern moderate in Japan meant something very different than for Woodward to iterate a similar thesis in the context of a liberal study of white southern racism. Woodward goes on to suggest that the nation should learn from the white South about the costs of colonialism; but Faulkner, for all his dislike of colonialism, uses global geopolitics to comment on local rights. By emphasizing that the white South and Japan know what it means to be "invaded," "defeated," and "devastated," Faulkner not only criticizes the federal government's interventions abroad, he also queries its current desire to engage in such activities at home. When one auditor asks Faulkner to comment on the idea that "Southern people" resent the criticism of the northerners, the Mississippian responds with a comment that well captures his tendency to view federally mandated desegregation as little more than colonial interference. It is "my belief," Faulkner states, "that one state, another precinct has no business compelling another state or precinct to correct its ills; that never works, but the precinct, the state itself must correct those ills" (128). Here the 1860s and the 1950s come together under the rubric of a southern tradition despoiled by state modernization.

It should come as no surprise that Faulkner's attempt to yoke together the white southern and Japanese colonial experiences didn't allow for a sustained engagement with questions of race.[42] Faulkner claims throughout *Nagano* that color is insignificant when compared to a love of freedom, a reiteration of the thesis so central to "On Fear"; alternately, he argues that white southern racism, while undeniable, has little to do with color and far more to do with a fear of economic privation. "He's afraid that the Negro will beat him at his own job," writes Faulkner of the white southern racist, "and he would feel the same toward anything that he believed would beat at him his economic level. It could be a piece of machinery"(168). Yet even as Faulkner attempts to downplay the significance of racial difference, his rejection of state-mandated modernization results in an othering of the African American, if only by default. Throughout *Nagano,* Faulkner rarely depicts African Americans in the U.S. South as a defeated and colonized people as he does with the Japanese and the white southerners. There is never any sense in his comments that African Americans would understand with white southerners or the Japanese what it means to feel that "the future offers . . . nothing but hopelessness" (186). To the contrary, in *Nagano* and other contemporary texts such as "On Fear" and "Letter to a Northern Editor," Faulkner gives the impression that in the aftermath of the *Brown* decision, black southerners have become part of the status quo, a black wing, if you will, of the same modernizing force that had in the past "defeated" and "despoiled" both the white South and Japan.[43] As he puts it in "Letter to a Northern Editor," "the underdog will not be the Negro since he, the Negro, will now be a segment of the topdog" (87). That Faulkner compares "the Negro" to "a piece of machinery" in his account of white racism only confirms all the more that the African American is, for this intellectual, aligned with the new technologies of modernity while still linked historically to the plantation complex from which he must be freed. In this fantasy, we may speculate, to focus on the suffering of African Americans would only help legitimate those forces hostile to Faulkner and his new Asian brethren.

Faulkner strove to find in Japan signs of home, from southern pastoral scenes to tragic reminders of the Lost Cause. Yet the uncanny discovery of Mississippi in Asia, of transracial traditionalism in the face of U.S. modernity, did not mean that he had eliminated or minimized the alterity of the Asian nation. However much he may have repressed it through cold war rhetorics of freedom and southern rhetorics of loss, for Faulkner Japan and the Japanese still seemed racially other. And how could it be otherwise? From Lafcadio Hearn's folklore to Ezra Pound's translations, white American men of letters long had considered Japanese culture and society exotic. For Faulkner, the difference of the Japanese spoke in a familiar racial register. The Japanese offered the white writer a means of celebrating the local and rural values of the white South, but these inheritors of the samurai and former opponents of British and U.S. troops also suggested to Faulkner a more disquieting characteristic of contemporary Mississippi life: the increasingly angry black demand for change.[44]

Shortly after he had left Japan, Faulkner responded to the recent murder of black teenager Emmett Till in a manner that foregrounded his fear of both blacks and Japanese. Circulated by the United States Information Service (U.S.I.S.), this commentary on the infamous Mississippi lynching suggests a very different "confederation" than that Faulkner articulated while in the land of the rising sun:

> When will we learn that the white man can no longer afford, he simply does not dare, to commit acts which the other three-fourths of the human race can challenge him for, not because the acts are themselves criminal, but simply because the challengers and accusers of the acts are not white in pigment?
>
> Not to speak of the other Aryan peoples who are already the Western world's enemies because of political ideologies. Have we, the white Americans who can commit or condone such acts, forgotten already how only 15 years ago, what only the Japanese—a mere eighty million inhabitants of an island already insolvent and bankrupt—did to us?
>
> How then can we hope to survive the next Pearl Harbor, if there should be one, with not only all peoples who are not white, but all peoples with political ideologies different from ours arrayed against us—after we have taught them (as we are doing) that when we talk of freedom and liberty,

we not only mean neither, we don't even mean security and justice and even the preservation of life for people whose pigmentation is not the same as ours. (*Essays,* 222–23)

Much of the press release illustrates the more liberal side of Faulkner's moderate vision. The writer indicts both the men who killed a fourteen-year-old boy and white racists more generally; he then goes on to point out that any society that relies on this sort of violence probably "won't survive." Yet, as is almost always the case, one also finds linked to Faulkner's democratic rhetoric a more xenophobic structure of feeling that emerges in distinctly racialist terms. The writer's willingness to refer to Till elsewhere in the press release as an "afflicted child"—an oblique reference to the idea that the black teenager had acted inappropriately in front of a white woman—suggests that, for all his purported tolerance, Faulkner understands the crime from the white southern perspective. And those regional concerns also inform his view of white survival in a world of color. White Americans should refrain from such racist murders, argues Faulkner, "not because the acts are themselves criminal, but simply because the challengers and accusers of the acts are not white in pigment." For this intellectual, the Till murder offers both a reminder of the pressing need for social change in the U.S. South and a warning to white Americans about the global consequences of domestic racist violence.

The latter point resonates in light of the writer's recent visit to Japan. By invoking much the same image of white vulnerability that he iterated in "On Fear: The South in Labor," Faulkner links domestic and global racial contexts in a manner that allows him to reimagine the Japanese not as brother confederates, but as frighteningly alien military opponents. "How . . . can we hope to survive the next Pearl Harbor?" asks Faulkner. "Have we . . . forgotten already . . . what only the Japanese—a mere eighty million inhabitants of an island already insolvent and bankrupt—did to us?" When linked to angry African Americans, the Japanese represent the aggressive racial other to whom no white southerner would ever feel connected. With this brief response to the most notorious lynching of the decade, Faulkner reveals that internationalism has not so much broadened his sensitivity to difference as intensified his anxieties over how federally mandated desegregation—modernization by decree—would destroy his natal zone. His moderate stance on segregation had always existed as a contradictory vision, but Faulkner's citation of the Pearl Harbor attack suggests that the attempt to resolve such tensions through the dream of a transracial confederation had the unfortunate effect of making him more rather than less conscious of the racial divide, at home and abroad.

"My Life Has Given Me Some Keys"

> "We ain't white, 'cause our skins got color
> in 'em; and we ain't black no more. Now
> white folks call us 'colored'; but ain't that
> 'cause they don't know *what* to call us. . . .
>   I think we done got to be another race,
> mebbe something like them Indonesians."
>
>   Mrs. Lamb speaking to Fishbelly,
>   Richard Wright, *The Long Dream* (1957)

Unlike Faulkner, Wright devoted a fair amount of his late work to Asia. Curious about both Japanese militarism and Indian rebellion during the 1930s and 1940s, Wright would with his growing postwar awareness of decolonization develop a more pronounced interest in the East.[45] His work of the 1950s includes *The Color Curtain*, letters and short comments on Asian geopolitics, and no less than ten thousand haiku. Yet Wright's Asian turn is important not only because it testifies to his Afro-orientalist sensibility, as Bill Mullen has recently argued, but also because it provided the writer with a new way of pondering the international meaning of the southern material with which he inaugurated his career (59–68). When Mrs. Lamb, a black Mississippian in *The Long Dream*, ponders the difficulty of fixing an African American identity and then proposes that the Indonesian example might provide something of a solution, one senses Wright's curiosity about how another community of color, one separate from the African diaspora, might offer some important insights into the vexed issues of race and power in the southland.[46] For Mrs. Lamb, the Indonesian, neither black nor white but brown, offers an alternative to the racial opposition that structures the oppressive Jim Crow regime. This isn't so much to suggest that Wright found in Indonesian identity a solution to the American dilemma, as it is to acknowledge that the writer understood how East Asians were, in their growing postcolonial prominence, transforming how Americans thought about race and place. Although, in *The Town*, Charles Mallison finds the lone Chinese American man a reassuring reminder that Asians are too distant to affect local racial issues, Mrs. Lamb takes up the Asian question to argue the opposite: the Indonesian example might offer a model with which to redefine not only African American identity, but also southern and national racial politics.

To emphasize that Wright took seriously the black South as a topic during his late period may seem odd, as most of the scholarly work on his 1950s texts has tended to emphasize his newfound identity as a postcolonial critic *avant la lettre*. From J. Saunders Redding's bitter claim that

Wright "cut the emotional umbilical cord through which his art was fed" to Paul Gilroy's celebration of Wright's turn to a black internationalist perspective, the most influential examinations of the writer's late career have tended to define him as an intellectual concerned with global, not black southern issues.[47] Yet as Wright himself noted in a 1958 letter, he was a "Southerner," and even if he tended to provide an international frame for the contemporary racial crisis in the U.S. southeast, as he did in a 1955 *France-Soir* interview about the Emmett Till murder, this hardly suggests a lack of interest in the region, but instead demonstrates a sensitivity to how the domestic problem of the color line spoke to its international counterpart.[48] As Wright made evident when he complained about the U.S. government's attempt to repress the circulation of "cruel pictures of how Negroes live," he was fully aware that Jim Crow was a global topic of considerable import during the era of decolonization.[49] His contemporary work attests to a complicated effort to integrate his experience and knowledge of the Jim Crow South into a new third world subject matter.

The Color Curtain exemplifies how Wright approached that challenge. Aptly identified by Amritjit Singh as the Asian counterpart to *Black Power* (1954), *The Color Curtain* takes as its subject the historic 1955 meeting in Bandung where pioneering figures such as Gamal Abdel Nasser, Jawaharlal Nehru, Kwame Nkrumah, and Sukarno gathered the representatives of twenty-nine sovereign nations of color in the spirit of cold war neutrality and anticolonial solidarity.[50] Captivated by the idea of a transnational Afroasian gathering, Wright viewed the Bandung conference as an unprecedented opportunity for newly independent nations of color to find a political "third way" in the midst of the cold war.[51] As he puts it in the first chapter of the volume, "This smacked of something new, something beyond Left and Right."[52] That the Bandung conference offered an inspiring vision of transracial and transnational connection no doubt rendered the event even more appealing to Wright, an intellectual who long had been fascinated by the idea of a global coalition of the oppressed.[53] Non-alignment, that signature concept of Bandung, proves central to *The Color Curtain* partly because it names the desire of sovereign nations of color to resist both the Soviet Union and the United States. But Bandung went beyond cold war politics to denote for Wright a more thoroughgoing resistance to the normative western alignment of race, religion, and politics, a refusal to heed the words of a Frenchwoman who asks, "What on earth have African Negroes and Burmese Buddhists in common?" (17). For Wright, Bandung may have been "a kind of judgement upon [the] Western world," but it was also a rejection of the innumerable cultural codes through which Europeans and Americans had categorized and thus separated Asians and Africans (12).

The Color Curtain offers a rich and multifarious indictment of various aspects of Western political and economic life. Capitalism, colonialism, and Communism all receive their fair share of criticism; indeed, no one reading Wright's closing rejection of Soviet and Chinese Communism can ever doubt his desire to distinguish himself from his former political creed. At the same time, importantly, *The Color Curtain* hardly endorses African and Asian traditions of culture, religion, and social organization. To the contrary, in this book, as in *Black Power*, Wright rejects what he considers the irrationalism and tribalism of non-Western peoples in favor of Western modernization. "Today as never before," he states, "it can be seen that the future of national cultures will reside in the willingness of nations to take up modern ideas." That he understood modernization as a complicated task cannot be overstated. Wright knew that modernity and colonialism often went hand in hand, and recognized as well that the urge to modernize had been perceived by many Africans and Asians as an attack on natal ties and local sovereignty. Yet Wright also insisted in various ways that an African and Asian affirmation of the local and the premodern in the name of anticolonialism would only render those chaotic societies vulnerable to Communist entreaties on the one hand and to fantasies of what he called "global racial revenge" on the other. As Kevin Gaines has recently argued, for Wright, the fact that modernization often came with colonial or, indeed, anti-Communist and capitalist baggage hardly legitimated the African and Asian rejection of "the virtues of Western modernity—secularism, scientific method, reason, individual rights, and artistic freedom."[54] In Wright's view, the newly decolonized nations had no choice but to take from the West the best aspects of modernization if they sought not only to protect, but also to improve the lives of their citizens. Despite significant challenges, these new nations might be able to foster their own third world or peripheral version of modernity.

That such a quest placed black Americans—racially oppressed citizens of that quintessentially modern empire, the United States—in a particularly odd position was hardly lost on Wright, and the hesitancy with which he articulated black U.S.–Asian connections suggests as much. Insofar as they were fellow victims of white oppression, African Americans resembled Asians and Africans. Yet as citizens of the West's paradigmatic modern nation and new global hegemon, African Americans were also connected to the very forces of colonial modernity with which postcolonial Asians and African had to contend. As Wright put it in an interview, the African American is "intrinsically a colonial subject, but one who lives not in China, India, or Africa but next door to his conquerors, attending their schools, fighting their wars, laboring in their factories."[55] In Wright's view, African Americans have been exposed to the ideals and advantages of Western development even as they are fully aware of the fact that, in the hands of whites, Western modernity is more often than not colonial modernity, which is to say deeply implicated in the exploitation and violence of imperialism.[56] If race-conscious African Americans have a stake in the Bandung attempt to reimagine color and internationalism beyond cold war polarities, they also inadvertently represent the modernization project he sees as integral to the postcolonial future. For Wright, in other words, African Americans maintain an agonistic relationship to the West and its modernism that cannot help but place them in what a somewhat contradictory if not impossible position when seeking to find common ground with decolonized peoples. Or, as Sam, a young black Mississippian in *The Long Dream* bitterly informs his friends during a discussion about national belonging, "You live Jim Crow . . . You can't live like no American, 'cause you ain't no American! And you ain't African neither! So what is you? Nothing! Just *nothing*!" (35).

That Wright was himself an exile several times over—a man who left the South for Chicago, New York for Paris, and, in an intellectual sense, Europe for the third world—only rendered him more sensitive to the splits and contradictions that attended any attempt to figure the African American's place in the postcolonial world. Paul Gilroy has argued that "in several essays and almost every book, Wright turned back to this problem of his own hybrid identity as a modern man," and one finds this preoccupation particularly evident in the writer's travel works.[57] In *Black Power*, for example, one senses Wright's self-consciousness as a displaced African American modern when he poses a potential agrarian link between the South and Ghana. "The soil was a rich red like that of Georgia or Mississippi and, for brief moments, I could almost delude myself into thinking that I was back in the American South" (36). Faulkner, we may remember, was willing to draw direct connections between the rice paddies of Mississippi and the rice paddies of Japan. Wright, however, proves much more circumspect about such claims—claiming, in fact, that they are delusional. In *The Color Curtain*, he pursues the possibility of a connection between African Americans and the Bandung group in a more intense but no less anxious manner, stressing both the importance of African Americans to any coalition eager for anticolonial modernization and the marginal status of a population whose contemporary civil rights struggle sometimes seemed like "child's play" compared to the great Asian and African struggles of the age (178).

This is hardly to claim that the postcolonial Wright had jettisoned the natal material so central to his first literary efforts. At several places in *The Color Curtain*, Wright insists on the importance of his own experiences in forging a connection with Asians. For example, when his wife,

Ellen, asks him how he will report on the many nations gathered at Bandung, Wright responds by saying, "I don't know. But I feel that my life has given me some keys to what they would say or do. I'm an American Negro; as such, I've had a burden of race consciousness" (15). The "burden of race consciousness" depicted so powerfully in such works as *Black Boy* (1945) would help him understand the Asian struggle and report it to the West. And, to be sure, the sensitivity to racial oppression informing much of *The Color Curtain* offers ample evidence that Wright did in fact turn to the African American experience in an attempt to understand Indonesians and other Asians in particular. Journalist Mochtar Lubis, one of Wright's main Indonesian interlocutors, would later complain in the periodical *Encounter* that Wright had drawn too deeply on his own autobiography and had, as a consequence, misrepresented the island nation. "I am afraid," writes Lubis, "while he was here in Indonesia, he had been looking through 'coloured-glasses', and had sought behind every attitude he met colour and racial feelings. Colour or racial problems are just not our problems."[58] In Lubis's view, Wright's embrace of a black southern perspective was such that it undermined his ability to understand the combination of economic, cultural, and so-cio-religious, and colonial oppressions that shaped the experience of Asian nations.

One can hardly deny that Wright misrepresents Indonesians and other Asians in *The Color Curtain*. As Mullen has argued recently, Wright tends to engage in his own version of Orientalism when describing the "Asian personality" (20).[59] Yet it is also important to note that at other moments he seems almost shy about claiming ethnographic insight. When Wright comments explicitly on how his life has given him certain keys to understanding the Bandung dynamic, he tends toward terse-ness and brevity, wary of slipping into the sort of delusion he had named in *Black Power*. He might acknowledge at one point that "American Negroes . . . shared a background of racial experience that made them akin to the Asian" or claim at another that "Negroes have been made ashamed of being black. Dark Hindus feel the same way"; but such statements, while sensitive to the omnipresence of white colonial oppression, do not hazard larger claims that might bridge vast histori-cal, geographic, and social differences (78; 186). Indeed, Wright offers only a qualified invocation of African American / Asian connections; he acknowledges shared suffering at the hands of white Westerners only to then insist that even this bond breaks down in face of the African American's modernity. Wright will argue that African Americans and Asians have nothing "in common" other than "what their past relationship to the Western world had made them feel," but this circumspect claim then founders on his refusal to imagine the African American as less than

American (12). For all their ongoing oppression by whites, African Americans still seem too much a part of the West to invoke such traumas as the ground of transracial connection.

Wright's most sustained examination of how the domestic problem of the color line bears upon its Asian counterpart takes place in the chapter entitled "Racial Shame at Bandung." Focusing at the outset of the chapter on the conference attendees themselves, Wright emphasizes that those disparate peoples of color can find common ground only by invoking the white enemy; the fact that all have endured white oppression offers them a kind of "negative unity" that will, Wright hopes, transmute into a more productive type of bonding. (One cannot help but think of Faulkner's claim that familiarity with despair links the white southerner to the Japanese.) Wright's portrait suggests the possibilities for transracial connection that an experience of white-induced shame can inadvertently produce:

> Living for centuries under Western rule, they had become filled with a deep sense of how greatly they differed from one another. But now, face to face, their ideological defenses dropped. . . . Day after day dun-colored Trotskyites consorted with dark Moslems, yellow Indo-Chinese hobnobbed with brown Indonesians, black Africans mingled with swarthy Arabs, tan Burmese associated with dark brown Hindus, dusty nationalists palled around with yellow Communists, and Socialists talked to Buddhists. But they all had the same background of colonial experience, of subjection, of color consciousness. (176)

The various allegiances to the cold war superpowers that these participants necessarily brought to Bandung have, in Wright's opinion, faded away to be replaced with a rich spectrum of "color consciousness." This isn't to claim that the question of ideology disappears entirely from Wright's account; it does not. It is rather to suggest that Wright understood how, in the absence of white colonialists and Communists, people of color could more boldly pursue a new internationalism. The color curtain might never completely obscure or cover the iron curtain, but Asians and Africans could still create a fledgling coalition that might affect their future treatment at the hands of modernized Western powers, Communist and capitalist alike. Indeed, we may speculate that in his most hopeful moments Wright imagines that the Bandung conference might in fact instantiate a new conception of modernization disconnected from the horrors of colonialism.

At the same time a "curtain" of difference also hangs between the unimaginably diverse colonial peoples at Bandung. Wright suggests as much when he segues almost immediately from the account of the hob-

nobbing Africans and Asians to a description of how Bandung constituted a "call of race" heard by African Americans as well. "I cite the case
of an American Negro," states Wright shortly after he concludes his
sketch of transracial bonding at the conference, and then goes on to relate not one but three examples of African Americans who had traveled
to Indonesia: a mechanic from Los Angeles named Mr. Jones, an anonymous black female journalist, and Congressman Adam Clayton Powell,
Jr. (176).[60] Wright interweaves these three anecdotes with accounts of
how the Dutch taught Indonesians self-hatred, and how the Indonesians still wrestle with that painful legacy. The chapter thus suggests
through its form that African Americans, while not officially part of the
event, may also partake of the "negative unity" underwriting the rain-
bow coalition at Bandung. The burden of white racism can prove a powerful common denominator indeed.

Or so it seems. For if the global power of "color consciousness" appears capable of uniting oppressed African Americans and Asians,
Wright's three portraits of his erstwhile compatriots suggest otherwise.
None of the three African Americans Wright represents seems capable
of establishing a meaningful connection with either the Indonesians or
the conference attendees. These colored subjects seem somewhat con-
strained in various ways by their connection to a modern U.S. society.
The first, Mr. Jones, may have spent his entire life savings to heed the
call of race and attend this conference of colored peoples, but, in
Wright's view, this African American's need to belong to "a 'colored' nation" suggests ignorance and confusion. If Jones find in Bandung an opportunity to "feel a fleeting sense of identity, of solidarity, of religious
oneness with the others who shared his outcast state," he is also "be-
fuddled," an American innocent among international cosmopolites
(177; 176). Wright's account of Jones emphasizes the hollowness of this
African American's notion of "solidarity" and "religious oneness" by
unmaking the idealized image of a coalition of color that opens the
chapter. Various shades of skin color once had cohered as an impressive
spectrum, but now they splinter apart: "And *brown* Mr. Jones, watching
the wily moves of *tan* Nehru and *yellow* Chou En-lai, understood absolutely nothing of what was going on about him" (177, emphasis
added). With the appearance of the African American comes the bitter
reminder that "negative unity" cannot completely eliminate the power
of modernity at Bandung. For Wright, we may surmise, the racist United
States has rendered Jones a subject more colonial than modern—a figure whose geopolitics has left him vulnerable to irrational fantasies or,
better, delusions that Wright refuses to indulge in himself.

In the case of the female African American attendee, who makes an
appearance only through her white roommate's conversation with

Wright, the contradictions of a black female U.S. identity also conspire to eliminate meaningful African American–Asian connection. Having learned from her roommate that the black woman, a journalist, devotes hours to straightening her hair and lightening her skin in their Bandung hotel room, Wright expounds on what he understands as nothing less than a missed opportunity for transracial connection: "I leaned back and thought: here is Asia, where everybody was dark, that poor American Negro woman was worried about the hair she was born with. Here, where practically nobody was white, her hair would have been acceptable; no one would have found her 'inferior' because her hair was kinky; on the contrary, the Indonesians would perhaps have found her different and charming" (186). In Wright's view, U.S. society has convinced this black woman to commit "psychological suicide," and this leaves her incapable of recognizing the social possibilities in Bandung (187). The reporter's racial shame is so strong that the very idea of bonding with dark-skinned foreigners would most likely prove anathema to her. Hers is a near-total dedication to whiteness—a dedication whose cathexis to colonial modernity emerges only in strange and irrational behavior. Ultimately, her white roommate imagines the journalist's use of Sterno (for hair straightening) is a sign of voodoo ritual, for such is her investment in the totemic idol of whiteness that her putative modern American identity has disappeared into "magic" practices (184).

Wright's deft sketches of these two very different African Americans illustrate how the U.S. version of racial shame can, when transplanted into the Asian context, prove more of a problem than a boon. But the same holds true for his third African American "case," a man who seems for Wright not to manifest any racial shame at all: New York congressman Adam Clayton Powell, Jr. If the black female journalist seems to descend into the depths of the irrational in her quixotic pursuit of the great white god, Powell seems to represent the worst excesses of the modern African American. Wright purports to be "delighted" that the black congressman "felt the call" of the Bandung conference and that he insisted on attending despite the protests of the U.S. State Department. But Wright quickly qualifies his initial wonder and respect: "Congressman Powell flew to Bandung, coming as far as the Philippines in a United States bombing plane; there he teamed up with the Philippine delegation and, while en route to Bandung, began holding press conferences to 'defend the position of the United States in relation to the Negro problem'" (178). In Wright's view, Powell has come to Bandung with a specific purpose in mind: to explain to the African and Asian attendees that this most modern of capitalist nations had solved its racial dilemma. Thanks to the *Brown* decision, argues Powell, the Jim Crow regime in the South will soon be a thing of the past.

Powell's "white" skin proves something of a problem for some of the "black," "brown," and "yellow" attendees, but for Wright it is hardly a melanin deficiency but rather an uncritical investment in U.S. (colonial) modernity that renders the Harlem congressman objectionable. In his unpublished diary of the trip, Wright focuses on Powell's inept diplomatic style as indicative of the politician's Western faith in the discourse of capitalism: Wright quotes Congressman Powell as saying that in America, racism is on the way out. Wright compares these words to a slogan similar to one that would be invented to sell a bar of soap and concludes that nobody was convinced by these words except those already pro-American.[61] By comparing Powell's comments on the *Brown* decision to Madison Avenue advertising, Wright doesn't only make the obvious point that for the U.S. representative promoting democracy is like selling a product; he also offers a more subtle argument that soap, one of the more typical emblems of the Western modernizer, is no more reliable a sign of progress than the empty claims of Washington politicians. In *The Color Curtain*, Wright offers a more polite version of this point, suppressing his disagreement with the content of Powell's message—"I'm not critical of Congressman Powell's efforts"—only to indict the black politician's behavior: "his activities were not my style, smacking much too much of high-pressure salesmanship and public relations—two hardy, frisky arctic animals utterly unknown in the tropical latitudes of Bandung" (178). For Wright, Powell's "activities" recall aggressive U.S. business practices thoroughly alien to Indonesian society.[62] If the "arctic" Powell seems out of place in "tropical" Bandung, this has as much to do with the congressman's identification with an imperialist U.S. government as it does with his incapacity to appreciate a different way of life. Moreover, by linking Powell's "high-pressure" "arctic" style to the aggressive promotion of U.S. modernity, Wright quietly offers a critique of his erstwhile nation's attempt to neocolonize the world. Powell's presence in Bandung may testify to the powerful allure of such an event for African Americans, but his performance speaks more to the way a modern imperial power can coopt the subaltern than it does to the transracial and transnational connections denoted by the idea of non-alignment.

These three portraits testify to the failure of African American–Asian bonding, but at the same time they alert the reader to the fact that such a failure is in large part a result of an unsolved American dilemma. These tales of race and power insist that, as a colonial subject who works in the colonizer's factories and fights his wars, the African American is never free from the white Westerner. As Wright reminds the white woman concerned about her roommate's "voodoo" practices, "The American Negroes are black and they live in a white country" (186). And even as Wright refers rather generously to "legislation against segregation" at one point, he also makes it very clear at several places in the text that "being 'colored' still means today in America that you can feel that you are in a lower category of the human race, that your hopes for freedom, for a redemption of your marked-off status, must be deferred" (177). And this is particularly true of African Americans in the Jim Crow South. The United States may be the world's great promoter of modernity—of rationalism, technology, and so on—but those modernist virtues are not bestowed upon African Americans living in the nation's most racially fraught region. The benefit allotted black southerners is a desegregation process so deliberate, so painfully slow, that it amounts to nothing less than an unwillingness to disturb white traditions of prejudice. We may speculate that the failure of the U.S. government and the white power elite to eliminate official and de facto segregation is, for Wright, a sign of how colonial modernity can evacuate itself of the modern itself and ironically promulgate atavistic social practices. When, in his contemporary travel volume *Pagan Spain* (1957), Wright draws a parallel between the conical headgear of Catholic monks and the hoods of the Ku Klux Klan, he deliberately draws our attention to ostensibly Western societies that seem willing to endorse, tacitly or otherwise, what he understands as irrational and primitive ritual.[63]

What is perhaps most extraordinary about Wright is that even as he is well aware of the horrors of white racism in the United States, he still believes in Western modernization and rejects the temptations of racial revenge. While waiting at the Ministry of Information for a press card, for example, Wright finds himself favored by an Indonesian official who ignores a white American newsman also in line. Wright understands that the Indonesian has recognized him as "one of his kind." As the writer explains, "I'd endured the humiliations that he and his people had endured" (114). But this gesture of transnational colored solidarity in the face of whiteness proves somewhat alarming to Wright, for it reminds him of the injuries of racism far more than it thrills him with the possibility of belonging to the dominant group. Referring to the Indonesian official's behavior, Wright shifts into a bitterly mnemonic mode: "It was racism. And I thought of all the times in the American South when I had had to wait until the whites had been served before I could be served" (114). To be acknowledged as "one of his kind" by the Indonesian official is to be embraced as a member of a racially defined group that now has the upper hand. "I got my press card at once," Wright states; "I was a member of the master race!" (114). He comes close to offering his own version of the Faulknerian disdain for belonging to the "topdog" group, but he does so not to reaffirm the value of the local or the subaltern, but rather to shore up his continuing faith in a modern state capable of functioning in a rational and impartial manner. The possibility of what fellow Bandung attendee Carlos Romulo dubbed "a lynch mob in reverse" disturbs Wright not only because of its threat of violence, in other words, but also because the threat of such violence attests to the impossibility of modernizing the new Asian and African nations.[64]

Wright's insistence on the paramount importance of modernization has a distinctly U.S. referent, and this emerges during an encounter with a U.S. development official. Wright introduces the man as a "highly competent official" who "was a reformed American of the Old South." "His grandfather had owned slaves," writes Wright, "and he was eagerly willing to own up to what had happened in history and was most committed to try to do something about it" (210). By emphasizing his white interviewee's southern background and then claiming that the man was "committed" to confronting slavery and its legacies, Wright raises the expectation that he will devote some portion of this scene to a discussion of social change in the U.S. southeast. Yet after invoking the racial politics of the South in an explicit fashion, Wright then abandons the domestic front altogether, "narrowing" his questions to the Indonesian situation or what he calls a "baby nation and its case of measles" (210). Both he and the white southerner seem to understand social change as linked not to the domestic region from which they both hail, but rather to the developing world. The legacy of the peculiar institution is supplanted by the legacy of Dutch colonialism, and the vulgar modernization project advocated by Adam Clayton Powell is supplanted by international development. And yet the U.S. racial experience—a largely southern experience—deeply inflects and nuances Wright's position, setting him apart from the other Asian and African attendees, even from the other Americans at the conference.

In his discussion with the reformed white southerner, Wright emphasizes the dire nature of the "baby" nation's problem; in the case of Indonesia, however, his interlocutor is committed to a painfully slow process of development. The unnamed official's particular plan for improving Southeast Asia centers on educating a small number of Indonesians in the United States so that in "fifty or a hundred years" the nation would have an improved standard of living and would no longer be vulnerable to Communist appeals (211). His is a philosophy of noninterference. Or, as he puts it, "I'm a Jeffersonian Democrat. . . . We will help, but we won't interfere." The reference to a Jeffersonian Democrat in this context most likely refers to the yeoman credo of small farmers and a limited state apparatus. But given Wright's opening emphasis on the man's southern origin, we may be tempted to read a bit more into this invocation of the founding father. If the U.S. official, this scion of former slave-owners, identifies himself as a Jeffersonian Democrat to emphasize his belief in the value of autonomy for people, states, and nations, he also recalls how many white southern liberals defended the right of the southern states to desegregate themselves in their own manner and on their own schedule. The anonymous white official's suggestion that the improvement of life in such nations as Indonesia may well take "fifty or a hundred years" inadvertently reminds us of Faulkner's oft-cited advice that desegregationists "go slow"—or, to recall Wright's words, the idea that "being 'colored' still means today in America that you can feel that . . . your hopes for freedom, for a redemption of your marked-off status, must be deferred" (177).

Objecting to the official's lengthy timetable for modernization, Wright makes clear that he rejects a *longue durée* approach to ending racial oppression for a more proactive response geared toward the present needs of the third world. As he explains to the white southerner, development hardly constitutes interference, for, as he puts it, "we start interfering with a baby as soon as it is born"—a not so subtle reference to his earlier description of the Asian nation as an infant. In Wright's view there is no possibility of allowing the Indonesians to maintain their old way of life after colonialism; the United States should instead do what it can to bring this Asian people "up" into modernity without exploiting them. And if the Americans and their Western allies don't pursue such a course, Wright argues, the Chinese in particular are only too happy to volunteer: "If the West spurns this call. . . . remember that Mr. Chou En-lai stands there, waiting, patient, with no record of racial practices behind him" (202).

Such a position may prove somewhat surprising given that Wright is, as we have seen, quite sensitive to the colonial dimensions of U.S. and Western modernity. Yet if we consider that he is in this argument debating the timetable of federal intervention with an avowed white southerner, albeit one of reformed sentiments, then the black writer's position becomes clearer. For Wright, we may speculate, the policy of non-interference in the developing nations of Africa and Asia reflects and supports the domestic policy of benign neglect in the U.S. South as well. To offer a vocal critique of the former is to offer a quiet indictment of the latter. The U.S. role in Asian modernization, while seemingly distant from the concerns of black Mississippians, may in fact bear upon precisely the sort of racial questions with which Wright began his career. As this intellectual well knew, modernization was a two-edged sword, one capable of eliminating the imprisoning traditions of foreign nations on the one hand and challenging his United States' own terrible investment in rituals of racism and violence on the other. When Wright alludes to the murder of Emmett Till during the lynching of Chris in *The Long*

Dream, he not only refers to the most notorious racist murder of the decade, but also paints a scathing portrait of a horribly backward Jim Crow South—of a region where the best aspects of modernization had had little purchase. The brutalization and murder of a young black man in this novel reminds us that Wright's lurid condemnation of Communism at the end of *The Color Curtain* also constitutes something of critique of an imperial United States as well. "MUST THIS TRAGIC METHOD, WITH ITS SECULAR RELIGIOSITY OF HORROR AND BLOOD, BE REPEATED ON THE BODY OF THE HUMAN RACE?" asks Wright on the last page of his Asian volume, the capitalization screaming for our attention. That the answer to this terrible question, a question written in the lexicon of lynching, never comes reminds us that Wright, like Faulkner, could not fully resolve all the contradictions of locating Mississippi in the Pacific.

In 1965, Malcolm X would claim that Mississippi could be found anywhere in the United States south of the Canadian border—a claim that extended the racism associated with the South to the entire nation. Yet as the eminent black leader well knew, in an era of U.S. attempts to modernize African and Asian nations, Mississippi had become more than another name for the United States; potentially, it named any part of the world in which the nation asserted its extraordinary power. For U.S. modernization, while ostensibly intended to uplift the backward and oppressed peoples of the African, Asian, and Latin American periphery, often functioned in a converse manner. Rather than rendering those places sovereign and self-sufficient, it colonized them anew, not through territorial conquest, but rather through the cooptation of hearts, minds, and markets. To engage in modernization during the cold war was to resist international Communism through a neocolonial strategy that often seemed designed to turn other nations, even allegedly independent nations, into places not unlike Mississippi itself, where a local elite would oppress and violate a peasant populace with the tacit blessing of the distant imperial metropole.

Faulkner and Wright approached the challenge of what we might call global Mississippi from very different perspectives. The white writer's moderate stance on desegregation at once reflected and helped generate his equally divided attitude on decolonization and Asian power. He would bond with the Japanese over resistance to compulsory modernization even as he wrestled with the notion that such peoples might serve as a metonym for African Americans rebelling against the Jim Crow regime. Wright's experience with the "secular religiosity" of Jim Crow violence didn't allow for his understandable concerns about colonial modernity to emerge through a wholesale critique of modernization as such. Instead, Wright's experience in the South forced him to appreciate the ideal of a rational, scientific, and democratic state willing to develop recalcitrant parts of the nation, even the world; that this ideal often collapsed back into the federal government's tacit endorsement of atavistic ritual and irrational thought could not eliminate his abiding investment in the modern. Both of these southern intellectuals attempted to find in alien cultures a new way of responding to the domestic center-periphery crisis that now appeared writ large across the globe. For them, we might say, borrowing from Mary Louise Pratt, modernity "comes into view . . . not as an agent that grants freedom but as an agent that sets in motion certain conflicts and that is itself constituted by those conflicts."[65] That Mississippi itself continued to provide ample reason to query the limit and meaning of the modern would preoccupy both men until the end of their lives.

EPILOGUE

Alice Walker and the Lost Cause

For all its influence with liberals and moderates, "cold war civil rights" gained little ground among white southerners.[1] Concern about the nation's reputation might have compelled elements of the federal government grudgingly to support desegregation, but many whites of the region, Faulkner's relatives included, tended to reject such global thinking in favor of an exclusionary investment in the local. For the Citizens Councils and their supporters, an era of federally mandated progress demanded a violent defense of sovereign white community and an affirmation of white southern tradition.[2] During the late 1960s and early 1970s, the mnemonic investments of a recalcitrant white South seemed most visible at the Confederate memorial carved into Stone Mountain, a granite monolith located some twenty miles north of Atlanta. First claimed by white supremacists in 1909, when Helena Plane of the Daughters of the Confederacy proposed a Confederate memorial for the site, the mountain soon grew infamous as the place where William Simmons would revive a moribund Ku Klux Klan in 1915.[3] The Klan's long-standing connection to the site would result in the frequent use of the mountain for cross-burnings and other terror tactics of white vigilantism, but the Confederate memorial itself long proved an abortive enterprise.[4] Initial efforts petered out by the early 1930s, and partisans of the Lost Cause would have to wait until 1964 for resumption of work on the memorial. Backed by the state of Georgia, which by then owned the mountain, sculptors and construction crews took to the project with vigor, and the vast majority of this tribute to Confederate leaders was soon completed. By the end of the 1960s, the city of Martin Luther King,

Jr.'s birth had become the site of a massive memorial to slavery and secession. Nothing could be further from the State Department's public displays of U.S. democracy.[5]

White Atlantans and white southerners were hardly alone in celebrating the newly completed memorial. Other white Americans also embraced the bas-relief on Stone Mountain, and some of those Americans were powerful indeed. On May 9, 1970, Vice President Spiro Agnew officially dedicated the memorial. Speaking with the granite figures of Robert E. Lee, Stonewall Jackson, and Jefferson Davis looming behind him, Agnew defended the South against its detractors. "The nation cannot afford to discriminate against the South," he declaimed to a crowd of thirty thousand."[6] Yet this affirmation of the South had to compete with his indictment of liberals, "peaceniks," and Communists. For the notoriously conservative Agnew, we may suspect, performing the dedication had less to do with honoring white southern tradition—however much he may have paid lip service to that notion—than it did with celebrating a reactionary conception of American identity emblematized by a clichéd image of the region. The event at Stone Mountain was not an opportunity for Agnew to participate in a white southern "community of shared loss" so much as it was a chance to transform Dixie affect into far-right exultation: in this scenario, the memorial would through the vice president's appearance become nothing less than a symbol for a national renewal of a distinctly reactionary kind.[7]

This was President Nixon's notorious "southern strategy": a political tactic that on the one hand sought to manipulate white voters through a bald-faced appeal to southern racism and on the other attempted to exploit "Dixie' as a national emblem for tradition in mortal danger from an insidious counterculture.[8] *Life* magazine addressed the historical dimensions of the administration's regionalism when it published a caricature of Nixon, Agnew, and Attorney General John Mitchell as latter-day versions of Lee, Jackson, and Davis as they appear on the Stone Mountain memorial (Figure 10). The cartoon's caption vivifies the point: "A more contemporary trio of Southern strategists have not yet been able to carve their stratagems into enduring stone. So we preserve them in full regalia . . . for the benefit of some ambitious memorialist of the future."[9] The image suggests that the GOP sought to make itself as permanent a part of the southern landscape as Stone Mountain itself—not to honor the South, needless to say, but rather to appropriate glory for the "silent majority" revolution. The administration had little interest in becoming part of any Lost Cause; instead it wanted to exploit that cause for its own future political success. What white southerners named a memorial—in Arthur Danto's words, "a segregated enclave where we

Figure 10. From "Parting Shots," *Life Magazine,* May 22, 1970

honor the dead"—the president and his cohort designated a monument, a means of honoring themselves.[10]

Nixon was hardly the first well-known member of the GOP to abandon the Lincoln legacy for an opportunistic identification with the Lost
Cause. As we have seen in our examination of President William McKinley, modern U.S. politicians and intellectuals have long located in Dixie
an inspiring source of conservative energies. Yet in the 1960s, such open
valuation of the Confederate legacy found new opposition in the wave
of liberal thinking that characterized the decade, and Agnew's presence
at Stone Mountain suggests as much. President Nixon had planned to
dedicate the memorial until news of the shootings at Kent State University forced a change of plans.[11] Ready to rally his white southern supporters, the president instead found he had to avoid further alienating
the many Americans who already had rejected his domestic and foreign
policies.[12] The enormous outcry over both the secret bombing campaign
of Cambodia and the murder of student protestors made clear that
many Americans would likely view Nixon's "southern strategy" not as
a gesture of respect, but rather as a manifestation of his desire to estab-

lish a historical connection to a white supremacist regime. For the president to celebrate Stone Mountain in the era of the Vietnam War was to suggest that the state should exert power over people of color and their supporters in nothing less than an imperial manner.

African Americans familiar with the memorial had long understood that Stone Mountain commemorated the white will to power. When Martin Luther King, Jr., included the line "Let Freedom ring from Stone Mountain of Georgia" in his speech at the Lincoln Memorial (1963), he emphasized that what seemed to some a dignified memorial to fallen heroes was to many others a terrible sign of how strenuously the South had exercised white supremacy since Appomattox. Not only did many African Americans grasp that slavery and Jim Crow segregation constituted a form of internal colonialism, they also understood that domestic white supremacy bore important connections to U.S. imperialism overseas. For them, that is, memorials to the Lost Cause "looked away" to the U.S. presence in Southeast Asia, and the behavior of some white military personnel only confirmed this assumption. White soldiers and sailors had flown the Stars and Bars before, but during the Vietnam War they would sometimes display the Confederate flag in tandem with the wearing of Klan robes and the burning of crosses.[13] In one of the most egregious incidents, white sailors at the U.S. naval base at Cam Ranh Bay staged a Klan rally to express their delight at the assassination of King himself (1968). Some black military personnel responded by joining the Black Panthers. African Americans hardly needed the historical proximity of the Kent State murders and the Confederate memorial dedication to recognize how the administration's claim on the South had global resonance. Stone Mountain might have been in Georgia, but its affirmation of white supremacy reverberated in the farthest reaches of the U.S. imperium.[14]

Given the administration's attempt to claim "Dixie" as its own, it should come as no surprise that African American writers of the era regularly linked Jim Crow abuses at home to the United States' continued prosecution of an imperial war abroad. Figures from Eldridge Cleaver to Margaret Walker mapped various local and global manifestations of the white expansionism in their public statements, but arguably no African American intellectual proved as capable as Alice Walker in transforming these anti-imperial insights into a new vision of the South. Walker's *Meridian* (1976), a novel about the civil rights movement, engages with much the same issues of memorialization, Jim Crow racism, and U.S. power that informed the administration's interest in Stone Mountain. And one chapter of the novel in particular offers a powerful riposte to the GOP's attempt to exploit the Lost Cause during what Walker dubbed "the criminal Vietnam-American War."[15] In "Indians and Ecstasy," Walker examines the complex and slippery correspondences between the contemporary African American struggle for democracy and the United States' decimation of the continent's indigenous people. That she does so by attending carefully to the politics and poetics of a burial mound suggests her sensitivity to those unusual spaces where memory lives and the past seems omnipresent. At once commemorating the dead and mapping future generations, speaking historically and resonating geographically, the Indian memorial offers Walker a basis for reconstructing democracy in the wake of the Nixon presidency.

When a Cherokee named Walter Longknife tells the young Meridian of his travels from Oklahoma to the South, he provides the reader with an atypical perspective on the notorious granite monolith with which we began: "He had started out in an old pick-up truck that broke down in the shadow of Stone Mountain. He abandoned it, and was glad . . . to walk through the land of his ancestors."[16] Longknife's passing encounter with Stone Mountain occurs in the mid-1950s, some fifteen years before Agnew's speech. Yet to recognize this temporal disjunction is hardly to undercut Stone Mountain's status as a political signifier. By having Longknife begin walking "in the shadow of Stone Mountain," Walker reterritorializes the white supremacist shrine that the administration is so eager to claim as Native American land—a fact borne out by the historical record. Native Americans inhabited this portion of Georgia from the early Woodland period (c. 2000 B.C.E.) until roughly 1838, when they were forced to vacate the area and move to Oklahoma along the Trail of Tears. During the seventeenth to nineteenth centuries, the Creeks and the Cherokees predominated in the state, with the latter tribe dominating the northern part of Georgia by the early eighteenth century. Stone Mountain most likely lay in Creek territory during this period, but the peak also functioned as something of an important nodal point for Native Americans of various tribes. Trails crisscrossed the mountain, suggesting its importance in the transportation network of the era. Thus even though the mountain isn't recognized as a Native American memorial, it had a certain economic and social significance to indigenous people that Longknife's walking tour of Georgia makes palpable. That Longknife undertakes his journey in the 1950s before the state of Georgia completed the Confederate memorial renders the granite monolith all the more available for a radical reterritorialization within the world of the novel.

What renders Longknife's reverse passage of the Trail of Tears directly relevant to the plot of Walker's civil rights text is his encounter with Meridian's father, a man obsessed with commemorating the white extermination of local Native Americans. The chapter begins with Meridian watching her father recover an earlier geographic formation: "Her father sat at a tiny brown table poring over a map. It was an old map, yellowed and cracked with frayed edges, that showed the ancient settlements of Indians in North America" (46). By invoking this "old map" and these "ancient settlements" in her civil rights novel, Walker urges her readers to remember the long history that predates contemporary battles over race and citizenship. White racists and black civil rights activists may debate questions of democracy in the southland, but this contest depends upon the removal of the region's native inhabitants whom, as Walker put it in her contemporary poem, "Eagle Rock" (1973), "the/National Policy slew."[17] And even as most modern Americans, black and white, have forgotten this terrible fact, Meridian's father manifests an almost obsessive need to remember the loss. His small office offers a hodge-podge memorial to Native American suffering: "There were actual photographs . . . of Indian women and children looking starved and glassy-eyed and doomed into the camera . . . As she tiptoed closer to the bookshelves and reached to touch a photograph of a frozen Indian child (whose mother lay beside her in a bloody heap) her father looked up from his map, his face wet with tears" (46–47). If most African Americans living in the South during the early 1950s had all they could do to survive poverty and racism, Meridian's father finds in himself untold reserves of empathy for the original targets of white expansion in the hemisphere.

That his sensitivity to the Native American past stems not from books, but from his land, renders these feelings of grief all the more potent. The family farm, first purchased by Meridian's great-grandfather after the Civil War, includes a burial mound—a "five-hundred-yard Sacred Serpent that formed a curving, twisting hill beyond the corn" (50). The fact that the hard-won farm rests on a Native American "cemetery" inspires Meridian's father to register the somatic implications of history. As he reminds his skeptical wife, their cabbages and tomatoes grow "healthy from the iron and calcium of . . . [Indian] bones"; the nourishment of the entire family depends in part on soil physically enriched by their predecessors' bodies (47). These African Americans have grown physiologically—and, by extension, historically and politically—thanks to the suffering and loss of a fellow people of color. And it is this realization, far more than any ancient maps or historical texts, that moves Meridian's father to think of himself as linked to Native Americans, those long dead and those still living. The fact that his family's life depends in part on the chemical residues of indigenous peoples isn't only proof of unwitting collusion with empire; it is also proof that land can function as an inadvertent crucible of hybrid identity.[18] By attempting to understand history from the bottom up, this black man redefines southern agrarianism as a form of radical commemoration; celebrating the southern farm no longer seems a stereotypical reactionary gesture but rather a first step toward a grassroots reconstruction of the region.

To be sure, U.S. intellectuals have often found in Native American burial mounds a mysterious phenomenon that seemed to challenge conventional notions of history. Many Americans attributed the mounds to a lost biblical tribe or to the ancient people of Atlantis in order to avoid acknowledging the accomplishments of First Peoples.[19] Walker herself may have been exposed to some myths and half-truths about the mounds while growing up in Georgia, for her hometown of Eatonton (located seventy miles from Stone Mountain) includes an extraordinary effigy mound, the 120-foot-long Rock Eagle. (Other parts of the state are home to burial mounds that include the deep central pit so important to Walker's depiction of the Sacred Serpent memorial in *Meridian*.[20]) Walker certainly accepts the notion that these memorials exceed normative Western notions of history—not because mythic foreign peoples created them, but rather because they remind all Americans about a loss that defies calculation. These earthen art works testify to the unfathomable costs of so-called progress. "Without [the Indian]," writes Walker, "the landscape of America seems lonely, speechless."[21]

In certain respects, Walker's interest in these memorials recalls the work of Faulkner, another southern writer who found in the burial mound a challenge to conventional notions of community and history. Faulkner's most famous engagement with this issue in "The Fire and Hearth" focuses on Lucas Beauchamp's complex attempt first to locate in the Indian mound his rightful McCaslin patrimony and then, when his alienation takes hold, to try to profit from the comic situation that ensues. The story draws together themes of race, genealogy, and capitalism in a rich meditation on southern rural life that frames the burial mound as a quintessentially American figure. Yet if Lucas Beauchamp's experience with a native memorial reflects his obsession with a much-valued white male ancestry, Walker's African American hero engages with his burial mound in a manner that sets aside any discussion of white inheritance in favor of affirming a radical connection between the red and the black. The fact that Beauchamp imagines that he will find in the burial mound the treasure denied him by the Jim Crow South could not be more different from the way in which Meridian's father locates in his burial mound a hybrid sense of the past that cannot be quantified by the calculus of modern capitalism. For Meridian's father, as we shall see, money has little if anything to do with the Sacred Serpent upon his land; to the contrary, the burial mound has the capacity to distance him from all such quotidian considerations as it endows him with a larger and more mystical sense of being.

Meridian shares her father's deep attachment to the Sacred Serpent. Like Feather Mae, a long-dead ancestor most likely based on Walker's great-grandmother, both father and daughter have the capacity to find within the forty-foot-deep walls of the burial mound a radical detachment from normative experience. For those subjects open to the possibility, the Serpent provides a means of decentering the self—of dislocating the subject from a conventional understanding of space and time. When Meridian first enters the mound, she feels tremendously isolated: "She was a dot, a speck in creation, alone and hidden. She had contact with no other living thing; instead she was surrounded by the dead" (52). But her feelings of insignificance and alienation soon give way to a new sense of empowerment as she senses herself leaving her body and adopting a new perspective on the world: "It was as if the walls of earth that enclosed her rushed outward, leveling themselves at a dizzying rate, and then spinning wildly, lifting her out of her body and giving her the feeling of flying" (52). She is still a "speck," but a "speck" that has a stunning aerial view of her environment. Houses, trees, flowers, people: all are suddenly available to her in this mystical experience. Her father believes that the mound gives one a sense of dying and becoming pure spirit, but Meridian argues the opposite; in her view, the mound enabled "the living . . . to expand the consciousness of being alive" (53). For all their differences on this issue, however, both characters understand that the decentered experience available in the burial mound bears directly upon their sense of a "tangible . . . connection to the past."

One senses that this might be Walker's impulse as well. If her account of the Sacred Serpent testifies to a longstanding investment in Native American shamanistic traditions, it also shores up an equally significant commitment to recovering neglected memorials to the subaltern, particularly in her native region.[22] By enabling Meridian and her father to leave behind their African American bodies and develop a mystical connection to the long-dead objects of U.S. empire, the Sacred Serpent stands opposed to the Confederate Memorial at Stone Mountain, the memorial to a war fought in defense of white supremacy and black slavery. Yet this opposition is not a matter of racial politics alone; it also emerges through the differences in the memorials. Stone Mountain portrays and names specific heroes; the Sacred Serpent engages in a far more anonymous and communal act of commemoration. Like the Rock Eagle effigy mound of Eatonton, Georgia, the Sacred Serpent doesn't focus on particular deaths.[23] To the contrary, the burial mound proves powerful precisely because it rejects conventional notions of personhood and identity in favor of commemorating an exterminated people.

Meridian's father attempts to honor what he has learned from the burial mound and his land by engaging in his own act of reparation. Moved by compassion for Indians "dead centuries before he was born," he gives the deed to the farm to Walter Longknife, the wandering Chero-kee who has abandoned his broken truck at Stone Mountain. The fam-ily may have acquired the land legally after the Civil War, but in his opinion he had only been "holding it" for its rightful owners, the Indi-ans. Meridian's father chooses to return the land not out of guilt for hav-ing benefited from the crimes of U.S. empire, although, as he reminds his wife, no American is innocent, "everybody's been a part of it for a long time" (49). Rather, he wishes to engage in his own remapping of the region: returning his postage-stamp-sized bit of northern Georgia to Native American ground. That this is a quixotic act soon becomes ap-parent. Having decided "to move on," Longknife returns the deed to Meridian's father. Shortly after the Native American's departure, "army green" trucks appear to begin the process of transforming the land into a segregated public park. The family farm is seized in the name of the state of Georgia; Meridian's father has his commemorative work "stolen away" (50). White power, conspicuously rendered in military form, challenges the new connectedness between red and black, past and present, and renders the Sacred Serpent a very different type of space indeed. The radical meaning of this soil, this gritty memorial to hybrid-ity and a palpable past has been eliminated. This seizure in the name of Jim Crow Georgia cannot help but recall the Confederate visages on the nearby granite monolith—another white monument created out of what was once Native American land, another example of how white empire can transform the rocks and earth into signs of its own power and permanence.

Yet if the novel reminds us that in the modern U.S. South no response to loss, past or present, can completely escape Jim Crow, this African American act of reparation suggests a way of responding to the presi-dent's southern strategy and its exploitative relationship to the Lost Cause. For Meridian's father insists through his compassion for Native Americans that the southland is the site of many lost causes: "that what had already and forever been lost" was not only antebellum white slave-holding society, but also societies far more crucial to the spiritual and political health of the republic (54). To celebrate acts of commemoration in Georgia is not only to bolster the imperial conception of state power in an age of Vietnam and Kent State, it is also to reconstruct this portion of the South in a manner that resists easy appropriation by white politi-cians. We may speculate that for Alice Walker, the sacred serpent, hum-ble and earthy, ever-vulnerable, talks back to Nixon's regionalism, demonstrating that subaltern grief has the capacity to render the South less a touchstone for empire than a potential source of its undoing. To reconstruct this region is to render it a sign for all that radical democ-racy has to offer, in different places and in different times.

NOTES

Introduction

1. For a concise summary of this journalistic trend see Gaurav Desai, Letter, *MLA Newsletter* 37 (Winter 2005): 5–6.

2. The U.S. census currently includes sixteen states in its definition of the South, the thirteen expected states plus Kentucky, Maryland, and Oklahoma. I realize of course that such a definition hardly captures the diversity and heterogeneity of this sprawling region. There are many "Souths." In this book, I have sacrificed the benefits of a more in-depth analysis of particular "Souths" for the advantages of assessing how the imagined region in its entirety functioned as an imperial signifier during the twentieth century. That is, while we will touch upon particular states and cities—Wilmington, North Carolina, or Columbus, Georgia, for example—we will for the most part interpret the figure of the South in its broadest parameters.

3. See W. J. Cash, *The Mind of the South* (New York: Vintage, 1991 [1940]), vii. For one of the most influential representations of the South as somehow "alien" to the nation, see Louis Hartz, *The Liberal Tradition in America* (New York: Harcourt, 1955), 53. This tradition has stemmed to an extent from what was up until the end of the twentieth century the region's subordinate position as an economically dependent and economically exploited part of a modern capitalist nation. Even as we register this history, however, it is crucial to recognize that the South's subaltern status was profoundly uneven. The white southern elite may have found themselves in a colonial relationship to a wealthier and more powerful North, but that same local elite adopted a fundamentally colonial attitude toward African Americans and poor whites. For an interesting account of the South as an internal colony, see Joseph Persky, *The Burden of Dependency: Colonial Themes in Southern Economic Thought* (Baltimore: Johns Hopkins University Press, 1992).

4. See Anne Norton, *Alternative Americas* (Chicago: University of Chicago Press, 1986), 6.

5. Throughout this study I will treat *race* not as an essential attribute, but rather as a cultural and social construction that has at various times taken on the authority of nature and science. To put it another way, I will stress the degree to which racial identity often emerges through identifications and cross-identifications that are at once performative and historical.

6. Ida B. Wells, *A Red Record* (1895) reprinted in Wells, *On Lynchings* (New York: Arno Press, 1969), 97; H. L. Mencken, "The Sahara of the Bozart," *The American Scene*, ed. Huntington Cairns (New York: Knopf, 1977), 157–68; Carl Carmer, *Stars Fell on Alabama* (New York: Literary Guild of America, 1934), iv.

7. For example, see "Tu Do Street" in Yusef Komunyakaa, *Neon Vernacular: New and Selected Poems* (Middletown, CT: Wesleyan University Press, 1993), 147.

8. See C. Vann Woodward, *The Burden of Southern History*, rev. ed. (Baton Rouge: Louisiana State University Press, 1960), 230. Needless to say, other figures, primarily white southern intellectuals, tended to associate the region with European civilization. As John Crowe Ransom argued over seventy years ago, "The South is unique on this continent for having founded and defended a culture which was according to the European principles of cultures; and the European principles had better look to the South if they are to be perpetuated in this country." See "Reconstructed but Unregenerate," in *I'll Take My Stand* (New York: Harper and Row, 1930), 3. We might note at the same time that white southerners from Thomas Jefferson to Thomas Nelson Page tended to link their region to Mediterranean Europe, to, that is, a part of the continent viewed as not quite white by many Americans of Anglo-Saxon stock.

9. Allen Tate, "Faulkner's Sanctuary and the Southern Myth," *Memories and Opinions* (Chicago: Swallow, 1975), 146.

10. By spatial scales, I refer to a way of delineating differently sized geographic formations, from the body to the home, the city to the world, and understanding their relationship. See Neil Brenner, "The Limits to Scale? Methodological Reflections on Scalar Structuration," *Progress in Human Geography* 15, no. 4 (2001): 525–48; Sally Marston, "The Social Construction of Scale," *Progress in Human Geography* 24, no. 2 (2000), 219–42; and Neil Smith, "Contours of a Spatialized Politics: Homeless Vehicles and the Production of Geographical Scale," *Social Text* 3 (1993): 55–81. Much of the current work on spatial scale reflects recent interest in constructivist approaches to geography. As will become clear in what follows, *Reconstructing the World* like much post-nationalist American Studies scholarship depends to a large degree on the work of such cultural geographers as David Harvey, Henri Lefebvre, Doreen Massey, and Edward Soja. That is, my thoughts on the South, the nation, and the world have benefited greatly from various formulations of the idea that space is made in and through cultural, social, and economic means. As Harvey puts it, "beneath the veneer of common-sense and seemingly 'natural' ideas about space and time there lie hidden terrains of ambiguity, contradiction, and struggle." See *The Condition of Postmodernity* (Oxford: Blackwell, 1989), 205.

11. I generally agree with Stephen Krasner that the modern Western state is best understood as a "set of roles and institutions [that] have peculiar drives, compulsions, and aims of their own that are separate and distinct from the interests of any particular societal group. These goals relate to general material objectives or ambitious ideological goals related to beliefs about the ordering of society." But I also believe that in many instances, the state looks out for the interests of capital, even when particular capitalist blocs are aligned against it. See Krasner, *Defending the National Interests: Raw Materials Investments and U.S. Foreign Policy* (Princeton: Princeton University Press, 1978), 10–11. I also have been influenced by Theda Skocpol's important claim that the state is "Janus-faced, with an intrinsically dual anchorage in class-divided socio-economic structures and an international system of states." See Skocpol, *States and Social Revolutions* (Cambridge: Cambridge University Press, 1979), 32. For an invaluable overview of the many Marxist and neo-Marxist perspectives on the relationship between the state and capitalism, see David Held, *Political Theory and the Modern State* (Cambridge: Polity Press, 1989).

12. To be sure, expansionist states have from the classical period claimed to liberate and assist the very peoples they conquered and dominated. Yet the historical proximity of the

nation-state's refusal to address the black question in the South and its assumption of new expansionist ambitions rendered this topic particularly vital for Americans as they confronted an increasingly globalized modernity.

13. See "Behold this Land" in *W. E. B. Du Bois: A Reader,* ed. Meyer Weinberg (New York: Harper and Row, 1970), 152–53,

14. I borrow the term "U.S. empire studies" from Susan Kay Gillman. See "The New, Newest Thing: Have American Studies Gone Imperial?" *American Literary History* 17 (2005): 196.

15. See Edward Said, *Culture and Imperialism* (New York: Vintage, 1993), 9. Needless to say, this is only one definition of imperialism, but it well captures a typical historical understanding of the term. Like many scholars of imperialism, Said draws in his work on the pioneering early twentieth-century studies of J. A. Hobson and Vladimir Lenin. Both men argued, albeit in somewhat different ways, that imperialism was the highest stage of Western capitalism inasmuch as it named the need of European and U.S. industrialists to push aggressively and competitively into new global territories (e.g., Africa) in search of resources, labor, and markets when domestic options seemed exhausted. See Hobson, *Imperialism: A Study* (New York: James Pott, 1902) and Lenin, *Imperialism, the Highest Stage of Capitalism* (New York: International Publishers, 1939 [1916]). David Harvey has recently reminded us, however, that other left thinkers, most notably Hannah Arendt, argued that the need for bourgeois control over the state and the military resources required for global initiatives rendered fin-de-siècle imperialism "the first stage in the political rule of the bourgeoisie rather than the last stage of capitalism." See Harvey, *The New Imperialism* (Oxford: Oxford University Press, 2003), 127.

16. Richard Van Alstyne, *The Rising American Empire* (New York: Oxford University Press, 1960), 4.

17. See Amy Kaplan, "Black and Blue on San Juan Hill," in her *Anarchy of Empire in the Making of U.S. Culture* (Cambridge: Harvard University Press, 2002), 121–45; and Nikhil Singh, *Black Is a Country: Race and the Unfinished Struggle for Democracy* (Cambridge: Harvard University Press, 2004).

18. To put it another way, for all the justifiable interest in Michael Hardt and Toni Negri's important book *Empire* (2000), few contemporary Americanists concerned with such issues have tended to agree that one can completely separate a U.S.-derived notion of decentered Empire from a traditional European definition of imperialism.

19. With respect to matters of definition, I follow Benedict Anderson's to my mind unparalleled description of "nation" as "an imagined political community—and imagined as both inherently limited and sovereign." See *Imagined Communities: Reflections on the Origin and Spread of Nationalism* (New York: Verso, 1991), 5.

20. See Anna Brickhouse, *Transamerican Literary Relations and the Nineteenth-Century Public Sphere* (Cambridge: Cambridge University Press, 2004); Kaplan, *The Anarchy of Empire;* Lisa Lowe, "The International within the National: American Studies and Asian American Critique," *Cultural Critique* 40 (1998): 29–47; Donald Pease, "National Identities, Postmodern Artifacts, and Postnational Narratives," in *National Identities and Post-Americanist Narratives,* ed. Pease (Durham: Duke University Press, 1994); John Carlos Rowe, "Post-Nationalism, Globalism, and the New American Studies" in *Post-Nationalist American Studies,* ed. Rowe (Berkeley: University of California Press, 2000), 23–38; Ramón Saldívar, "Looking for a Master Plan: Faulkner, Paredes, and the Colonial and Postcolonial Subject," in *The Cambridge Companion to William Faulkner,* ed. Philip Weinstein and Philip Wadlington (New York: Cambridge University Press, 1995), 96–120; and Malini Johar Schueller, *U.S. Orientalisms: Race, Nation, and Gender in Literature, 1790–1890* (Ann Arbor: University of Michigan Press, 1998).

21. We should note, however, that scholars in other disciplines have found the notion

of a more expansive version of Americanist scholarship somewhat troubling to say the least. Latin Americanists have offered the most powerful critiques of the idea of a post-nationalist American Studies. See, for example, José David Saldívar, *The Dialectics of Our America* (Durham: Duke University Press, 1991); Ramón Saldívar, "Looking for a Master Plan"; and Walter Mignolo, *The Darker Side of the Renaissance: Literacy, Territoriality, and Colonization* (Ann Arbor: University of Michigan, 1995).

22. See Pease, "National Identities," 3.

23. We should recognize, of course, that these scholars have drawn from and helped contribute to a now thirty-year-old interdisciplinary emphasis on challenging white male dominance in the literary, cultural, and historiographic canons.

24. See Jeffrey Belnap and Raul Fernández, "Introduction," in their edited volume *José Martí's "Our America"* (Durham: Duke University Press, 1998); Vicente L. Rafael, "White Love: Surveillance and Nationalist Resistance in the U.S. Colonization of the Philippines," in *Cultures of United States Imperialism,* ed. Amy Kaplan and Donald Pease (Durham: Duke University Press, 1993), 185–218; and Kate Baldwin, *Beyond the Color Line and the Iron Curtain: Reading Encounters between Black and Red, 1922–1963* (Durham: Duke University Press, 2002). These examples well suggest the enormous debt post-nationalist American Studies owes to postcolonial studies.

25. As Homi Bhabha puts it, counter-narratives of the nation "that continually evoke and erase its totalizing boundaries—both actual and conceptual—disturb those ideological maneuvers through which 'imagined communities' are given essentialist identities." See "Dissemination" in *Nation and Narration,* ed. Bhabha (London: Routledge), 300.

26. The one major exception is Amy Kaplan's recent exploration of how "representations of U.S. imperialism were mapped not through a West/East axis of frontier symbols and politics, but instead through a North/South axis around the issues of slavery, Reconstruction, and Jim Crow segregation." See *The Anarchy of Empire,* 18.

27. See Neil Smith, "Contours of a Spatialized Politics: Homeless Vehicles and the Production of Geographical Scale," *Social Text* 33 (1993): 55–81.

28. There is an opposing school of thought on the question of regional writing, a school that insists regionalism is in fact radical and subversive; or, as Stephanie Foote has argued, "regionalism in its broadest terms" functions "as a critique of the universal subject." See Foote, *Regional Fictions* (Madison: University of Wisconsin Press, 2001), 13. Regionalism for these scholars names nothing less than the challenge of the local to corporate or state power. This argument is important to a host of intellectuals from Americanists intent on reclaiming and revaluating nineteenth-century women writers to anti-globalization scholars eager to identify sources of grassroots resistance to late twentieth-century transnational flows of capital. Yet even though Foote and a few others do address international issues, I believe that this view of regionalism "as a critique of the universal subject" has played only a minor role in U.S. empire studies.

29. See Rowe, "Post-Nationalism, Globalism, and the New American Studies."

30. This approach recalls the internal colony thesis that had its heyday in the late 1960s and 1970s. As Robert Blauner, one of the best-known proponents of the internal colony thesis, puts it in *Racial Oppression in America* (New York: Harper and Row, 1972), "communities of color in America share essential conditions with third world nations abroad: economic underdevelopment, a heritage of colonialism and neocolonialism, and a lack of real political economy and power" (72). For a critique of the internal colony thesis as dangerously imprecise, see Michael Omi and Howard Winant, *Racial Formation in the United States* (New York: Routledge and Kegan Paul, 1986).

31. See Richard Slotkin, *Regeneration through Violence* (New York: Hill and Wang, 1973); Kenneth Frampton, "Towards a Critical Regionalism: Six Points for an Architecture of Resistance" in *The Anti-Aesthetic,* ed. Hal Foster (Port Townsend, WA: Bay Press, 1983), 16–30.

32. See Caroline Levander, "Confederate Cuba," *American Literature* 78, no. 4 (December 2006), 821 45; and John Matthews, "Reading the West Indies: From Yoknapatawpha to Haiti and Back," *American Literary History* 16, no. 2 (2004): 238–62.

33. See Jon Smith and Deborah Cohn, "Introduction: Uncanny Hybridities," in *Look Away! The U.S. South in New World Studies*, ed. Smith and Cohn (Durham: Duke University Press, 2004), 13.

34. See Louis Althusser, "Ideology and the Ideological State Apparatus," in *Lenin and Philosophy and Other Essays* (London: New Left Books, 1977). The notable exception here is Houston Baker's important analysis of the relationship between the plantation legacy and the twentieth- and twenty-first-century prison-industrial complex. See *Turning South Again* (Durham: Duke University Press, 2001), 94. Colin Joan Dayan's argument that the current administration's attempt to legitimate torture draws on the rhetoric of antebellum slave codes also provides a nice example of how one can attend to both the legacy of the U.S. South and the politics of U.S. empire in a statist vein. See Dayan, *The Story of Cruel and Unusual* (Cambridge: MIT Press, 2007).

35. Robert Penn Warren certainly thought so. The eminent southern writer devoted a book-length poem to the struggles of the Nez Perce, *Chief Joseph and the Nez Perce* (New York: Random House, 1983).

36. See C. Vann Woodward, *The Origins of the New South* (Baton Rouge: Louisiana State University Press, 1971); and Kevin Phillips, *The Emerging Republican Majority* (New York: Harper, 1969).

37. What I am stressing here is the state's capacity to foster capitalism by creating certain types of geographies and, conversely, its ability to generate particular geographic formations by supporting capital. As R. J. Johnston argues with reference to the United States, "the need for a unitary business environment, in which capitalism can flourish, has meant that . . . the federal government defined economic and social policy and provides the financial ability and stimulus for State and local governments to operate that policy." See *Geography and the State: An Essay in Political Geography* (London: Macmillan, 1982), 189. This isn't to say that the regions and other sub-national spaces don't shape and, at times, resist such policies; they do. Yet it is equally important to recognize that capitalism generates uneven development within and without a national space only by acceding, however intermittently, to the power of a federal state apparatus.

38. If this book were 150 pages longer, it would include chapters on Mark Twain, Woodrow Wilson, Katherine Anne Porter, and Zora Neale Hurston. I also might have devoted a chapter to the U.S. occupation of Haiti. Yet with the notable exception of Porter, these figures and issues have already received a fair amount of attention from post-nationalist Americanists.

39. See "Negro Art and Literature," in *The Oxford W. E. B. Du Bois Reader*, ed. Eric Sundquist (New York: Oxford University Press, 1996), 315.

40. For Gramsci's account of the organic intellectual, see *Prison Notebooks* (New York: Columbia University Press, 1992).

41. See Eric Foner, *Reconstruction: America's Unfinished Revolution* (New York: Harper and Row, 1988), 23.

42. For an important analysis of the South's double-edged colonial crisis, see John T. Matthews, "This Race Which Is Not One: The 'More Inextricable Compositeness' of Faulkner's South," in *Look Away!*, ed. Smith and Cohn, 221–22. For an older and less racially aware engagement with similar issues, see Rupert Vance, *The Human Geography of the South* (Chapel Hill: University of North Carolina Press, 1935).

43. See Michael Lind, *Made in Texas: George W. Bush and the Southern Takeover of American Politics* (New York: Basic, 2002), 25.

44. See Hall, "Gramsci's Relevance for the Study of Race and Ethnicity," in *Stuart Hall:*

Critical Dialogues in Cultural Studies, ed. David Morley and Kuan-Hsing Chen (London: Routledge, 1996), 437.

45. See Timothy Brennan, "The National Longing for Form," in *The Post-Colonial Studies Reader,* ed. Bill Ashcroft et al. (New York: Routledge, 1995), 170–75.

Chapter 1. The Geography of Reunion

1. C. Vann Woodward points out that President McKinley's relationship with the white South wasn't very substantive: While "McKinley made two rather successful tours of the South, the appeal he made to the people was largely sentimental in nature." See *The Origins of the New South* (Baton Rouge: Louisiana State University Press, 1971), 462. For my purposes, however, it is precisely the affective dimensions of the president's southern tours that are relevant to understanding the place of the South in the contemporary culture of U.S. imperialism.

2. It's worth noting that McKinley served as a major in an Ohio regiment during the Civil War. William McKinley, *Speeches and Addresses* (New York: Doubleday, 1900), 370. All future citations are included in the text.

3. See David Blight, *Race and Reunion: The Civil War in American Memory* (Cambridge: Harvard University Press, 2001); Paul Buck, *The Road to Reunion, 1865–1900* (Boston: Little, Brown, 1937); Kathleen Diffley, *Where My Heart Is Turning Ever: Civil War Stories and Constitutional Reform, 1861–1876* (Athens: University of Georgia Press, 1992); Carol Reardon, *Pickett's Charge in History and Memory* (Chapel Hill: University of North Carolina Press, 2003); Nina Silber, *The Romance of Reunion: Northerners and the South, 1865–1900* (Chapel Hill: University of North Carolina Press, 1997).

4. See David Starr Jordan, *Imperial Democracy* (New York: D. Appleton, 1901), 7. Fellow anti-imperialist George Boutwell also made this argument: "It is a boast that the war has cemented the Union, and that the South has shown its capacity in war. The Union was compacted and firm when the war opened." See *The Crisis of the Republic* (Boston: D. Estes, 1900), 119. In linking anti- and pro-imperialist white Republicans to a common investment in white sectional reunion, I recall Christopher Lasch's well-known argument that the detractors of expansion were no less racist than its promoters. See "The Anti-Imperialists, the Philippines, and the Inequality of Man," *Journal of Southern History* 24 (August 1958): 319–31. At the same time, we should note that historian James McPherson takes issue with Lasch's characterization of the anti-imperialists, arguing that the legacy of abolition, "the ancestral cause," inspired a genuinely democratic form of anti-imperialism. See *The Abolitionist Legacy* (Princeton: Princeton University Press, 1975), 325–31.

5. In effect, a new appreciation of regional exceptionalism helped shore up national exceptionalism. Donald Pease recently made a similar point in the context of a lecture on twenty-first-century U.S. foreign policy, "American Studies after U.S. Exceptionalism: The Responsibility of the Intellectual," given at the Intellectuals and the Nation-State Conference, November 30, 2005, University College, Dublin.

6. For an important recent overview of white northern affection for plantation culture at the fin de siècle, see Shelley Fisher Fishkin, "Race and the Politics of Memory: Mark Twain and Paul Laurence Dunbar" *Journal of American Studies* 40(2006): 284–86. For a valuable assessment of the response to both the new immigration and the new imperialism, see Matthew Jacobson, *Barbarian Virtues* (New York: Hill and Wang, 2001).

7. See Lothrop Stoddard, *The Rising Tide of Color against White Supremacy* (New York: Scribner's, 1920).

8. This isn't to deny the force of, for example, Justice Harlan's dissent in Plessy, a statement that challenged the constitutionality of the majority decision, or other courageous outbursts by aging Abolitionists (e.g., William Lloyd Garrison and Thomas W. Higgin-

son). It is, however, to recognize with most African American intellectuals of the era that the 1890s represented the nadir of U.S. democracy.

9. See *Contending Forces* in *The Magazine Novels of Pauline Hopkins* (New York: Oxford, 1988), 248.

10. For the classic articulation of this argument see Frederick Turner's "The Significance of the Frontier in American History," first delivered at the meeting of the American Historical Association in Chicago at the World Columbian Exposition, July 12, 1893.

11. The impending social disaster provoked great concern; indeed, as Richard Slotkin has argued, the violent contemporary South seemed to many "an important 'predictor' of what a post-Frontier society might become." See *The Fatal Environment* (New York: Atheneum, 1985), 141.

12. Native Americans, attacked by federal troops released from Reconstruction-era assignments in the South, also had reason to worry about this legacy.

13. It's important to note that Mark Twain was arguably the most famous figure aware of how the new vogue for imperialism might intensify rather than resolve racial and sectional tensions. But Twain's comments, while astute, tended for the most part to avoid direct engagement with the contemporary southern question even as they offered pointed criticism of McKinley's expansionist designs. See Twain, *Weapons of Satire: Anti-Imperialist Writings on the Philippine-American War,* ed. Jim Zwick (Syracuse: Syracuse University Press, 1992).

14. Both men had their novels read by influential U.S. congressmen. However, Chesnutt had to mail the text to politicians while Dixon could rely on his work's extraordinary popularity to ensure its dissemination in the halls of power. According to Helen Chesnutt, the writer's daughter and biographer, at least one (unnamed) congressman commented on the fact that Dixon and Chesnutt had "entirely different points of view" on the question of race. For this passage and a brief account of Chesnutt's decision to send *The Marrow of Tradition* to the Washington elite, see Helen M. Chesnutt, *Charles Waddell Chesnutt: Pioneer of the Color Line* (Chapel Hill: University of North Carolina Press, 1952), 179–80.

15. To be sure, for all their interest in contemporary issues of race and space, Chesnutt and Dixon may appear unlikely bedfellows. The current critical consensus suggests as much. While both figures have provoked a good deal of scholarly interest in recent years, Chesnutt rightly has been affirmed as a major literary figure, and Dixon has been condemned as a white supremacist propagandist. Eric Sundquist canonizes Chesnutt with an enormous chapter in his volume *To Wake the Nations: Race and the Making of American Literature* (Cambridge: Harvard University Press, 1993), 271–454; Sandra Gunning suggests a similar impulse in pairing Chesnutt with Mark Twain in her book *Race, Rape, and Lynching: The Red Record of American Literature, 1890–1912* (New York: Oxford University Press, 1996). Conversely, Walter Benn Michaels lumps Dixon with Thomas Nelson Page in *Our America: Nativism, Modernism, and Pluralism* (Durham: Duke University Press, 1995) while Susan Gillman links the white supremacist to the less-than-canonical African American writer Sutton Griggs in *Blood Talk: American Race Melodrama and the Culture of the Occult* (Chicago: University of Chicago Press, 2003). For an exception to this rule, see Judith Jackson Fossett's important article "The Civil War Imaginations of Thomas Dixon and Charles Chesnutt: Or, North Carolina, 'This Strange World of Poisoned Air'," *North Carolina Literary Review* 8 (1999): 107–20. We also should note that William Andrews contrasts Chesnutt's novel with the spate of plantation romances and Reconstruction tales produced by Joel Chandler Harris, Thomas Nelson Page, and Thomas Dixon. See *The Literary Career of Charles W. Chesnutt* (Baton Rouge: Louisiana State University Press, 1980), 182–87.

16. Although I don't have the space to pursue this idea in the more theoretical terms it demands, it's worth pointing out that both Dixon and Chesnutt insist on imagining the South as a place where unsettling questions of gender and sexuality will not be denied.

That is, if the United States like many nations was often imagined in terms of what Benedict Anderson has famously dubbed "a deep, horizontal comradeship," the fin-de-siècle attempt to factor an implicitly "raced" and feminized South into this white fraternal equation proved somewhat problematic. See Anderson, *Imagined Communities* (New York: Verso, 1983), 7. For more specifically Americanist work on this topic, see Mason Stokes, *The Color of Sex* (Durham: Duke University Press, 2001); and Tara MacPherson, *Reconstructing Dixie* (Durham: Duke University Press, 2002).

17. For an alternate, but politically sympathetic, conception of such a trans-sectional white fraternity, one that incorporates white western men into the dynamic, see Theodore Roosevelt's *The Rough Riders: A History of the First United States Volunteer Cavalry* (New York: Scribner's, 1899).

18. As my reference to "national manhood" should suggest, this chapter owes a considerable debt to Dana Nelson's superb study, *National Manhood* (Durham: Duke University Press, 1998). Future citations to this book will be included in the text. For a more wide-ranging examination of how issues of gender and sexuality impact issues of nationhood (and vice versa), see Andrew Parker et al., eds., *Nationalisms and Sexualities* (New York: Routledge, 1991).

19. Chesnutt, *The Marrow of Tradition* (New York: Penguin, 1993 [1901]), 42. All further citations will be included in the text.

20. See Michaels, *Our America,* 17–23; Eric Love, *Race over Empire: Racism and U.S. Imperialism, 1865–1900* (Chapel Hill: University of North Carolina Press, 2004).

21. See Paul Kramer, *The Blood of Government: Race, Empire, the U.S., and the Philippines* (Chapel Hill: University of North Carolina Press, 2006), and Michael Salman, *The Embarrassment of Slavery: Controversies over Bondage and Nationalism in the American Colonial Philippines* (Berkeley: University of California Press, 2001) for important examinations of the racial politics of the Filipino question.

22. See Lasch, "The Anti-Imperialists," for the classic account of how racism informed northern anti-imperialism. We also should note with Edward Ayers that some southern politicians objected to the annexation of the Philippines because they were opposed to any form of U.S. imperialism. See *The Promise of the New South* (New York: Oxford University Press, 1992), 332–33.

23. Tillman delivered this speech on February 7, 1899.

24. See *Journal of the Executive Proceedings of the Senate,* 55 Cong. 1284 (February 6, 1899). As Gaines Foster puts it, "The [southern] opponents of annexation acted less from sympathy for the Philippine cause than out of racist fears that the Filipinos would become part of the United States and thereby destroy it" (152). See *Ghosts of the Confederacy: Defeat, the Lost Cause, and the Emergence of the New South, 1865–1913* (New York: Oxford University Press, 1987), 149.

25. As the Preacher explains to the New England reformer Susan Walker in *The Leopard's Spots,* the North views southerners as "heathens" in need of "missionary" assistance (46).

26. See Woodward, *Origins of the New South, 1877–1913* (Baton Rouge: Louisiana State University Press, 1971), 369. Indeed, no less a figure than Donald Davidson, the fiercely anti-Northern Agrarian, admitted that "even the South, that most persistent example of sectionalism, seemed quiet and pliable" during the era "of McKinley imperialism." See *The Attack on Leviathan* (Chapel Hill: University of North Carolina Press, 1938), 16.

27. For a powerful theoretical analysis of how "woundedness" can provide a sense of identity, see Wendy Brown, *States of Injury: Power and Freedom in Late Modernity* (Princeton: Princeton University Press, 1995).

28. See Raymond A. Cook, *Thomas Dixon* (New York: Twayne, 1974), 40–41.

29. Indeed, the Academy of Music, where Dixon held his Church of the People services,

soon became known as an important gathering spot for those supportive of the Cuban cause. See ibid., 46.

30. See *Dixon's Sermons* (New York: F. L. Bussey, 1899), 29, 5. All future citations will be included in the text.

31. Joel Williamson argues that Dixon's attendance at a 1901 staging of *Uncle Tom's Cabin* inspired him to write *The Leopard's Spots*. See *The Crucible of Race: Black-White Relations in the American South since Emancipation* (New York: Oxford University Press, 1984), 161. While Stowe's novel and its cultural and political legacy are undeniably important to Dixon's text—supplying the white supremacist with a host of characters from George Harris to Simon Legree—the allure of Republican expansion plays an equally important role in the narrative. Indeed, as I demonstrate in what follows, Dixon's pro-imperialist and pro-GOP sermons inform much of the novel.

32. It's worth recalling the important place of Great Britain in contemporary discourses of imperial white unity. Many pro-imperialists imagined that the new U.S. imperialism would reconnect the two Anglophone nations. As Paul Kramer has argued, "both the 1898 war and the U.S. annexation of the Philippines could be read as expressions of Anglo-Saxonism: Through England, it seemed, America was speaking to the world." Dixon, however, while hardly unaware of the British example, insisted on a very different geographic scenario: through the white South, America was speaking to the world. See Kramer's valuable essay "Empire, Exceptions, and Anglo-Saxons: Race and Rule between the British and the United States Empires, 1880–1910" *Journal of American History* 88 (March 2002): 1315–53.

33. *The Leopard's Spots* (New York: Doubleday, 1902), 413. All future citations will be included in the text.

34. While I don't have the space to address this issue, the generic shift from sermon to novel, from a performative mode to a printed work, plays an important role in Dixon's political intervention.

35. I have learned a great deal about Dixon and his first novel from the following critics: Cook, *Thomas Dixon*; Williamson, *The Crucible of Race*; Michaels, *Our America*; Maxwell Bloomfield, "Dixon's *The Leopard's Spots*: A Study in Popular Racism," *American Quarterly* 16, no. 3 (Autumn 1964): 387–401; Michael Rogin, "'The Sword Became a Flashing Vision': D. W. Griffith's *The Birth of a Nation*," in *The Birth of a Nation*, ed. Robert Lang (New Brunswick: Rutgers University Press, 1994), 250–93; Gunning, *Race, Rape, and Lynching*; Lawrence Oliver, "Writing from the Right during the 'Red Decade': Thomas Dixon's Attack on W. E. B. Du Bois and James Weldon Johnson in *The Flaming Sword*," *American Literature* 70, no. 1 (March 1998): 131–52; and Amy Kaplan, *The Anarchy of Empire in the Making of U.S. Culture* (Cambridge: Harvard University Press, 2002), 121–24, 161–62. Late in the drafting of this chapter, I came across Scott Romine's related argument in "Things Falling Apart: The Postcolonial Condition of *Red Rock* and *The Leopard's Spots*" in *Look Away! The U.S. South in New World Studies* ed. Jon Smith and Deborah Cohn (Durham: Duke University Press, 2004), 175–200.

36. For an important assessment of how Dixon rewrites Stowe, see Leslie Fiedler, *The Inadvertent Epic: From "Uncle Tom's Cabin" to "Roots"* (New York: Simon and Schuster, 1979).

37. Bluford Adams has pointed out that Dixon's use of the name "Hambright" recalls the town of Hamburg, North Carolina, where blacks and whites fought over the right to drive down a particular road.

38. It may seem strange to describe the body as a spatial scale. For many of us the body seems to exist before or beyond the geographic. Yet to adopt this view is to ignore the potential of the body to constitute a site, a space or place of contestation. As Robyn Longhurst argues, "bodies exist *in* places; at the same time they *are* places." For important work on

this question see Longhurst, "Situating Bodies," in *A Companion to Feminist Geography*, ed. Lise Nelson and Joni Seager (Oxford: Blackwell, 2005), 337–49; and Linda McDowell, *Gender, Identity, and Place: Understanding Feminist Geographies* (Oxford: Polity Press, 1999).

39. We should note at the same time that on at least one occasion Dixon celebrates a vague idea of amalgamation so long as it does not include African Americans. Speaking mainly of new European immigrants in his sermon "Destiny of America," Dixon claimed, "We have demonstrated our power to amalgamate and unite all races, from all climates and conditions of the human race. This is the continued evidence of immortal life in the make-up of the American nation" (78).

40. To be sure, Dixon downplays the miscegenation that has occurred through white male relations with black females. As the Preacher explains to a visiting Boston clergyman who notices the "many evidences of a mixture of blood," mixed-race people have "no social significance" if they are the product of "polygamous" white men and black women. Only children resulting from black male and white female union have the potential to undermine the region and the nation's "racial life," a concern that warrants passionate protection of white womanhood (336).

41. See Kaplan, *The Anarchy of Empire*, 121–22. Walter Benn Michaels makes a related point about the unifying effect of "Negrophobia" for white men; see *Our America*, 43.

42. See Nelson, *National Manhood*, 19. For another important engagement with issues of race, gender, and citizenship, see Robyn Wiegman, *American Anatomies: Theorizing Race and Gender* (Durham: Duke University Press, 1995).

43. See Gunning, *Race, Rape, and Lynching*, 31.

44. Rogin, "'The Sword Became a Flashing Vision,'" 254.

45. See Wiegman, *American Anatomies*, 97.

46. It is important to acknowledge that Dixon distinguishes between the burning of Dick by a white mob and the far more quiet and nocturnal hanging of Tim Shelby by robed Klansmen. While Dixon suggests that both black men should die, the former is killed in too uncivilized and spectacular a manner; this is a vulgar lynching that should have no place in the new South.

47. See Gunning, *Race, Rape, and Lynching*, 34.

48. Dixon would devote far more attention to the Klan in the next two volumes of his trilogy.

49. Indeed, we might say, to borrow from David Lloyd, that *The Leopard's Spots* offers us an example of the desire of regionalism for the state. See *Ireland after History* (South Bend: University of Notre Dame Press, 2000), 27.

50. For an example of national grief over Bagley's death, see J. B. Bernadou, "The Winslow at Cardenas" *The Century Magazine* 57 (1899): 705–6.

51. Of course, Dixon knows his southern audience too well to let a critique of the Lost Cause stand without some compensatory gesture. Thus even as he distinguishes the New South's awareness of nation and world from the Old South's obsessive localism, he has Gaston reaffirm the value of the local as that scale which enables the creation of a white American community capable of conquering the globe: "I love mine own people. . . . I hate the dish water of modern world-citizenship. A shallow cosmopolitanism is the mask of death for the individual. It is the froth of civilization, as crime is its dregs. Race, and race pride, are the ordinances of life. The true citizen of the world loves his country. His country is part of God's world" (441). Dixon opposes a heartfelt connection to his "own people" to "shallow cosmopolitanism" precisely because the latter encourages a certain cultural tolerance while the former shores up a faith in "race and race pride." Indeed, for Dixon to love one's "country"(read: section) is to be a citizen not of the fallen secular world, but instead of "God's world." Yet this gesture, however important to Dixon's autochthonous feeling, stands out as unusual in that it refuses to link local sentiment to Anglo-Saxon global power.

52. If the need to rethink spatial and temporal consciousness in light of the metropole-colonial dialectic might have informed the origins of European modernism, as Edward Said has argued, we might speculate that a very different kind of sensitivity to these issues played a role in the emergence of a new U.S. culture of empire at roughly the same time. See Said, *Culture and Imperialism* (Cambridge: Harvard University Press, 1993), 225–29. For a related and more specifically American engagement with similar issues of race, space, and modernity, one that attends brilliantly to the place of alternative spirituality in the dynamic, see Gillman, *Blood Talk.*

53. For an important examination of how the persistence of slavery in the U.S.-occupied archipelago did in fact offer U.S. anti-racists some slight chance of reviving debates over color and democracy, see Salman, *The Embarrassment of Slavery.*

54. See Willard B. Gatewood, Jr., *Black Americans and the White Man's Burden, 1898–1903* (Urbana: University of Illinois Press, 1975), 100.

55. The Grimke letter is quoted in ibid., 210.

56. This isn't to deny his anti-imperialist sentiments, only to argue that Chesnutt tended to suppress his opinions for pragmatic reasons. Chesnutt thus chose not to publish the essay "Liberty and the Franchise" (written 1899), an angry critique of the North's willingness to be "absorbed in money getting" and annexation, and let "the fruits" of Emancipation "become ashes on the lips of those whom they meant to benefit." But he did publish a far more circumspect explanation of why African Americans had to suppress their anti-imperialist feelings and support Theodore Roosevelt in the 1904 election: "It is a great pity that Negro men should not feel free to choose their political party in the same way as other voters do. There would doubtless be some pronounced difference of opinion among them on the questions, for instance, of Philippine independence, and the course of the administration in respect to the Panama Canal. . . . But vital as these questions are, they fade into insignificance beside the issue of Negro rights—human rights—which the Democratic party has injected into this campaign, and which it has put to the front in every recent state election." See "Liberty and the Franchise" and "For Roosevelt," *Charles W. Chesnutt: Essays and Speeches*, ed. Joseph R. McElrath, Jr., et al. (Palo Alto: Stanford University Press, 1999), 107, 209.

57. The full passage reads: "I should like to feel that I had been able, in the form of a widely popular work of fiction . . . to win back or help retain the popular sympathy of the Northern people, which has been so sorely weakened by Southern deviltry in the past decade." See Charles Chesnutt, *"To Be an Author": Letters of Charles W. Chesnutt, 1889–1905 by Charles W. Chesnutt*, ed. Joseph R. McElrath, Jr., and Robert C. Leitz (Princeton: Princeton University Press, 1989), 159–60.

58. See *The Journals of Charles W. Chesnutt*, ed. Richard H. Brodhead (Durham: Duke University Press, 1993), 157.

59. Smith quoted in Andrews, *The Literary Career of Charles W. Chesnutt*, 206.

60. *Chesnutt: Essays and Speeches*, 122–23. All further citations will be included in the text.

61. See Wegener, "Charles Chesnutt and the Anti-Imperialist Matrix of African American Writing, 1898–1905," *Criticism: A Quarterly for Literature and the Arts* 41, no. 4 (1999): 465–93. I also have benefited from the work of the following Chesnutt critics: William L. Andrews, "William Dean Howells and Charles W. Chesnutt: Criticism and Race Fiction in the Age of Booker T. Washington," *American Literature* 48 (1976): 327–39; Keith Byerman, "Black Voices, White Stories: An Intertextual Analysis of Thomas Nelson Page and Charles Waddell Chesnutt," *North Carolina Literary Review* 8 (1999): 98–105; Fossett, "The Civil War Imaginations of Thomas Dixon and Charles Chesnutt"; William Gleason, "Voices at the Nadir: Charles Chesnutt and David Bryant Fulton," *American Literary Realism* 24, no. 3 (Spring 1992): 22–41; Ellen J. Goldner, "(Re)Staging Colonial Encounters: Chesnutt's Critique of Imperialism in *The Conjure Woman*," *Studies in American Fiction* 28,

no. 1 (2000); John Lowe, "Reconstruction Revisited: Plantation School Writers, Postcolonial Theory, and Confederates in Brazil," *Mississippi Quarterly: The Journal of Southern Cultures* 57, no. 1 (2003): 5–26; Sundquist, *To Wake the Nations*, 271–454; and Bryan Wagner, "Charles Chesnutt and the Epistemology of Racial Violence," *American Literature* 73, no. 2 (2001): 311–37.

62. We should note that Chesnutt slyly injects a slight complication into his seeming endorsement of the GOP's penchant for expansionism, and he does so through a strategic use of the word "fusion." As Chesnutt knew, to define amalgamation as "racial fusion" necessarily referenced the ill-fated attempt to construct a more iconoclastic political party of Republicans and Populists in the South. The short-lived Fusion party, referenced in *Marrow* and elsewhere in Chesnutt's work, hardly advocated amalgamation, but in its desire to resist the racism of southern Democrats and the Jim Crow regime in the name of citizens' rights, it recalls the more inclusive nation to which Chesnutt hopes amalgamation will lead. For Chesnutt, African American support for Republican policy wasn't simply a matter of resisting the likes of Ben Tillman, it was also a matter of countering the power of figures like Indiana senator Albert Beveridge, a politician whose vocal enthusiasm for Anglo-Saxon expansion rendered him nothing so much as a northern Republican counterpart to the notorious racist from South Carolina.

63. Manly published his editorial in the *Wilmington Daily Record,* the paper he edited for the African American community.

64. Sundquist, *To Wake the Nations,* 275.

65. See Matthew Wilson, *Whiteness in the Novels of Charles Chesnutt* (Oxford: University of Mississippi Press, 2004), 135–37.

66. As the narrator informs us, Belmont walks "with the leisurely step characteristic of those who have been reared under hot suns" (31). It's worth noting that Belmont is the only member of the white supremacist trio who recognizes the power of the federal government. He argues that any attempt to depose the federally appointed African American "collector of the port" would "bring the government down upon" the Big Three and their allies (251).

67. We also should note that Chesnutt may be thinking of another North Carolinian here, the mid-century politician and diplomat John Hill Wheeler. Wheeler was the U.S. ambassador to Nicaragua in the 1850s and reputedly contributed some pro-slavery statements to William Walker's speeches as the short-lived filibuster president of the Central American nation.

68. Thousands of Igorots wielding bows and arrows were slaughtered by U.S. troops in one of the first clashes between Filipinos and their erstwhile protectors.

69. Barbara Ladd has made a related point about race, bodies, and scale in the fin de siècle. Writing of lynching and empire, Ladd argues insightfully, "One might read the hysteria of radical racism as an appropriation on the domestic front of the imperialistic agenda of redemption, the burnings and dismemberments of black bodies a dramatization on the physical body of the effects of colonization on the black cultural bodies of Cuba, Puerto Rico, and the Philippines, acquired by the United States in the Spanish-American War." See *Nationalism and the Color Line in George W. Cable, Mark Twain, and William Faulkner* (Baton Rouge: Louisiana State University Press, 1996), 148–49.

70. See John T. Matthews, "This Race Which Is Not One: The 'More Inextricable Compositeness' of William Faulkner's South," in *Look Away!* 218.

71. See Wagner, "Charles Chesnutt and the Epistemology of Racial Violence."

72. See Eliza Scidmore, "China: The River of Tea," *The Century* 58, no. 4 (August 1899): 549.

73. See "Why I am a Republican," in *Chesnutt: Essays and Speeches,* 97.

Chapter 2. Up from Empire

1. James Weldon Johnson, *The Autobiography of an Ex-Colored Man,* in *The Selected Writings of James Weldon Johnson,* vol. 2, ed. Sondra K. Wilson (New York: Oxford University Press, 1995 [1912]). All citations are included in the body of the text.

2. William Sydney Porter (O. Henry) introduced the offensive term "banana republic" in *Cabbages and Kings* (1904), a linked short story collection that takes Central America as its subject.

3. I have learned a great deal about "big stick diplomacy," "dollar diplomacy," and other manifestations of early twentieth-century U.S. imperialism in the hemisphere from Scott Nearing, *Dollar Diplomacy* (New York: Viking Press, 1925); Peter Smith, *Talons of the Eagle: Dynamics of U.S.-Latin American Relations* (Baton Rouge: Louisiana State University Press, 1990); and Richard H. Collins, *Theodore Roosevelt's Caribbean: The Panama Canal, the Monroe Doctrine, and the Latin American Context* (New York: Oxford University Press, 2000).

4. We should note that this argument inverts the more typical scholarly understanding of the relationship between the Civil War and turn-of-the-century imperialism. Richard Hofstader, Christopher Lasch, Michael Rogin, and others have argued that in the eyes of many white Americans, north and south, the conquest of Cuba, Puerto Rico, and the Philippines provided an opportunity to defuse lingering sectional tensions through a common investment in empire.

5. It is important to remember that Johnson refrained from any overt critique of the brutal U.S. campaign in the Philippines. For important insights on Johnson and imperialism, see William E. Gibbs, "James Weldon Johnson: A Black Perspective on 'Big Stick' Diplomacy," *Diplomatic History* 8 (1984): 329–47; and Lawrence J. Oliver, "James Weldon Johnson's *New York Age* Essays," in *Critical Essays on James Weldon Johnson,* ed. Lawrence J. Oliver and Kenneth Price (New York: G. K. Hall). For biographical material on Johnson, I rely on Eugene Levy's useful book *James Weldon Johnson: Black Leader, Black Voice* (Chicago: University of Chicago Press, 1971), and Johnson's autobiography *Along This Way* (New York: Viking, 1933). All citations from the latter are included in the body of the text.

6. See Kevin Gaines, "Black Americans' Racial Uplift Ideology as 'Civilizing Mission': Pauline E. Hopkins on Race and Imperialism," in *The Cultures of U.S. Imperialism,* ed. Amy Kaplan and Donald Pease (Durham: Duke University Press, 1993), 436–38.

7. Johnson himself barely escaped lynching by Florida National Guardsmen in 1901.

8. For more work on the turn-of-the-century African American response to U.S. imperialism, please see Willard B. Gatewood, *Black American and the White Man's Burden* (Urbana: University of Illinois Press, 1975); George P. Marks, ed., *The Black Press Views American Imperialism* (New York: Arno Press, 1971); Brenda Plummer, *Rising Wind: Black Americans and U.S. Foreign Affairs, 1935–1960* (Chapel Hill: University of North Carolina Press, 1996); and Amy Kaplan, "Black and Blue on San Juan Hill," in *The Anarchy of Empire in the Making of U.S. Culture* (Cambridge: Harvard University Press, 2002), 121–45.

9. The one partial exception is Eugene Levy's brief interpretation of *The Autobiography* in his biography of Johnson. Briefly put, Levy argues that the *café con leche* racial dynamic of Venezuela disturbed Johnson inasmuch as it seemed to offer mestizos or mulattoes full citizenship at the cost of claiming a black identity. See pp. 110–12. Among the many articles on *The Autobiography,* I have found the following to be most useful: Neil Brooks, "On Becoming an Ex-Man: Postmodern Irony and the Extinguishing of Certainties in *The Autobiography of an Ex-Colored Man,*" *College Literature* 22, no. 3 (1995): 17–29; Cheryl Clarke, "Race, Homosocial Desire, and 'Mammon' in *Autobiography of an Ex-Colored Man,*" in *Professions of Desire: Lesbian and Gay Studies in Literature,* ed. George E. Haggerty and Bonnie Zimmerman (New York: Modern Language Association of America, 1995), 84–97; Euge-

nia W. Collier, "The Endless Journey of an Ex-Coloured Man," *Phylon* 32 (1971): 365–73; Robert E. Fleming, "Irony as a Key to Johnson," *American Literature* 43 (1971): 83–96; Samira Kawash, *"The Autobiography of an Ex-Colored Man:* (Passing for) Black Passing for White," in *Passing and the Fictions of Identity,* ed. Elaine Ginsberg (Durham: Duke University Press, 1996), 59–74; David Levering Lewis, "Dr. Johnson's Friends: Civil Rights by Copyright during Harlem's Mid-Twenties," *Massachusetts Review* 20 (1979): 501–19; Jennifer L. Schulz, "Restaging the Racial Contract: James Weldon Johnson's Signatory Strategies," *American Literature* 74, no. 1 (2002): 31–58; Joseph T. Skerrett Jr. "Irony and Symbolic Action in James Weldon Johnson's *The Autobiography of an Ex-Colored Man,*" *American Quarterly* 32 (1980): 540–58; and Kenneth W. Warren, "Troubled Black Humanity in *The Souls of Black Folk* and *The Autobiography of an Ex-Colored Man,*" *The Cambridge Companion to American Realism and Naturalism: Howells to London,* ed. Donald Pizer (Cambridge: Cambridge University Press, 1995), 263–77.

10. See Brent Edwards, *The Practice of Diaspora* (Cambridge: Harvard University Press, 2003); and Michelle Stephens, *Black Empire* (Durham: Duke University Press, 2005).

11. See Deborah Cohn, *History and Memory in the Two Souths* (Nashville: Vanderbilt University Press, 1999), 3.

12. See, for example, ibid.; George Handley, *Postslavery Literatures in the Americas* (Charlottesville: University Press of Virginia, 2000); and Edouard Glissant, *Faulkner, Mississippi* (New York: Farrar, Straus and Giroux, 1999).

13. Glissant, *Faulkner, Mississippi,* 29.

14. Kirsten Silva Gruesz makes a similar point about the non-contiguous border in her fine recent article, "The Gulf of Mexico System and the 'Latinness' of New Orleans," *American Literary History* 18 (2006): 468–95.

15. To be sure, a black Latina subject would seem far less exotic in Florida or in coastal Alabama or Mississippi than she would in Virginia.

16. White southern textile manufacturers also looked to China and the Far East as a growing market for their products. This southern interest in Asia helps explain why such white southern politicians as John Tyler Morgan were among the most passionate proponents of the proposed Panama Canal—the waterway that would expedite sea travel from the Atlantic United States to Pacific Asia. For an important overview of this topic, see Tennant S. McWilliams, *The New South Faces the World* (Baton Rouge: Louisiana State University Press, 1988).

17. Excerpts from the letter by James Weldon Johnson to Grace Nail Johnson dated August 31, 1912, are reprinted here by permission of Dr. Sondra Kathryn Wilson, Executor for the Estate of Grace and James Weldon Johnson, and may be found in the James Weldon Johnson Archive at the Beinecke Library, Yale University.

18. Johnson's delight over the attentions of Admiral Southerland echoes his better-known relationship to Dr. Thomas Osmond Summers, the affluent white eccentric who hired the writer as a secretary in Jacksonville. The fact that both of these white/black relationships find their fictional analogue in the ex-colored man's erotically charged relationship to the white millionaire suggests the extent to which Johnson conceived of interracial male friendship as somehow always already queer.

19. The ex-colored man's excited response to Shiny's invocation of Toussaint L'Ouverture looks ahead to Johnson's passionate description of the black Haitian leader Henry Christophe in *Along This Way.* See Mary Renda, *Taking Haiti: Military Occupation and the Culture of U.S. Imperialism* (Chapel Hill: University of North Carolina Press, 2001), 193–94, for an interesting interpretation of Johnson's investment in Christophe.

20. Timothy Brennan has argued that the tradition of U.S. liberal pluralism owes a great debt to Latin American creole culture and society. See "Cosmo-Theory," *South Atlantic Quarterly* 100, no. 3 (2002): 125–62.

21. For a fascinating examination of racial politics in late nineteenth-century Cuba, see Ada Ferrer, *Insurgent Cuba: Race, Nation, and Revolution* (Chapel Hill: University of North Carolina Press, 1999).

22. "The cigarworkers in Florida not only provided political support to launch the PRC [the Cuban Revolutionary Party]," writes historian Louis Perez, "they also supplied the financial base to sustain its activities through the full six years of its existence." See *José Martí in the United States: The Florida Experience* (Tempe: ASU Center for Latin American Studies, 1995), 4. Johnson suggests as much when he characterizes the ex-colored man's landlord as "a prominent member of the Jacksonville junta" responsible for collecting money "to buy arms and ammunition for the insurgents" (302).

23. See "Our America," in *Our America: Writings on Latin America and the Struggle for Cuban Independence,* trans. Elinor Randall, Juan de Onis, and Roslyn Held Foner, ed. Philip S. Foner (New York: Monthly Review Press, 1977), 93–94.

24. The ex-colored man's landlord does not mention Martí, but this omission seems to have more to do with a passion for the overtly military leaders of the movement than with a particular political point. While indispensable to the Cuban independence struggle, Martí was celebrated for his intellectual contribution, not his military prowess.

25. There is a tragic irony to Johnson's invocation of Cuban racial idealism in the year 1912 for this date witnessed the slaughter of black former Cuban independence fighters by their erstwhile white comrades.

26. Lectors were often the source of radical political education in Latin American factories; their role as public readers placed them in the position of teacher and potential leader, with enormous implications for the creation and maintenance of oppositional social movements.

27. While we must heed Joseph Skerrett and not collapse the distinction between character and creator, we also must register the important parallels between biography and novel. See Skerrett, "Irony and Symbolic Action."

28. See Levy, *James Weldon Johnson,* 107.

29. Johnson will also critique the place of Native Americans in the creation of an indigenous popular culture in his *New York Age* editorial "American Music" (1916). He writes, "When [skilled musicians] have striven to be original they have gone to Indian themes and legends, but here they have worked sterile soil." Johnson seems to find the Native American a potential competitor for the throne of U.S. cultural originality.

30. The ex-colored man expounds on the global power of ragtime in an effort to counter contemporary white U.S. critiques of the musical form. Ragtime was, as the protagonist puts it, a cultural form that "originated in the questionable resorts about Memphis and St. Louis"—and thus represented to many Americans of the era the most disreputable aspect of the Jim Crow South (314). See Edward Berlin, *Ragtime* (Berkeley: University of California Press, 1980), for an important history of this music.

31. For a brilliant argument about the relationship of black music and U.S. popular culture, see Eric Lott, *Love and Theft* (New York: Oxford University Press, 1993).

32. Paul Gilroy and Brent Edwards have both offered acute "black atlanticist" readings of this scene. My reading tends to diverge from both of theirs in emphasizing the relationship between the imperial implications of the German's dismissive action and the regional denouement of the encounter. See Paul Gilroy, *The Black Atlantic* (Cambridge: Harvard University Press, 1993), 130–32; and Brent Edwards, *The Practice of Diaspora* (Cambridge: Harvard University Press, 2003), 40–43.

33. See Ross Posnock, *Color and Culture* (Cambridge: Harvard University Press, 1998), 76. Tom Lutz also engages with the cosmopolitanism of the ex-colored man in *Cosmopolitan Vistas* (Ithaca: Cornell University Press, 2004), 123–27.

34. As Johnson would himself argue in his articles on the U.S. occupation of Haiti, New

York banks and investment houses both exploited and provoked U.S. military domination south of the border from the turn of the century well into the 1930s.

35. As Michael Hanchard has written, "U.S. blacks lie at the vortex of conquest and decimation. And so does the hyphen between 'African' and 'American'." See "Identity, Meaning, and the African American," in *Dangerous Liaisons: Gender, Nation, and Postcolonial Perspectives*, ed. Anne McClintock et al. (Minneapolis: University of Minnesota Press, 1997), 230–39.

36. For an important assessment of Johnson's critique of white southern racism, see Lawrence J. Oliver, "James Weldon Johnson's *New York Age* Essays on *The Birth of a Nation* and the 'Southern Oligarchy.'" *South Central Review* 10, no. 4 (Winter 1993): 1–17.

37. See "Why Latin American Dislikes the United States," *Selected Writings of Johnson*, vol. 2, ed. Wilson, 197.

38. See "The Truth about Haiti," *Selected Writings of Johnson*, vol. 2, ed. Wilson, 251.

Chapter 3. *"Take Your Geography and Trace It"*

1. *Darkwater: Voices from within the Veil* (New York: AMS Press, 1969 [1920]), 86; *Color and Democracy* (New York: Harcourt, 1945), 4.

2. For some examples of fine recent work on the transnational Du Bois, see Paul Gilroy, *The Black Atlantic: Modernity and Double Consciousness* (Cambridge: Harvard University Press, 1993), 111–45; Amy Kaplan, *The Anarchy of Empire in the Making of American Culture* (Cambridge: Harvard University Press, 2003), 171–212; Bill Mullen, *Afro-Orientalism* (Minneapolis: University of Minnesota Press, 2004), 1–41; Ross Posnock, *Color and Culture* (Cambridge: Harvard University Press, 1994); John Carlos Rowe, *Literary Culture and U.S. Imperialism* (New York: Oxford University Press, 2000), 195–216; Kenneth W. Warren, "An Inevitable Drift? Oligarchy, Du Bois, and the Politics of Race between the Wars" *boundary 2* 27, no. 3 (2000): 153–69; and Alys Weinbaum, "Reproducing Racial Globality: W. E. B. Du Bois and the Sexual Politics of Black Internationalism," *Social Text* 19, no. 2 (Summer 2001): 15–41. We should note that Dohra Ahmad's "More than Romance": Genre and Geography in *Dark Princess*," (*ELH* 69, no. 3 [2002]: 775–803) does engage briefly with Du Bois's notion of a "global South." For a recent suggestion that we should take seriously Du Bois's interest in the U.S. South, see Riche Richardson, "The World and the U.S. South" *American Literature* 78, no. 4 (December 2006): 722–24.

3. Indeed, Gilroy goes so far as to claim that Robert Stepto's regionalist analysis of *The Souls of Black Folk* impedes a full appreciation of the text's Black Atlantic sensibility. See *The Black Atlantic*, 138.

4. See Davis's valuable essay "Expanding the Limits: The Intersection of Race and Region," *Southern Literary Journal* 20, no. 1 (Spring 1988): 3–11.

5. Of course, other spaces, particularly Africa, also held enormous status in Du Bois's conception of this struggle.

6. See "Shall the Negro Be Encouraged to Seek Cultural Equality" in *W. E. B. Du Bois Speaks*, ed. Philip Foner (New York: Pathfinder Press, 1970), 54.

7. My language here draws on Arnold Rampersad's insightful point about the tension between the spiritual and the secular in *Dark Princess*. See *The Art and Imagination of W. E. B. Du Bois* (Cambridge: Harvard University Press, 1976), 202–18. For another important take on these issues, see Keith Byerman, *Seizing the Word: History, Art, and Self in the Work of W. E. B. Du Bois* (Athens: University of Georgia Press, 1994).

8. To put it another way, those critics who understand Du Bois's response to the U.S. South solely in terms of an internationally significant "black belt" ignore the fact that for him the global meaning of this geographic formation cannot be understood without recognizing its intimate relation to a conventionally defined domestic region.

9. See W. E. B. Du Bois, *The Souls of Black Folk* (New York: Oxford University Press, 2007 [1903]), 123. All further citations will be included in the text; and W. E. B. Du Bois, *The Quest of the Silver Fleece* (Chicago: Mclurg Publishers, 1911), 55. All further citations will be included in the text.

10. See "Behold the Land" in *W. E. B. Du Bois: A Reader,* ed. Meyer Weinberg (New York: Harper and Row, 1970), 152–53.

11. It is important to note that Frampton's approach to regionalism doesn't so much endorse "simple-minded attempts to revive the hypothetical forms of a lost vernacular" as suggest that a "critical self-consciousness" about the regional can destabilize and undermine a nation or a corporation's "universalist" claims to reconstruct the world in its own image. See his "Critical Regionalism: Toward an Architecture of Resistance," in *The Anti-Aesthetic: Essays on Postmodern Culture* ed. Hal Foster (Port Townsend, WA: Bay Press, 1983), 16–30.

12. For the classic account of pastoral critiques of urban life (and vice versa), see Raymond Williams, *The Country and the City* (Oxford: Oxford University Press, 1973).

13. See Robert L. Dorman, *Revolt of the Provinces: The Regionalist Movement in America, 1920–1945* (Chapel Hill: University of North Carolina Press, 2003).

14. See John Dewey, "Americanism and Localism," *The Dial* 68 (June 1920): 686.

15. See Sauer's influential essay "The Morphology of Landscape" (1925) in *Land and Life: A Selection from the Writings of Carl Otwin Sauer,* ed. John Leighly (Berkeley: University of California Press, 1963), 315–50.

16. See Frank, "Foreword" in Jean Toomer, *Cane* (New York: Norton, 1988 [1923]), 139. *Cane* also includes representations of life in Washington, D.C., and Chicago.

17. In *The Oxford W. E. B. Du Bois Reader,* ed. Eric Sundquist (New York: Oxford University Press, 1996), 324.

18. Du Bois, "Liberia and Rubber," *New Republic* 44 (November 18, 1925): 326.

19. Ibid.

20. See "Worlds of Color" in *Writings by W. E. B. Du Bois in Periodicals Edited by Others,* ed. Herbert Aptheker (Millwood, NY: Kraus-Thomson, 1982 [1925]), 256.

21. "Liberia and Rubber," 329.

22. Marcus Garvey and the United Negro Improvement Association were also interested in Liberia as an important site of black diasporic empowerment, but the relationship between the West Indian's organization and the West Africans grew sour by the mid-1920s. I have benefited greatly from recent historical work on African Americans and Liberia. See Tamba E. M'Bayo. "W. E. B. Du Bois, Marcus Garvey, and Pan-Africanism in Liberia, 1919–1924," *The Historian* (2004), and Ibrahim Sundiata, *Brothers and Strangers: Black Zion, Black Slavery, 1914–1940* (Durham: Duke University Press, 2003).

23. "Liberia, the League, and the United States," in *Writings by Du Bois in Periodicals Edited by Others,* 332.

24. See Warren, "An Inevitable Drift?"

25. The next Pan-African Conference co-organized by Du Bois would take place in 1945.

26. See Michelle Stephens, *Black Empire* (Durham: Duke University Press, 2005), 5.

27. David Levering Lewis, *W. E. B. Du Bois* (New York: Henry Holt, 2000), 124. It's worth considering that the legacy of the U.S. South in Liberia—evident in surnames, architecture, and forms of punishment—may have ironically enough contributed to Du Bois's rediscovery of the region.

28. For a longer passage from this letter, see ibid., 209.

29. See "Worlds of Color" in *Writings by Du Bois in Periodicals Edited by Others,* 255.

30. Rampersad, *The Art and Imagination of W. E. B. Du Bois,* 208.

31. W. E. B. Du Bois, *Dark Princess* (Millwood, NY: Kraus-Thomson, 1974 [1928]), 4. All further citations appear in the text.

32. In *Darkwater,* Du Bois describes the skin tones of African Americans in the South in similar ways: "Around me sat color in human flesh—brown that crimsoned readily; dim soft-yellow that escaped description; cream-like duskiness that shadowed to rich tints of autumn leaves" (228).

33. See W. E. B. Du Bois, "Postscript," *The Crisis* 34, no. 1 (March 1927): 33–34.

34. See Weinbaum, "Reproducing Racial Globality"; and Mullen, *Afro-Orientalism,* 16–19. For an important overview of these issues, see Cedric J. Robinson, *Black Marxism* (London: Zed Press, 1983).

35. In "The Negro Mind Reaches Out" (1925), Du Bois refers to the Soviet interest in African Americans: "Russia has been seeking a rapprochement with colored labor. . . . Claude McKay, an American Negro poet travelling in Russia, declares: 'Lenin himself grappled with the question of the American Negroes and spoke on the subject before the Second Congress of the Third International. He consulted with John Reed, the American journalist, and dwelt on the urgent necessity of propaganda and organization work among the Negroes of the South.'" Du Bois learned even more about the Communist position on the Negro question during his 1926 trip to the Soviet Union.

36. See Gilles Deleuze and Félix Guattari, "On the Refrain," in *A Thousand Plateaus,* trans. Brian Massumi (Minneapolis: University of Minnesota Press, 1987), 310–50.

37. Indeed, given that it is a contemporary Egyptian who inadvertently pushes Matthew into performing "Go Down, Moses," we may speculate that Du Bois is making a point about how people of color also can engage in oppressive practices.

38. "What Is Civilization? Africa's Answer," in *Du Bois: A Reader,* ed. Weinberg, 380.

39. Quoted in John Bassett, *Harlem in Review: Critical Reaction to Black American Writers, 1917–1939* (New York: Susquehanna University Press, 1992), 99.

40. It's worth noting here that Du Bois refers to Chicago in similar terms when he writes of its "brute might" in "Of Beauty and Death," one of the chapters of *Darkwater* (1919), 237.

41. In thinking about this debate between Matthew and Kautilya I have benefited from much of the recent transnational work on Du Bois cited above.

42. See Weinbaum, "Reproducing Racial Globality," 38.

43. I have benefited from Charles C. Lemert's insightful essay "The Race of Time: Du Bois and Reconstruction," *boundary 2* 27, no. 3 (Fall 2000): 215–48. To my knowledge the only scholar who has recognized and examined the anti-imperialist dimensions of *Black Reconstruction* is John Carlos Rowe; see his fine argument in "W. E. B. Du Bois's Tropical Critique of U.S. Imperialism," in *Literary Culture and U.S. Imperialism,* 198–200.

44. Thanks are due John Carlos Rowe for this point.

45. See, for example, Karl Marx and Friedrich Engels, *The Communist Manifesto* (New York: International Publishers, 1948 [1848]), 17–18.

46. We should note that Du Bois, while moving steadily to the left during the early 1930s, still disapproved of the way the Communist Party–USA hijacked the defense of the Scottsboro Boys from the NAACP.

Chapter 4. "Members of the Whole World"

1. For two representative examples, see Louis Rubin, "Carson McCullers: The Aesthetics of Pain," *Virginia Quarterly Review* 53 (1977): 265–83, and Sarah White-Gleeson, "Revisiting the Southern Grotesque: Mikhail Bakhtin and the Case of Carson McCullers," *Southern Literary Journal* 33 (Spring 2001): 108–24.

2. McCullers, *The Heart Is a Lonely Hunter* (Boston: Houghton Mifflin, 1940), 254. All further citations from this volume will be included in the text.

3. McCullers, "The Russian Formalists and Southern Literature," in *The Mortgaged*

Heart, ed. Margarita Smith (New York: Mariner Books, 2001), 258. All further citations from this volume will be included in the text.

4. To be sure, McCullers was hardly the only U.S. intellectual of the late 1930s and 1940s to point out the disturbing parallels between the South and other disenfranchised parts of the world. As Robert Brinkmeyer has argued recently, a wide range of intellectuals—W. J. Cash, Eleanor Roosevelt, Gunnar Myrdal—registered the unnerving connections between the Jim Crow South and fascist regimes abroad. Conservatives such as Richard Weaver and Allen Tate argued conversely that the U.S. South represented the opposite values in its steadfast insistence on regional sovereignty and autonomy. See Brinkmeyer, "Faulkner and the Democratic Crisis," in *Faulkner and Ideology,* ed. Donald M. Kartiganer and Ann J. Abadie (Oxford: University of Mississippi Press, 1995), 70–94.

5. I have benefited enormously from Virginia Carr's biography of McCullers, *Lonely Hunter* (New York: Doubleday, 1975). All further citations will be included in the text.

6. Yaeger, *Dirt and Desire: Reconstructing Southern Women's Writing, 1930–1990* (Chicago: University of Chicago Press, 2000), 52. All further citations will be included in the text.

7. See Rachel Adams, "'A Mixture of Delicious and Freak': The Queer Fiction of Carson McCullers," *American Literature* 71, no. 3 (September 1999): 551–83; Elizabeth Freeman, *The Wedding Complex* (Durham: Duke University Press, 2002), 45–69; Charles Hannon, "The Ballad of the Sad Café and Other Stories of Women's Wartime Labor," *Genders* 23 (1996): 97–119; Thadious M. Davis, "Erasing the 'We of Me' and Rewriting the Racial Script: Carson McCullers's 'Two Member[s] of the Wedding,'" in *Critical Essays on Carson McCullers*, ed Beverly Lyon et al. (New York: Hall, 1996), 206–20; McKay Jenkins, *The South in Black and White* (Chapel Hill: University of North Carolina Press, 1999), 147–84. Leslie Fiedler linked McCullers to the female and queer southern writers published by pioneering editor George Davis in *Harper's Bazaar* during the late 1930s and early 1940s. See *Love and Death in the American Novel* (New York: Criterion, 1966 [1960]), 476–78.

8. In 1951, McCullers claimed that if "had it not been for the Tuckers, *The Member of the Wedding* would not have been written" (qtd. in Carr, 350).

9. Fiedler dubs Frankie a "good bad tomboy" in his Twain-inflected analysis of *Member*. See *Love and Death in the American Novel*, 334.

10. I have learned a great deal about the role of the military in the transformation of the South from Schulman's indispensable volume, *From Cotton Belt to Sunbelt: Federal Policy, Economic Development, and the Transformation of the South, 1938–1980* (New York: Oxford University Press, 1991). More recently, revisionist scholars have argued that the militarization of the South began before 1940, and that it paled in comparison with federal military investment in other parts of the country, particularly California and New England. See, for example, David L. Carlton, "The American South and the U.S. Defense Economy," in *The South, the Nation, and the World*, ed. Carlton and Peter A. Coclanis (Charlottesville: University Press of Virginia, 2003), 151–62.

11. The subsequent expansion of Columbus—the town's population would triple during the war—offered additional proof that the region's future lay with the military-industrial complex.

12. One suspects, however, that her father's jewelry store most likely benefited from the increased population of male soldiers and their occasional need for engagement rings and Valentine's Day presents.

13. As biographer Virginia Carr puts it, Carson's "sense of differentness having been curried by her mother since infancy, she was made to believe that she was *in fact* a genius" (144).

14. In dubbing the young McCullers a tomboy, I don't mean to ignore or suppress the fact that she was bisexual later in life.

15. For an important take on McCullers and the discourse of the freak see Adams, "'A Mixture of Delicious and Freak.'"

16. Carson McCullers, *Illumination and Night Glare*, ed. Carlos L. Dews (Madison: University of Wisconsin Press, 1999), 55, 65. All further citations will be included in the text.

17. Richard Wright, "Inner Landscape," *New Republic* 103 (August 5, 1940): 195.

18. See, for example, Cynthia Enloe, "Feminists Thinking about War, Militarism, and Peace," in *Analyzing Gender: A Handbook of Social Science Research*, ed. Beth B. Hess and Myra Marx Ferree (London: Sage, 1987), 526–47; and bell hooks, "Feminism and Militarism," in *Talking Back: Thinking Feminist, Thinking Black* (Boston: South End Press, 1989). One can draw an analogy between McCullers's experience and those of contemporary queer men and women during World War II. Alan Berube argues that the mass military mobilization during the war had the paradoxical effect of bringing together gays and lesbians who might otherwise found themselves isolated in small towns and rural communities. See *Coming Out under Fire* (New York: Free Press, 2000).

19. See Catherine Lutz, *Homefront: A Military City and the American Twentieth Century* (Boston: Beacon, 2001), 39.

20. See *Reflections in a Golden Eye* (New York: Houghton Mifflin, 1940), 3.

21. See Lutz, *Homefront*, 114.

22. For a valuable history of the base, see Sharyn Kane and Richard Keeton, *Fort Benning: The Land and the People* (Fort Benning: SEAC, 1998).

23. The vexed place of African Americans in the U.S. war effort has been the subject of a number of important historical studies. See Neil Wynn, *The Afro-American and the Second World War* (London: Paul Elek, 1976); Patrick Washburg, *A Question of Sedition: The Federal Government's Investigation of the Black Press during World War Two* (New York: Oxford University Press, 1986); and Nikhil Pal Singh, *Black Is a Country: Race and the Unfinished Struggle for Democracy* (Cambridge: Harvard University Press, 2005).

24. The letter sent to the newspaper makes clear that the unnamed base is Fort Benning. I have learned a great about the Hall lynching and the generally deplorable conditions at the base in the early 1940s from the NAACP papers. See The NAACP Archives: The Anti-Lynching Campaign, 1912–1955 (Bethesda: University Publishers).

25. While it is unclear whether McCullers knew of the racist atrocities perpetrated at Fort Benning, white southern liberal Jonathan Daniels's article on the Hall lynching would most likely have caught her eye. See "The Army Camp Mystery," *Nation*, May 31, 1941. Indeed, the title to Daniels's article recalls the original title and general spirit of McCullers's contemporary novel *Reflections in a Golden Eye*.

26. The phrase "empire of bases" comes from Chalmers Johnson. It's worth quoting the relevant passage in full: "What is most fascinating and curious about the developing American form of empire . . . is that in its modern phase, it is solely an empire of bases, not of territories, and these bases now encircle the earth." See *Blowback: The Costs and Consequences of American Empire* (New York: Holt, 2000), 188.

27. It is important to remember that before the German invasion of the Soviet Union on June 21, 1941, American Communists and fellow travelers often argued that imperialism motivated U.S. involvement in the war. McCullers lived for a short time during the early 1940s with Auden and Wright, among other "lefties," in a Brooklyn Heights brownstone nicknamed "February House." For an interesting account of this experiment in artistic life, see Sherrill Tippins, *February House* (New York: Houghton Mifflin, 2005).

28. McCullers finished part one in 1942, but didn't complete the second portion until 1945, or publish it until 1946. The entire novel would first appear in *Harper's Bazaar* and then be issued by Houghton Mifflin later the same year.

29. McCullers certainly witnessed the military presence in Columbus during her wartime visits home, but she also may have drawn on letters from her erstwhile husband,

Reeves, when he worked at Camp Wheeler, Georgia, training novice infantrymen, after his return from the European theater. As Reeves describes it, the southern military town is a site of tension and movement: "Macon is a crowed army war time town with thousands of men and hundreds of officers due for overseas duty soon trying to snatch a few last days or weeks with their wives and families" (*Illumination*, 151). For historical work on gender politics and domestic life during the war, see Karen Anderson, *Wartime Women: Sex Roles, Family Relations, and the Status of Women during World War II* (Westport, CT.: Greenwood, 1981); and Susan Hartmann, *The Home Front and Beyond: American Women in the 1940s* (Boston: Twayne, 1982).

30. For an autobiographical analysis of this dynamic, see Lillian Smith, *Killers of the Dream* (New York: Norton, 1949), 28–29.

31. For an important theoretical account of this sort of crisis, see Fredric Jameson, *Postmodernism, or the Cultural Logic of Late Capitalism* (Durham: Duke University Press, 1991), 51–54. While he links this sort of crisis to postmodernism, I would argue that one can locate traces of this type of cognitive instability in the total war of the 1940s. The fact that maps and globes were of particular fascination to many Americans during this era attests to a frustrated desire to reestablish a sense of normative space. For an important account of cartography and the 1940s, see Susan Schulten, *The Geographical Imagination in America, 1880–1950* (Chicago: University of Chicago Press, 2001), 226–27. Thanks are due Keith Wilhite for bringing this book to my attention.

32. In the second stanza of her 1948 poem "When We Are Lost," McCullers offers an even more extreme description of a crisis in orientation.

> The terror. Is it of Space, of Time?
> Or the joined trickery of both conceptions?
> To the lost, transfixed among the self-inflicted ruins,
> All that is non-air (if this indeed is not deception)
> Is agony immobilized. While Time,
> The endless idiot, runs screaming around the world. (*Mortgaged Heart*, 287)

33. McCullers in effect offers a negative recasting of the argument of Tom Lutz's important recent book, *Cosmopolitan Vistas* (Ithaca: Cornell University Press, 2004). Regionalism and cosmopolitanism are indeed linked, but in fearful and imprisoning ways.

34. This draft is included in Box 11, Folder 8, of the Carson McCullers Collection at the Harry Ransom Research Library, the University of Texas–Austin. My thanks to the UT librarians and the Carson McCullers Estate for their help.

35. Billie Holiday recorded Meeropol's song in 1939, and it soon became a protest classic.

36. For a concise account of Smith's ideas on spatial scale, see "Contours of a Spatialized Politics," *Social Text* 33 (1992).

37. My account of unstable borders and boundaries in this scene has benefited from Patricia Yaeger's wonderful reading of *Member* as a surrealist text. See *Dirt and Desire*, 159–61.

38. Freeman, *The Wedding Complex*, 81.

39. For an important analysis of the temporal and spatial meanings of the concept "the American Century," see Neil Smith's valuable book *American Empire: Roosevelt's Geographer and the Prelude to Globalization* (Berkeley: University of California Press, 2003).

40. Mason Stokes, *The Color of Sex* (Durham: Duke University Press, 2001), 20.

41. Berenice's four failed marriages (all to African American men) suggest all the more that in this world, only white weddings have the capacity to signify hegemonically.

42. I take the phrase "war without mercy" from John W. Dower's fine book, *War without Mercy: Race and Power in the Pacific War* (New York: Pantheon, 1987).

43. George Lipsitz, *The Possessive Investment in Whiteness* (Philadelphia: Temple, 1998), 75. Robert Westbrook makes the complementary point that Rita Hayworth was less pop-

ular with white soldiers in large part because the Latina star was understood to be not quite, not white. See "I Want a Girl, Just Like the Girl That Married Harry James," *American Quarterly* 42 (December 1990): 587–614.

44. We also might note that at one point in her wandering through the town, Frankie imagines that Jarvis and Janice are behind her, but when she looks down an alley she sees instead "two colored boys . . . something about the angle or the way they stood . . . had reflected the sudden picture of her brother and the bride" (75). This African American double for the wedding couple well suggests how the wedding must exile both blackness and homosexuality in order to function as a successful ritual of national belonging.

45. Alaska wouldn't achieve statehood until 1959.

46. Amy Kaplan, *The Anarchy of Empire in the Making of U.S. Culture* (Cambridge: Harvard University Press, 2002), 16.

47. For interesting historical work on this issue, see John Morton Blum, *V Was for Victory: Politics and American Culture during World War II* (New York: Harcourt Brace Jovanovich, 1976), 302–22; and Dana Polan, *Power and Paranoia: History, Narrative, and the American Cinema, 1940–1950* (New York: Columbia University Press, 1986).

48. See Luce, *The American Century* (New York: Farrar and Rinehart, 1941), 36. In this line Luce glosses the reference to freedom of movement in the seventh point of the Atlantic Charter (1941): "Seventh, such a peace should enable all men to traverse the high seas and oceans without hindrance." President Roosevelt and Prime Minister Churchill collaborated on the charter.

49. See Wilkie, *One World* (New York: Simon and Schuster, 1943), 190.

50. Jean-François Darlan was a French admiral who, despite working with the Vichy government, was appointed civil and military chief of French North Africa by General Eisenhower after the Allied takeover. Pietro Badoglio—McCullers's spelling is off—was notorious as the Italian army officer who sanctioned the use of poisonous gas against Ethiopians and was later made Duke of Addis Ababa for his efforts. Despite his record, he succeeded Mussolini as prime minister of Italy in 1943 and signed an armistice with the Allies in September of that year. McCullers, we may speculate, no doubt found these men objectionable both as fascists and as white colonialists. The idea that the Allies would deal with such figures horrified her.

51. Although McCullers's fellow southern intellectual Allen Tate would take similar aim at U.S. internationalism in his essay "The New Provincialism" (1945), the author of *Member* stakes out her opposition to this jejune imperialism not by applauding the oppositional power of white southern culture as Tate does, but rather by endowing a black housekeeper with the power of critique. See "The New Provincialism" *Virginia Quarterly Review* 21 (Spring 1945): 262–72.

52. As this passage suggests, McCullers's account of what Du Bois dubbed "double consciousness" is resolutely spatial.

53. For a fascinating account of African American movement northward during the 1940s, see Nicholas Lemann, *The Promised Land: The Great Black Migration and How It Changed America* (New York: Random House, 1995). For a more culturally oriented perspective on the Great Migration, see Farah Jasmine Griffin, *"Who Set You Flowin'?": The African American Migration Narrative* (New York: Oxford University Press, 1994).

54. This passage may be found in an incomplete draft of *Member* in Box 11, Folder 8, in the Carson McCullers Collection, University of Texas–Austin.

55. Frankie's reference to "pictures of Cubans and Mexicans" recalls Henkie Adams's citation of a picture of the beach at Rio de Janeiro in "Correspondence" (1941). Henkie Adams, a forerunner to Frankie Addams, is the prepubescent protagonist of McCullers's short story. See "Correspondence" in Carson McCullers, *The Collected Stories* (Boston: Houghton Mifflin, 1987), 119–24.

56. Nikhil Singh has brilliantly analyzed the differences between Wallace's notion of a "people's century" or a "century of the common man" on the one hand, and the black internationalist idea of a "peoples' century" on the other. See *Black Is a Country*, 159.

57. Mary McLeod Bethune, *Building a Better World*, ed. Audrey Thomas McCluskey and Elaine M. Smith (Bloomington: Indiana University Press, 2000), 253. For a valuable account of Bethune's life, see Rackham Holt, *Mary McLeod Bethune: A Biography* (Garden City, NY: Doubleday, 1964).

58. McCullers herself would affirm this vision of the postwar world in her *Mademoiselle* essay "Our Heads Are Bowed" (1945). A short piece on the meaning of Thanksgiving at the end of war, "Our Heads" reminds its primarily female readership that it isn't enough to honor those who have risked their lives to combat the Axis powers; Americans also must bow their heads and pray for the humility needed to build a peaceful, just, and democratic postwar world. McCullers calls for Americans to recognize that "we have grown mighty, not through prejudice and insularity, but by the peoples of many nations and the genius of varied racial strains. . . . We pray that our pride will be free of all bigotry" (*Mortgaged*, 229). For McCullers, the end of the war offers the United States the power and the responsibility to create a better world than that which preceded the conflict.

59. Frankie's continuing investment in the privileges accorded a member of this white nuptial ritual leads her, however, not to a swift tour of the world but to another challenge to her imperialistic vision of travel: one articulated not by a beloved black housekeeper, but by an anonymous white soldier. In this penultimate turn of the plot, the disturbingly alien qualities of the military return as Frankie goes on a date with a soldier and in the process almost loses her sense of cognitive mapping once more.

Earlier in the novel, Frankie has initiated a rapport with this nameless military man. Seeing him on the street, she offers him a meaningful look meant to register that they both are "friendly, free travelers" (313). Not surprisingly he reads her glance in a very different way, asking her "are you going my way or am I going yours?" a pick-up line that signifies only geographically to Frankie (313). In her view, "The soldier was joining with her like a traveler who meets another traveler in a tourist town" (313). Thrilled at the prospect of meeting a fellow traveler, Frankie tags along, asking about his place of origin and his future destinations. That he hails from Arkansas, a southern state of no particular interest, disturbs her a bit, but she reassures herself with the thought that as a soldier he might be sent anywhere at all. "Here we are sitting here at this table," Frankie exclaims, "and in a month from now there's no telling where on earth we'll be. Maybe tomorrow the army will send you to Alaska like they sent my brother. Or to France or Africa or Burma. And I don't have any idea where I'll be. I'd like for us to go to Alaska for a while, and then somewhere else" (315). Ignorant of the sexual implications of her statements, Frankie misunderstands her budding relationship with the soldier as the camaraderie of white Americans eager to experience the world.

Yet her later "date" with the soldier suggests otherwise. However much she may claim adult white privilege through her imagined connection to the wedding, from the perspective of the military she is still beyond the pale. When the soldier makes a pass at Frankie, the military's power to go anywhere, to make the world available for the nation, appears transmuted into brutal rapacity of a particularly pedophilic kind. Her standing as a white bourgeois girl in a white southern town cannot protect her from this predatory military man. She exists outside the white fraternity of the U.S. military and, as such, represents little more than another potential territory to be conquered, another space to occupy. Frankie's physical response to the soldier is suitably defensive and successful—she hits him over the head with a glass pitcher. But her intellectual response to his behavior proves more complex. In an effort to reclaim her own status as a member of the white imperial wedding, the unit that will speed through the world welcomed at every turn,

Frankie attempts to distinguish the would-be rapist from the globe-trotting military of which he is a part: "Now she was seeing him altogether as a single person, not as a member of the loud free gangs who for a season roamed the streets of town and then went out into the world altogether. . . . She could not see him any more in Burma, Africa, or Iceland, or even for that matter in Arkansas" (371). Separated from the military, isolated and alone, this "single person" no longer suggests either local or international movement. Like "the Wild Nigger" at the fair, supposedly from an exotic island but most likely from Selma, the soldier exists as someone adrift, alone, nowhere; both the performer and the soldier are disturbing figures whose freakishness derives as much from a lack of destination as from a lack of belonging.

60. See Bethune, *Building a Better World*, 187.

Chapter 5. Mississippi on the Pacific

1. As Thomas Borstelmann has put it, "the Germans' and Japanese' lurid but often accurate stories of lynchings and race riots targeted the nonwhite peoples of the European colonies, especially those in Asia." See *The Cold War and the Color Line: American Race Relations in the Global Arena* (Cambridge: Harvard University Press, 2001), 36.

2. Brenda Plummer argues that "The Cold War had altered the meaning of internationalism and bought time and space for racism to predicate itself on presumed patriotism and orthodoxy. It provided a temporary oasis for colonialism in the name of global security." See *Rising Wind: Black Americans and U.S. Foreign Affairs, 1935–1960* (Chapel Hill: University of North Carolina Press, 1996), 239. As my account should suggest, I believe it is important to acknowledge that many white Americans did not share a liberal or even moderate perspective on the question of segregation and its relationship to U.S. global power. One can point to a variety of white conservatives from the "Asia First" members of the Republican party to the John Birch Society who linked the perpetuation of Jim Crow and U.S. expansion abroad. Indeed, the very name of the John Birch Society celebrates a bigoted white southern soldier who died in a conflict with Chinese Communists in 1945—a useful illustration of how the confluence of a belief in segregation and a dedication to rid Asia of Communism stood at the center of much 1950s conservative sentiment.

3. Von Eschen, *Race against Empire: Black Americans and Anticolonialism, 1937–1957* (Ithaca: Cornell University Press, 1997), 6.

4. Quoted in Mary Dudziak, *Cold War Civil Rights: Race and the Image of American Democracy* (Princeton: Princeton University Press, 2000), 77.

5. For an important analysis of the relationship between the cold war and anticolonialist insurrection, see Matthew Connelly, "Taking off the Cold War Lens: Visions of North-South Conflict during the Algerian War for Independence," *American Historical Review* 105 (June 2000): 739–69.

6. See Plummer, *Rising Wind*, 179.

7. Quoted in Christina Klein, *Cold War Orientalism: Asia in the Middlebrow Imagination* (Berkeley: University of California Press, 2003), 40.

8. See Dudziak, *Cold War Civil Rights*, 46–48.

9. For modernization theorists, Native Americans also constituted an example of a domestic group that seemed backward and underdeveloped.

10. Rostow made his feelings about segregation and modernity evident in the following description of an exhibit on the nation's "unfinished business" that he organized for the 1958 World Exposition in Brussels: "The presentation of American shortcomings, such as the history of race relations, would lend credibility to the exhibits, so long as they were contained within a progressive narrative, ending with new technological trends such as automated factories." By concluding the "progressive narrative" with "automated facto-

ries," Rostow suggests that the United States could fully enfranchise African Americans in much the same technocratic manner that it has improved slow and inefficient modes of manufacture. Technology and democracy would together produce the social engineering necessary to modernize the recalcitrant U.S. South. See Nils Gilman, *Mandarins of the Future: Modernization Theory in Cold War America* (Baltimore: Johns Hopkins University Press, 2003), 207, 210. It's worth noting that President Eisenhower and a host of white southern politicians took offense at the exhibit's candid representation of the Jim Crow regime and had it taken down.

11. While I don't have time to address directly this complex issue here, the relationship between literary modernism and modernization theory demands more attention.

12. See "Shingles for the Lord" in William Faulkner, *Collected Stories* (New York: Random House, 1950), 29.

13. See "The Tall Men" in William Faulkner, *Collected Stories* (New York: Random House, 1950), 59–60.

14. See *Lawd Today* in *Richard Wright: Early Works* (New York: Library of America, 1991 [1963]), 132.

15. See "Long Black Song" in *Uncle Tom's Children, Richard Wright: Early Works* (New York: Library of America), 352.

16. Wright understood that modernization was, as Michael Latham has argued, "a means for the continued assertion of the privileges and rights of a dominant power during an era in which the nations of Africa, Asia, and Latin America, and the Middle East increasingly demanded independence." See Michael Latham, *Modernization as Ideology: American Social Science and "Nation-Building" in the Kennedy Era* (Chapel Hill: University of North Carolina Press, 2000), 16.

17. *Faulkner at Nagano* is usually treated as a minor resource for scholars seeking to ascertain the writer's views on desegregation or the cold war. For critics who examine the text in more thorough terms, see Joseph Leo Blotner, *Faulkner: A Biography* (New York: Random House, 1984), 1550–61 and Frederick R. Karl, *William Faulkner: American Writer* (New York: Weidenfeld and Nicolson, 1989), 887–92. *The Color Curtain* has attracted more scholarly attention. I have learned a great deal from Addison Gayle, *Richard Wright: Ordeal of a Native Son* (Garden City, NY: Anchor, 1980), 258–60; Harold T. McCarthy, "Richard Wright: The Expatriate as Native Son," in *Richard Wright: A Collection of Critical Essays*, ed. Richard Macksey and Frank E. Moorer (Englewood Cliffs, NJ: Prentice-Hall, 1984), 68–86; Michel Fabre, *The Unfinished Quest of Richard Wright*, trans. Isabel Barzon (New York: William Morrow, 1973), 418–25; Cedric Robinson, *Black Marxism: The Making of the Black Radical Tradition* (London: Zed, 1983), 422–27; Paul Gilroy, *The Black Atlantic: Modernity and Double Consciousness* (Cambridge: Harvard University Press, 1993), 180–211; and Virginia Whatley Smith, ed., *Richard Wright's Travel Writings: New Reflections* (Jackson: University Press of Mississippi, 2001), 78–116.

18. See *All That Is Solid Melts into Air: The Experience of Modernity* (New York: Simon and Schuster, 1982), 15.

19. *The Town* (New York: Vintage, 1957), 306.

20. *Go Down, Moses* (New York: Vintage, 1940), 364.

21. Thanks are due Matthew Jones for the *Newsweek* citation. As Jones recently put it with reference to one federal advisory group, "in its analysis of the Far East, the Operations Coordinating Board (OCB) reported the 'persistent belief, despite U.S. professions to contrary, that [the] U.S. regards Asiatic people as inferior'." See "'Segregated' Asia? Race, the Bandung Conference, and Pan-Asianist Fears in American Thought and Policy, 1954–1955," *Diplomatic History* (2005): 841–68.

22. See *The Mansion* in *William Faulkner: Novels, 1957–1962* (New York: Library of America, 1999 [1959]), 579–80.

23. See Richard King, "Faulkner, Ideology, and Narrative," in *Faulkner and Ideology*, ed.

Donald M. Kartiganer and Ann J. Abadie (Oxford: University of Mississippi Press, 1995), 22–44; and Noel Polk, "'Polysyllabic and Verbless Patriotic Nonsense': Faulkner at Mid-century—His and Ours," in the same volume, 297–328.

24. See "Letter to a Northern Editor," in *William Faulkner: Essays, Speeches, and Public Letters*, ed. James B. Meriweather (New York: Modern Library, 2004), 91. All further citations to this volume will be included in the text with the title *Essays.*

25. Faulkner made this statement in an interview with British journalist Russell Howe. The interview first appeared in the London *Sunday Times* (March 4, 1956); slightly different versions were published in the *Reporter* (March 22) and the *New York Times* (March 22). Faulkner repudiated the interview, but Howe insisted on its legitimacy.

26. Communism, Faulkner would claim in a 1955 letter, "is dangerous." See *The Selected Letters of William Faulkner,* ed. Joseph Blotner (New York: Random House, 1977), 379.

27. As Joseph Blotner puts it when commenting on Faulkner's brief trip to the Philippines in 1955, "the conviction was growing upon him that America needed all the friends it could get" (*Faulkner: A Biography,* 609). All further citations of this work will be included in the text.

28. This celebration of freedom typified contemporary U.S. culture. As Eric Foner writes, "by the end of the 1950s, the idea that the love of freedom was the defining characteristic of American society had become fully incorporated into the popular consciousness" (*The Story of American Freedom* [New York: Norton, 1998], 260).

29. *Intruder in the Dust* (New York: Random House, 1948), 56.

30. See Joe Karaganis, "Negotiating the National Voice in Faulkner's Late Work," *Arizona Quarterly* 54 (1998): 53–81.

31. It's tempting to read Faulkner's use of the Alaska figure in light of Shreve McCannon's comment on the North and South poles in the closing moments of *Absalom, Absalom!* Pondering the significance of Jim Bond as the last surviving Sutpen, Shreve argues that as "the Jim Bonds" "spread towards the poles they will bleach out again like the rabbits and the birds do, so they wont show up so sharp against the snow. But it will still be Jim Bond." If the omnipresence of snow disguises racial difference in a manner that foreshadows Faulkner's argument in "On Fear," both Shreve and Quentin recognize that such fantasies of erasure cannot be sustained. See *Absalom, Absalom!* (New York: Vintage, 1986 [1936]), 302.

32. Polk argues that Faulkner's "world vision . . . seems to be marked out by a kind of xenophobia ("Man in the Middle: Faulkner and the Southern White Moderates," in *Faulkner and Race,* ed. Doreen Fowler and Ann J. Abadie [Jackson: University Press of Mississippi, 1987], 139).

33. See Frances Stonor Saunders, *The Cultural Cold War: The CIA and the World of Arts and Letters* (New York: New Press, 2000).

34. See Frederick Karl, *William Faulkner: American Writer* (New York: Grove Press, 1989), 920. Karl is correct to point out, however, that even as some of what Faulkner stated in Japan is unsystematic and confused, the speeches and addresses delivered do offer us an image of the writer attempting to come to terms with difficult issues of race, power, and nationhood (913).

35. Robert A. Jeliffe, ed., *Faulkner at Nagano,* 4th ed. (Tokyo: Kenkyusha, 1966 [1956]), 20. All further citations will be included in the text.

36. See Louis Hartz, *The Liberal Tradition in America* (New York: Harcourt, 1955), 53.

37. For another response to this portion of *Nagano,* see Edwin Arnold, "Japanese Views of the American South," *SAR* 65 (2000): 114–31.

38. In his description of this interaction, Blotner reports that one Japanese auditor "brought up a postwar outrage, and [Faulkner] responded sympathetically" (*Faulkner: A Biography,* 555).

39. Faulkner even made his concern with federal power known to the State Department itself, albeit in an oblique manner. Writing to his State Department contact, Harold E. Howland, in November 1955, Faulkner argues that the U.S. government's desire to keep Germany from "going" Communist has blinded the government to the greater importance of leaving the Germans alone to sort out their own affairs: "I wonder what would happen if we . . . said that a un-unified nation is such a crime against nature and morality both that, rather than be a party to it, we will allow Germany to withdraw from promise of NATO troops, and be united under any conditions they wish" (*Selected Letters*, 388). The notion that an "un-unified nation is . . . a crime against nature and morality" cannot help but recall the American Civil War that haunts virtually all of Faulkner's work. Yet it is in the writer's last phrase—"be united under any conditions they wish"—that we see the relevance of this statement on the German question to anxieties about the contemporary relationship between Washington and the South. For what is this plea for German sovereignty and American withdrawal but a comment on how the federal government should avoid the mistakes of Reconstruction and not impose its will on the South? What is this reference to German autonomy but a way of expressing the hope that the federal government would allow the American South to resolve the problem of the color line in its own fashion? As in his propaganda performances in Japan, Faulkner once again makes clear the degree to which he identifies the federal government with crude interventionism and a general disregard for local traditions and local rights.

40. See *Requiem for a Nun* (New York: Random House, 1951), 92.

41. See C. Vann Woodward, "A Second Look at the Theme of Irony," in *The Burden of Southern History* 3rd ed. (Baton Rouge: Louisiana State University Press, 1993 [1968]), 229–30.

42. Faulkner avoided commenting on the question of Japanese racism toward the Koreans.

43. I thus disagree with David Minter's claim that foreign travel gave Faulkner the freedom needed "to proclaim the moral repugnance and mounting danger of racism without having to recommend caution and patience" (*William Faulkner: His Life and His Work* [Baltimore: Johns Hopkins University Press, 1980], 233).

44. That the World War II–era Japanese had created their own version of an Asian anticolonial coalition in the form of The Greater East Asia Co-Prosperity Sphere suggests all the more their relevance to white fears of colored insurrection.

45. Bill Mullen has recently reminded us that Wright describes the African American fascination with newspaper images of Japanese generals during the 1930s in his essay "How Bigger Was Born." See *Afro-Orientalism* (Minneapolis: University of Minnesota Press, 2004), 48. All further citations will be included in the text. Amrijit Singh has recovered the fact that Wright met with Vijaylakshmi Pandit, Nehru's sister, during the mid-1940s; see Singh, "Afterword," Richard Wright, *The Color Curtain* (Oxford: University of Mississippi Press, 1995 [1956]), 239. For important studies of African American interest in Asia see, as well as Mullen's book, Jervis Anderson, *Bayard Rustin: Troubles I've Seen* (New York: Harper Collins, 1997), 130–35, and Marc Gallicchio, *The African American Encounter with Japan and China: Black Internationalism in Asia, 1895–1945* (Chapel Hill: University of North Carolina Press, 2000), 207–8. For an indispensable overview of African American critiques of white imperialism from the 1930s to the 1950s see Von Eschen, *Race against Empire*.

46. Richard Wright, *The Long Dream* (Oxford: University of Mississippi Press, 2000 [1958]), 198. All further citations will be included in the text.

47. See J. Saunders Redding, Review of *The Long Dream, New York Times Book Review,* October 26, 1958, reprinted in *Richard Wright: Critical Perspectives*, ed. Henry Louis Gates, Jr., and K. A. Appiah (New York: Amistad, 1993), 61; and Gilroy, *The Black Atlantic*, 186.

48. The letter is quoted in Michel Fabre, *The Unfinished Quest of Richard Wright,* 2nd ed. (Urbana: University of Illinois Press, 1993 [1973]), 470, 422.

49. The full line reads: "You see America as leader of the free world does not wish cruel pictures of how Negroes live shown to Africans and Asians. This is the way we fight Communism." Fabre cites this observation from Wright's letter to Paul Reynolds. See ibid., 619.

50. See Singh, "Afterword," 228.

51. We should note that the United States had already attempted to form its own anti-Communist Asian coalition one year earlier. In 1954, Australia, Britain, France, New Zealand, Pakistan, the Philippines, and Thailand founded the Southeast Asia Treaty Organization (SEATO).

52. *The Color Curtain,* 13. All further citations will be included in the text.

53. This wasn't the first time Wright had attempted to place the black American fight for justice in a global context. During his Communist phase, his concern with the black question was tempered by a need to see the African American struggle as part of an international fight against white racist capital: "My attention was caught by the similarity of the experience of workers in other lands, by the possibility of uniting scattered but kindred people into a whole . . . here at last, in the realm of revolutionary expression, Negro experience could find a home, a functioning value and role" (Richard Crossman, ed., *The God That Failed* [New York: Harper, 1949], 106). Wright's interest in the anticolonial struggle of Africans and Asians must be seen in a similar light; for him, the global struggle against white imperialism and colonialism was another movement in which African Americans might be able to "find a home." This isn't to say that Wright understood international Communism and global anticolonialism as equivalent; he did not. Rather, it is suggested that Wright's interest in another international movement of oppressed people illustrates his long-standing belief in the importance of situating African American activism in the context of global liberation.

54. Kevin Gaines, *American Africans in Ghana: Black Expatriates and the Civil Rights Era* (Chapel Hill: University of North Carolina Press, 2006), 59.

55. Quoted in Singh, "Afterword," 226.

56. As Paul Gilroy has argued, Wright's "work articulates simultaneously an affirmation and a negation of the western civilization that formed him" (*The Black Atlantic,* 186).

57. Ibid., 162.

58. Mochtar Lubis, "Through Coloured Glasses?" *Encounter,* March 1956: 73.

59. Mullen claims that "Wright's means of giving shape to this mass through a continued course of Western rationalization constituted an attempt to bleach it of its red, yellow, or even black excesses in order to reconfigure Asia itself in the image, and imagination, of the ambivalent Western interpreter. Wright, in short, accomplished his goal at Bandung of narrativizing his own displacement from the West" (*Afro-Orientalism,* 66). While I agree with Mullen that Wright depends on Orientalist discourse in his interaction with Asia and Asians, I find this assessment a bit harsh. As I hope to show in my analysis of Wright's portraits of African Americans at the conference, the writer was in many ways very sensitive to how such narratives might be constructed and undermined.

60. This emphasis on the "case" is typical of Wright's informal social science method in *The Color Curtain;* earlier in the volume, he uses a set of identical questions to interview a handful of Asians and Westerners about issues of race and colonialism (20–75).

61. See Wright's Indonesian diary, 137, James Weldon Johnson Collection, Beinecke Library, Yale University.

62. Needless to say, Wright's vision of Indonesia suggests his own lingering attachment to tropical clichés of Pacific Rim Asia.

63. Wright, *Pagan Spain* (Oxford: University of Mississippi Press, 2002 [1957]), 284.

64. Romulo used this phrase to describe the Bandung conference, an event he viewed

as anything but vengeful in tone. Yet the fact that Romulo invoked this phrase in the course of giving a lecture at the University of North Carolina gives its regional meaning more bite. See *The Meaning of Bandung* (Chapel Hill: University of North Carolina Press, 1956), 48.

65. See Mary Louise Pratt, "Modernity and Periphery: Toward a Global and Relational Analysis," in *Beyond Dichotomies*, ed. Elisabeth Mudimbe-Boyi (Albany: SUNY Press, 2002), 33.

Epilogue

1. I take the phrase "cold war civil rights" from Mary Dudziak, *Cold War Civil Rights: Race and the Image of American Democracy* (Princeton: Princeton University Press, 2002).

2. We should note, however, that some southern politicians, most notably Senator William Fulbright of Arkansas, continued to promote international connections during this era. See Randall Bennett Woods, "Dixie's Dove: J. William Fulbright, the Vietnam War and the American South," *Journal of Southern History* 60, no. 3 (August 1994): 533–52.

3. The Venable family gave the Klan a lien on their portion of the mountain in perpetuity. In order to block Klan rallies on the peak, the state of Georgia had to condemn the land and thus evacuate the lien.

4. In 1945, for example, the Klan etched a 300-foot-tall cross shape into the side of the mountain and then lit it ablaze with a mixture of sand and fuel oil. The resulting flames stood as a reminder to African Americans that the war was over and normal segregation had returned.

5. I have learned a great deal about the history of this granite monolith from David B. Freeman, *Carved in Stone: The History of Stone Mountain* (Macon, GA: Mercer University Press, 1997), and Grace Elizabeth Hale, "Granite Stopped Time: The Stone Mountain Memorial and the Representation of White Southern Identity," *Georgia Historical Quarterly* 82 (Spring 1998): 22–44.

6. See Jon Nordheimer, "Agnew Mellow in Talk Hailing Confederate Heroes," *New York Times*, May 10, 1970, p. 69.

7. See Marita Sturken, *Tangled Memories: The Vietnam War, the AIDS Epidemic, and the Politics of Remembering* (Berkeley: University of California Press, 1997), 184.

8. Ever since the 1968 Republican Convention in Miami, Nixon had done his best to curry favor with the white South. Most historians agree that without the assistance of Senator Strom Thurmond (R-South Carolina) and the segregationist contingent, Nixon wouldn't have won the GOP nomination and the presidency. Nixon's prospects seemed dim until he promised Thurmond at the party convention that, if elected, he would quietly decrease federal government support of desegregation and allow the white elite of the region increased autonomy in racial matters. Thurmond found Nixon's pledge credible and pulled the nomination away from Ronald Reagan, the front runner, to the other Californian on the party ballot. Although all previous postwar administrations had reluctantly subscribed to some notion of cold war civil rights, Nixon chose to follow an alternate path: one blazed not by such Democratic and Republican presidential predecessors as Eisenhower and Johnson, but instead by such maverick rightists as Thurmond, Senator Barry Goldwater (R-Arizona), and, most notoriously, Governor George Wallace of Alabama, a pro-segregationist Democrat. A segregationist "southern strategy," as GOP adviser Kevin Phillips dubbed the tactic, would prove central to Nixon's success in 1968 and, with few exceptions, the president would honor his racist credo and white southern allies throughout his first term.

9. Charles A. Thomas's e-book *Blood of Isaac* has proven very helpful. See Kent State University Library Special Collections, http://speccoll.library.kent.edu (accessed Oct. 10,

2006). See also "Parting Shots: Will the Southern Strategy Rise Again," *Life Magazine*, May 22, 1970, 78.

10. As Arthur Danto puts it, "the memorial is a special precinct, extruded from life, a segregated enclave where we honor the dead. With monuments we honor ourselves" (qtd. in Sturken, *Tangled Memories*, 47).

11. Ohio National Guardsmen shot and killed four Kent State University students protesting the U.S. bombing of Cambodia. The United States had started carpet-bombing Cambodia in the spring of 1968. The attacks were intended to deny the North Vietnamese safe haven in a neutral nation.

12. Millions of Americans already had rejected the administration's foreign policy in Southeast Asia; indeed, the largest anti-war protests of the era (the "Moratorium" demonstrations) occurred that year.

13. For an important history of this symbol see John M. Coski, *The Confederate Battle Flag* (Cambridge: Harvard University Press, 2005).

14. For African Americans, we might say, the "dixiefication" of the war had always been a foregone conclusion.

15. See "Cuddling" (1985) in Walker, *The Way Forward Is with a Broken Heart* (New York: Random House, 2000), 86.

16. Walker, *Meridian* (New York: Harcourt, 1976), 48. All further references will be included in the text.

17. Walker, *Revolutionary Petunias* (San Diego: Harcourt Brace, 1973), 20.

18. As Patricia Riley has recently reminded us, Walker herself has both Cherokee and African American ancestors. See "Wrapped in the Serpent's Tail: Alice Walker's African–Native American Subjectivity," in *When Brer Rabbit Meets Coyote: African–Native American Literature*, ed. Jonathan Brennan (Urbana: University of Illinois Press, 2003), 242.

19. The most famous exception to this white mythology is, of course, Thomas Jefferson's comments in *Notes on the State of Virginia*. For an important examination of Jefferson's thoughts on this topic, see Linda Bolton, *Facing the Other: Ethical Disruption and the American Mind* (Baton Rouge: Louisian State University Press, 2004), 101–103, 105. For a useful general history of the white response to the burial mounds, see George R. Milner, *The Moundbuilders: Ancient Peoples of Northeastern America* (London: Thames and Hudson, 2004).

20. The most famous example of a serpent effigy mound in the United States is actually in Ohio.

21. *The Way Forward Is with a Broken Heart*, 37.

22. It's no accident in this regard that Walker is famous for rediscovering the grave of Zora Neale Hurston.

23. In her contemporary poem "View from Rosehill Cemetery: Vicksburg" (1973), Walker emphasizes how the messiness of anonymous burial, of "unmarked graves atangled in the brush," may inadvertently suggest a provocative blurring of the lines between persons and identities: see *Revolutionary Petunias*, 25. For an interesting collection of essays on these issues, see Cynthia Mills and Pamela H. Simpson, eds., *Monuments to the Lost Cause: Women, Art, and the Landscape of Southern Memory* (Knoxville: University of Tennessee Press, 2003).

INDEX